Katharine Hepburn

George Cukor says she swept through Hollywood in 1932
like a hurricane insulting everyone in sight – a freckled, snotty
eccentric who wore men's clothes and fought senselessly with
everyone in sight. She was an immediate star.
'I had to or they would have had me playing whores or
discontented wives who always wonder whether they should go
to bed with some bore.' – Katharine Hepburn, interviewed
by Rex Reed, New York *Daily News*, 28th January 1979.

'A radical? She's a female Jacobin – she's a nihilist. Whatever
is, is wrong, and all that sort of thing. If you are going to dine
with her, you had better know it.'
'Oh, murder!' murmured the young man vaguely, sinking
back in his chair with his arms folded. – Henry James,
The Bostonians.

LANCASHIRE COUNTY LIBRARY
SOUTH EAST LANCS.

ANDREW BRITTON

Katharine Hepburn

STAR AS FEMINIST

STUDIO
VISTA

This edition first published in 1995 by
Studio Vista
a Cassell imprint
Wellington House
125 Strand
London WC2R 0BB

A Movie Book
Edited and designed by Ian Cameron

Produced by Cameron Books
PO Box 1, Moffat, Dumfriesshire DG10 9SU, Scotland

Copyright © Andrew Britton 1984
This edition © Movie 1995

All rights reserved. No part of this book may be reproduced or
transmitted in any form or by any means, electronic or mechanical,
including photocopying, recording or any information storage and
retrieval system, without prior permission in writing from the publishers
and the copyright owner.

Distributed in Australia
by Capricorn Link (Australia) Pty Ltd
2/13 Carrington Road
Castle Hill
NSW 2154

08929736**4** - 2|03

British Library Cataloguing-in-Publication Date
A catalogue record for this book is available from the British Library

ISBN 0-289-80139-7 (hardback)
ISBN 0-304-34657-8 (paperback

Stills by courtesy of The American Film Theatre, Avco Embassy,
British Film Institute, Cinerama, Columbia, ITC, MGM, Paramount,
RKO, Talent Associates-Norton Simon, Twentieth Century-Fox,
United Artists, Universal, Warner Brothers.

Filmography and bibliography updated by Ben Francis.

The lines quoted from the poem 'Spinster' from *The Colossus and other
poems* by Sylvia Plath are reprinted by permission of Faber & Faber Ltd.

Cameron Books wishes to acknowledge the help of Sheila Whitaker and
Linda Ramsay, and to thank Tyneside Cinema, which published the
first edition of this book under the title *Katharine Hepburn: The Thirties
and After*.

Half-title page: Hepburn as she appeared in Sylvia Scarlett.
Frontispiece: as Susan Vance in Bringing Up Baby, *with Fritz Feld as Dr
Lehmann.*
Title page: Hepburn during the shooting of Morning Glory.

Contents

Foreword

The reason for producing this new edition of Andrew Britton's book is in part as a memorial to a friend, but it is also to make more widely available a text that is outstanding among the literature of stardom. Using the films as his primary evidence, juxtaposed (where relevant) with contemporary journalistic coverage of Hepburn both as an actress and as a star personality, Andrew has set out to analyse the meaning of her screen persona.

One of the most consistent features of his writing was a refusal to look at movies as isolated works. Here, he finds antecedents for the Hepburn persona in the work of Henry James, and his treatment of her is illuminated by comparisons with two other equally individual stars, Greta Garbo and Bette Davis, relating, for example, Hepburn's star image in the 'thirties to that of Garbo, and her 'spinster' movies to those of Davis. In her one film with Ginger Rogers, he finds Hepburn playing the Fred Astaire part.

It is also characteristic of Andrew that, before embarking on the various stages of his analysis, he questions and places the terms to be used rather than simply taking them as read. This is, then, not just a book about Katharine Hepburn, the star, but a consideration of, among other things, genre, camp, bisexuality and spinsterhood, all feeding into a treatment of Hepburn's stardom as an embodiment of actual or potential female roles in (or against) a society that remains predominantly patriarchal.

This edition includes Andrew Britton's original text, substantially unmodified apart from the incorporation into the main sequence of the author's further thoughts on *State of the Union* and *Desk Set*, which previously appeared as an appendix. The bibliography and filmography have been updated, and a list of stage work has been added. The largest addition, however, is of over a hundred stills, which are intended to complement the text; their selection and their captions cannot, of course, be attributed to Andrew. I hope he would have enjoyed them.

Ian Cameron
September 1995

Why Hepburn?

The significance for feminist cultural studies of the great female stars of the Hollywood cinema lies in the contradictions they generate within narrative structures that are committed overall to the reaffirmation of bourgeois-patriarchal norms. While we are invited, at the end of *The Philadelphia Story*, to take comfort in the discovery by Tracy Lord (Katharine Hepburn) that 'men are wonderful' as a satisfactory resolution of the problems of the film, we have also previously been allowed to celebrate those very qualities which must be humbled to engineer this 'happy ending'. The contradiction – which embodies a conflict both of values and of possibilities of pleasure – is insoluble.

The cumbersome (and, happily, increasingly moribund) body of contemporary film theory which owes allegiance to Lacan has underwritten the seer's conviction – derived, despite disclaimers, from existentialism – that identification is a matter of misrecognition, alienation and self-loss. However, identification may also represent an intelligent affiliation to value. All works of art, clearly, seek to govern evaluation, both by foreclosing certain alternatives and discriminating amongst those they acknowledge; but because the determinants of a reading are by no means exhausted by the invitation of the work (readers have a history), the acceptance of the invitation is never guaranteed. A peculiar interest accrues, then, to works which have radically contradictory invitations – works which, in seeking to accommodate ideological disturbances, are compelled to allow them a space in which they become available to readers for purposes which the work as a whole cannot endorse. A project which is, in essence, conservative may be destabilised by the very mechanisms it adopts to achieve success.

In an article on 'Four Films of Lana Turner', Richard Dyer has argued:

'Stars frequently speak to dominant contradictions in social life – experienced as conflicting demands, contrary expectations, irreconcilable but equally held values – in such a way as to appear to reconcile them. In part, by simply being one indivisible entity with an existence in the "real world", yet displaying contradictory personality traits, stars can affirm that it is possible to triumph over, transcend, successfully live out contradictions' (*Movie* 25, Winter 1977/78, p.30).

The point might be adapted to the discussion of genre, and inasmuch as it works, the function Dyer describes is a conservative one – structural contradictions are reconcilable within the status quo. Yet the kind of analysis of the Hollywood cinema undertaken since the mid 'seventies has demonstrated (if it has demonstrated anything) the frequency with which it *doesn't* work. Even if one leaves aside the films of particular artists who, far from seeking to mediate, are concerned to present and articulate 'dominant contradictions in social life' (Fritz Lang, Alfred Hitchcock, Josef von Sternberg, Douglas Sirk and Vincente Minnelli are obvious cases in point), one is still confronted by numerous films in which a set towards reconciliation, more or less desperately signalled, succeeds only in demonstrating its impossibility.

With the exception of Sternberg's Marlene Dietrich, who clearly constitutes a special case, Katharine Hepburn is the only star of the classical cinema who embodies contradictions (about the nature and status of women) in a way that not only resists their satisfactory resolution in a stable, affirmable ideological coherence, but which also continually threatens to produce an *oppositional* coherence which is registered by the films as a serious ideological threat. There is no other star so many of whose films seem systematically dedicated to expressing animus against her, or offering her as a 'voice' which has to be placed.

I do not wish, it should be made clear at once, to argue either that Hepburn is an *auteur* or that any of her films embody anything like a 'radical' feminist position, although she was centrally involved in setting up a number of projects which explicitly address feminist politics (*A Woman Rebels*, *Woman of the Year*, *Adam's Rib*, for example), and it would be as absurd to fail to honour this achievement – unique in its time – as it would be to ignore its limitations. These limitations remain, to date, the condition for producing films which *openly* articulate the politics of feminism in Hollywood, and it could not be said, I think, that the 'seventies produced anything which, in this respect, goes further than *Adam's Rib*. They certainly didn't produce a *Stage Door* which, for all the problems created for it by Hepburn's persona, remains the most progressive of all women's pictures.

My argument will be, in fact, that Hepburn's presence is always more radical than her films, and that this suggests both why she is not an *auteur* in any significant sense and why she is so important: her presence forces her films to go in directions they cannot possibly follow, adopt strategies they cannot fully sustain, raise issues they cannot adequately resolve. She both generates the most fundamental contradictions, and impedes the films' access to their emergency exit.

Most importantly, she is not merely an object for academic study, interesting as this may be: I have not set out to produce 'one of those depressing "contributions to knowledge" which are so patently uninformed by any first-hand perception of why the subject should be *worth* study' (F.R. Leavis, *The Common Pursuit*). For Hepburn is also the most *useful* of the great stars: the tone of the persona, the strengths and values it embodies, the struggles to which it refers, have a very real and vital pertinence for a period in which the gay and women's movements have made the politics of sexuality a substantive – a *practical* – issue.

I wish to thank Sheila Whitaker, an old friend and colleague, for proposing the idea of the Tyneside Cinema Hepburn retrospective, which was the original occasion for this work, and for her patience and support during the vicissitudes of its composition. Without her labours and dedication, the season could not have taken place nor the book have been published. I have also discussed Katharine Hepburn with her at various times, though needless to say, she should not be blamed for the views I express.

This book is dedicated to John Fletcher and Ed Gallafent, with my love.

Andrew Britton.

1. An American Princess

The Hepburn persona can be related to an American tradition of feeling about women which finds its most significant expression in Henry James's image of the 'American princess'.

While Isabel Archer, the heroine of *The Portrait of a Lady*, has her antecedents (the eponymous protagonists of *Madame de Mauves* and *Daisy Miller*, Pandora Day in *Pandora*, Bessy Alden in *An International Episode*), she may be taken as the paradigm of the type. In the preface to the New York edition of the novel, James tells us that 'my dim first move towards *The Portrait* was exactly my grasp of a single character . . . Thus I had my vivid individual – vivid, so strangely, in spite of being still at large, not confined by the conditions, not engaged in the tangle, to which we look for much of the impress that constitutes an identity . . . The point is that this single small cornerstone, the conception of a certain young woman affronting her destiny, had begun with being all my outfit for the large building of *The Portrait of a Lady*.'

He goes on to try to explain how it can be that 'this slight personality, the mere slim shade of an intelligent but presumptuous girl,' is yet fit to take on 'the high attributes of a Subject':

'Millions of presumptuous girls, intelligent or not intelligent, daily affront their destiny; and what is it open to their destiny to *be*, at the most, that we should make an ado about it? . . . Challenge any such problem with any intelligence, and you immediately see how full it is of substance; the wonder being, all the while, as we look at the world, how absolutely, how inordinately, the Isabel Archers, and even much smaller female fry, insist on mattering. George Eliot has admirably noted it – "In these frail vessels is borne onward through the ages the treasure of human affection." '

There are three crucial emphases here – 'the conception of a certain young woman affronting her destiny', the question of 'what it is open for her destiny to be', and her status as a 'vessel' in which 'the treasure of human affection' is transmitted and preserved. We take note, also, of the simultaneous suggestions of strength ('affront') and vulnerability ('frail') in James's description of her, the significance of which comes out later, in the narrative itself, in the definition of the *nature* of Isabel's confidence:

'She spent half her time in thinking of beauty and bravery and magnanimity, she had a fixed determination to regard the world as a place of brightness, of free expansion, of irresistible action: she held it must be detestable to be afraid or ashamed . . . Altogether, with her meagre knowledge, her inflated ideals, her confidence at once innocent and dogmatic, her temper at once exacting and indulgent, her mixture of curiosity and fastidiousness, of vivacity and indifference, her desire to look very well and to be if possible even better, her determination to see, to try, to know, her combination of the delicate, desultory, flame-like spirit and the eager and personal creature of conditions: she would be an easy victim of scientific criticism if she were not intended to awaken on the reader's part an impulse more tender and more purely expectant.'

In terms of 'the international theme' Isabel is, of course, America, the descendant of Hudson in *Roderick Hudson* and Christopher Newman in *The American*: the change of gender suggests that a woman functions, for the male author, more adequately than a man as an emblem of the pathos of American innocence. For Isabel is doomed from the start: the confidence from which her strength derives has as its corollary the 'meagre knowledge' which leads her astray. While the defeat of the representative American figure is not necessarily pre-given in James's work, it is initiated in his first novel (Hudson is driven to suicide) and is obstinately recurrent: fundamentally, it is latent in the very terms of the opposition between American innocence and European experience. This is a peculiarly American blockage: again and again in American fiction, it is precisely the ideal social efficacy of the protagonist which, in the society which he or she confronts, entails defeat by or exclusion from it. Given that 'civilisation' is always already 'corruption', or tends towards it, the protagonist embodies a promise which is perpetually unrealisable. Part of the interest of *Taxi Driver* (Martin Scorsese, 1976) consists in the persistence of this pattern, and of an ambiguous allegiance to the protagonist, even when his 'innocence' is a form of psychosis and he clearly embodies no viable social possibility whatever; one may, indeed, trace a development from a model of American innocence which must either succumb to or 'light out' from 'civilisation', to another which increasingly appears, as in the films of Frank Capra, as the reflection of its corrupt antagonist.

But Isabel is also a woman, and the question of 'what it is open for her destiny to *be*' raises feminist issues. We never know the answer to the question in *The Portrait of a Lady*, because Isabel, 'with her meagre knowledge', opts for marriage half-way through. The marriage is a disaster, as we know from the beginning it will be, and at the end of the book she rejects both her husband and the importunities of her American suitor. Her cousin, who was also in love with her, has died. This narrative strategy has the effect of an indefinite postponement of the question of Isabel's destiny at the very moment when her meagre knowledge has been supplemented and the possibility has emerged of a destiny which is not contingent on men. Her 'innocence', clearly, is part of this strategy: it allows James to propose the theme of a woman having a destiny while building in an impediment to its realisation which is removed only when the story is over.

This structure recurs obsessively in James, most obviously in the tales and novellas which anticipate *The Portrait of a Lady*, and the impediments to the heroine's *effective* agency – to her power of using the knowledge she gains or exploring her destiny – subsequently grow ever more drastic: in *What Maisie Knew*, Maisie is a child, and the *donnée* of *The Wings of the Dove* is that Milly Theale is dying. More disturbingly, in the latter novel, the substantial force of

Isabel's impulse to 'affront her destiny' has been hived off into Kate Croy, the American Princess's European antagonist.

Turning back to *The Portrait of a Lady*, we note also that Isabel is juxtaposed with a number of women who *do* have destinies – Madame Merle, Mrs Touchett, Henrietta Stackpole. The first, who partially anticipates Kate Croy, is satisfactorily placed: she is allied to Isabel's future husband in a relationship the (brilliantly realised) complexities of which need not concern us here, but which effectively ties her agency, at once viciously and *self*-destructively, to a man who has destroyed *her*. In Mrs Touchett and Henrietta however, we have American women who have succeeded in defining independent professional and domestic lives apart from men, and James's reaction is to present them both with a parodic irony which, whether 'affectionate' or astringent, is essentially dismissive. Henrietta, most strikingly, is endowed – however 'amiably' – with all the qualities that James takes to be the negative side of American confidence and innocence ('loudness', vulgarity, lack of culture); and it is profoundly characteristic of his radical limitations as an artist that, in the preface to the New York edition, he can see in Henrietta only 'my tendency to overtreat' the subject – only an appendage which is 'almost inexplicable'. The later James would have failed to perceive in her a contradiction, let alone the possibility of another subject.

The problem here becomes most manifest in James's remarkable 'feminist' novel, *The Bostonians,* in which the contradiction I have tried to indicate is most rigorously followed through: the critique, on the one hand, of male paternalism and sexism and the social relations which generate them, and the association, on the other, of Olive Chancellor's feminism with 'the New England conscience' produces a stalemate in which nothing is left, at the end, but another appalling marriage. *The Bostonians* is the work in which James comes nearest to articulating the theme of what it is open for women to be, and in which its unrealisability – the blockage of articulation – is clearest. The 'destiny' which is left to Verena at the close is 'the tears' which mark her capture by Ransom and her loss of Olive: the novel can refuse the viability of bourgeois marriage, but the only terms in which Olive can be construed foreclose imagining an alternative to it, and we must make do, in that famous final sentence, with the cutting edge of authorial irony.

Even in *Washington Square,* the condition of the novel's ruthless analysis of bourgeois patriarchy is the fact that Catherine Sloper's sensibility is so limited that she can do nothing in response to her oppression except suffer – or, when she has become 'a middle-aged woman', put up at best a stubborn, stoic passive resistance. *The Portrait of a Lady* certainly goes beyond *Washington Square:* whereas Catherine, after rejecting Morris Townsend, can only sit down at her needlework again, 'for life, as it were', Isabel at least returns to the world. But James cannot say with what purpose or to what end: he can scarcely allow Isabel to speak in the final confrontation with Goodwood, and, while we are told after she has fled from him that 'she had not known where to turn; but she knew now', James can neither specify this knowledge nor do more, in accounting for her return to Italy, than retreat into enigma. Having got to the point at which the heroine rejects men, James can go no further.

In his analysis of the relationship between *The Portrait of a Lady* and George Eliot's *Daniel Deronda,* F.R. Leavis argues that Isabel Archer is Eliot's Gwendolen Harleth 'seen by a man':

'To say that, in the comparison, James's presentment is seen to be sentimental won't, perhaps, quite do: but it is, I think, seen to be partial in both senses of the word – controlled, that is, by a vision that is both incomplete and indulgent . . .' (*The Great Tradition*, Penguin, 1977, p.104).

This seems to me importantly true, and it has a political corollary: the qualities which James indulges represent the necessary condition for admitting her self-assertion, for they are the qualities which, in Europe, condemn her to entrapment and passivity. James needs both to think of Isabel as the promise of an affront to destiny and to inscribe its eternal delay: the pathos is produced by the delay (which the novel in fact requires) being experienced as 'tragic'. James could not possibly accept what a real affront to destiny would be, as Olive Chancellor is there to prove. He can create a heroine determined 'to see, to try, to know', because her flawed sensibility will allow him to go off at a tangent and reiterate – interminably – the negative consequences of the flaw. A full account of James would need to discuss this blockage in terms of James's own relation to his heroines – in terms of the historical situation of a gay man who feels and recreates, through them, his own powerlessness, and finds, through compassion for these frail yet resilient women, both a sense of his own strength and promise, and the pathos of a predicament in which what they might come to is unimaginable. The effect, for James's work, finds both formal and thematic expression in the obsessive preoccupation, in Leavis's phrase, with the 'doing' at the expense of the 'done', and in the succession of protagonists who have not had, and cannot have, their lives.

The Hepburn of *Morning Glory is* Isabel Archer: James's description of his heroine, and his account of the value we are to ascribe to her, can be applied directly to Eva Lovelace. This is to say that in the brief early period of Hepburn's stardom – the fifteen months in which the first three films were made – the persona's self-assertion is contained by, amongst other things, the tragic 'inevitability', and thus the pathos, of its defeat. Hepburn is to embody the magnificently impetuous and confident American girl whose affront to patriarchal destiny cannot, sadly and fortunately, be realised: and Hillary Fairfield (John Barrymore) in *A Bill of Divorcement* and the protagonist of *Christopher Strong* (Colin Clive) enact the function of Gilbert Osmond in *The Portrait of a Lady*, intervening to curtail the heroine's agency in a manner which is at once discredited and ideologically necessary. It will be seen that there are discriminations to be made: *Christopher Strong*, which is directed by a woman (Dorothy Arzner) goes infinitely further than *The Portrait*, and may be partly read, as I shall argue later, as an exposure and critique of the Jamesian narrative mechanisms in which the endowment of the heroine with a consciousness beyond Isabel's plays a crucial part. To this extent Arzner's film foregrounds, while also partly sharing, the ideological set of *A Bill of Divorcement* and *Morning Glory*, in which the use of Hepburn in James's manner is clearly dominant. There are the 'fixed determination to regard the world as a place of brightness, of free expansion, of irresistible action', the 'meagre knowledge and inflated ideals', the 'flame-like spirit' (an early publicity piece on Hepburn actually employs the same metaphor, in the same way); and there is the appeal to 'an impulse more tender

Still: Morning Glory – *Eva Lovelace (Hepburn) with Joseph Sheridan (Douglas Fairbanks, Jnr).*

and more purely expectant' – to a pathos the experience of which will pre-empt our recognition that the heroine must be defeated.

I shall attempt to explain the historical purchase of this image in the next chapter – the fact of its extraordinary contemporary potency is clear enough. No other star has emerged with greater rapidity or with more ecstatic acclaim. No other star, either, has become so unpopular so quickly for so long a time. Of the eleven Hepburn films between *Little Women* (1933) and *The Philadelphia Story* (1940), only two – *Alice Adams* (1935) and *Stage Door* (1937) – were box-office hits, and these (though the latter is crucially ambiguous) are the most anti-Hepburn of all her 'thirties films.

The significance of this development is that Hepburn's films increasingly demonstrate the fragility and contradictoriness of the popular ideological synthesis initially embodied by her persona. The potent image of mid 'thirties American confidence was provided by Shirley Temple – post-Depression audiences certainly did not want the pathos of defeat, yet without it, how are the latent class and feminist connotations of the image of the American Princess to be negotiated, or even made tolerable? The unfolding of internal incoherence apart, the context which deposited the image and gave it its cultural force simply disintegrated.

Hepburn's career is significant because her films act through a series of strategies, all of them more or less contradictory – all of them, crucially, resisted and disturbed by the very fact of Hepburn's presence – and designed to accommodate a woman's affront to destiny. How are the affront and the destiny to be reconciled? How is the affront to be punished, subdued, contained? The films are the most striking record in the popular cinema of the ideological struggles which these questions entail.

2. Publicity

The history of the Hollywood cinema provides numerous examples of a radical discrepancy between the nature of a star's popular image and the kinds of thing which, in the films themselves, the star actually does: Mandy Merck and her collaborators have documented just such a case in their analysis of the work of Doris Day (*Move Over, Misconceptions*, British Film Institute, 1980). Similarly, James Stewart is, as we all know, an embodiment of homely, middle-American integrity and moral earnestness, whose potency is actually guaranteed by an apparent impotence and disingenuousness (the metaphor is literally enacted in the gun imagery of *Destry Rides Again*): in this conception, his performances, for Anthony Mann and Alfred Hitchcock, as obsessional neurotics and 'action heroes' trembling on the brink of psychosis, simply do not exist. And Garbo's image of relentless doom and gloom had, by 1939, achieved such currency (indeed, the status of myth), that it was possible for MGM to sell her penultimate film, *Ninotchka* (Ernst Lubitsch, 1939), with the slogan 'Garbo Laughs!'

Clearly, it's not a question of the image having no material basis at all – if it didn't correspond to something in the films, it could not be sustained. What concerns us is how and why the selective appropriation which constitutes the current image is effected. The 'why' is easily answered: the image, in these cases, evacuates the ideological tensions embodied in the dramatic persona by suppressing contradictory terms or representing them as something else. Thus, for example, in Stewart's case, 'moral earnestness and integrity' are repeatedly defined by his post-war films as at once the expression and progenitor of an intense repressive violence, barely contained and constantly threatening to erupt. In Frank Capra's *It's a Wonderful Life* (1946), which marked Stewart's return to Hollywood after his war service, the 'two James Stewarts' – pillar of petit-bourgeois, Midwestern domesticity and disintegrating neurotic – form a crucial term in a series of congruent binary oppositions which the film both endorses and irretrievably undermines: the ideal patriarch and beneficent small capitalist is bought at the cost of accumulating desperation which issues, at the end of the film, in the smashing-up of the family home and an attempted suicide that can only be averted by the intervention of a *deus ex machina*. The same estrangement from domesticity is associated, in Stewart's work for Hitchcock, with a destructive investment in fetishistic romantic fantasy (*Vertigo*, 1958) or the acting out, through others, of private emotional frustration (*Rope*, 1948; *Rear Window*, 1954); and in the Mann westerns, the upright quester-hero becomes Captain Ahab, intent, with psychotic deliberation, on the satisfaction of drives which far exceed their ostensible object.

The meaning of the Stewart persona might be said to be: 'if you are the perfect, middle-class, heterosexual American male, you go mad'; though it scarcely needs saying that this is not the meaning of Stewart's popular image, from which the negative corollaries – so rigorously dramatised in the films – of a normative culture hero have been repressed. This significant amnesia was doubtless facilitated by the fact that the persona's 'dark' side emerged comparatively late, at a stage when the familiar image had already been consolidated: while Stewart's early work occasionally anticipates its subsequent trajectory (most fascinatingly, in *Mr Smith Goes to Washington*, Frank Capra, 1939), a radical change of emphasis undoubtedly takes place. It is also relevant to note that the Mann/Hitchcock period is interspersed with films which, while they are indelibly marked by the persona's disturbing new accretions, cast Stewart as emblematic American heroes – *The Glenn Miller Story, Strategic Air Command* (1954 and 1955, both also directed by Mann), Billy Wilder's *The Spirit of St Louis* (1957) – in whom obsessiveness is partially recuperated as noble patriotic enterprise, and the violence engendered by the action hero's *internalisation* of the settling/wandering conflict is softened and contained.

Nevertheless, the simplification of the Stewart persona in popular memory is also directly attributable to the reiteration, in publicity and promotion, of some of its aspects at the expense of others, and the assimilation of the image obtained into the beliefs and convictions of the star-as-person (Stewart's hawkish social patriotism, and his association with the right wing of the Republican party). The fact that the star himself may collaborate in the process only serves to authenticate it.

Thus the persona defined by the films and the image constructed by the vast apparatus of publicity may be more or less out of true; the latter may function so as to mystify the significance of the former, and in Stewart's case the mystification has been accomplished so successfully that the persona has become socially invisible. The dynamic tension of internal contradictions has congealed as a simple unity, which may then be read back on to the persona from which the homogeneous image has been extracted. This operation is germane to one of the fundamental ideological services provided by publicity and promotion – the continual reconstruction of films as commodities to be consumed (as opposed to texts to be read): contradiction is either eliminated, where possible, or inflected in a way that makes one's attitude to and investment in it less problematic.

Nothing is more remarkable in the Hepburn material that I wish to consider, than the *redundancy* with which it enforces the one or two simple motifs that are to govern the star's availability to the reader, and while these motifs may vary, or may fail to negotiate the star satisfactorily, they always effect a reductive 'clarification' of the persona, and always appeal for an explicit affirmation or disavowal of the image they produce. Alternatively, the failure to grasp the star at all may be offered as evidence of the star's 'mysteriousness', in which case his/her availability is defined in terms of 'unavailability' – the classic case, of course, is Garbo, that embodiment of unfathomable enigma, where the mystification of the star (which, again, has its purchase on *partial* properties of the films) appears as her defining characteristic. None of this implies that particular readers or spectators necessarily affiliate to a given star on these terms: precisely because the films themselves are more complex and contradictory, the star may be appropriated for very different purposes, some of which may be ideologically 'unsound' (a possibility dealt with later in the discussion of bisexuality in Chapter Four). The importance of publicity and promotion consists in the fact that they *seek* to define an orientation to the star – not that they succeed.

Hepburn's case is a peculiarly interesting one in this respect, both because her early publicity and promotion give evidence of quite extraordinary confusion about what she is supposed to represent, and about the way in which specific qualities (let alone contradictions) are to be defined, and because she went through a long period of unpopularity during which problematic elements in her persona, which previous publicity had sought to mitigate, suddenly became the focus for explicit animus and condemnation. Both the confusions and the shifts in evaluation are present in the films: the non-filmic material, because it is able to limit contradiction and control response more drastically, is equally cruder and more explicit about their social determinants.

Youthfulness

In an article entitled 'What her Birth Date means to Katharine Hepburn' (*Picturegoer*, 18th November 1933, p.13), the writer named as 'the Editor' begins:

'When Addison wrote:

> The stars shall fade away, the sun himself
> Grow dim with age, and Nature sink in years
> But thou shalt flourish in immortal youth,

he might almost have been prophecying the future of Katharine Hepburn, this epitome of immortal youth who has so swiftly flashed into the film public's orbit.'

In a later article ('Katharine Hepburn Talks About Herself', *Picturegoer*, 7th April 1934, pp.10-11), Gladys Baker also resorts to poetry in order to reach 'a closer understanding of [Hepburn's] complex personality' and 'discover the secret of . . . [the] physical appeal which has actually set a new vogue in Feminine beauty:

> 'For she shall catch the wind's young hands
> And run along the uplands of the sun,
> And down the valley of the Spring. . . '

Poetry, as a component of 'tony' culture, underwrites the distinctive class ethos of Hepburn's image. However, the dominant emphasis in both passages falls not simply on 'youthfulness', but on an essence, a spirit, an 'epitome' of youth. The yearning for a condition beyond the human – the human being associated with death, decay and transience – is a recurrent theme in bourgeois poetry, and these verses embody, albeit in a rhetorically debased and inflated form, preoccupations which find their most complex expression in the odes of Keats: like the nightingale, Youth/Hepburn 'wast not born for death'.

This lyrical tendency – associating Hepburn with a regenerative principle in nature, or elevating her to a 'sublime' which transcends it – is paralleled by an insistence on what Alice L. Tildesley (*Picturegoer*, 15th April 1933, pp.10-11) calls 'that schoolgirl look'. The two images are clearly closely related to one another, but their tone is quite different.

'The graceful gown of pale grey velvet which she had worn in the final scene of *The Lake* had been changed for a nondescript bath robe such as schoolgirls wear among themselves in not too fashionable dormitories, and Katharine Hepburn, the most discussed actress in America, was a madcap, freckle-faced gamin; laughing, chatting slangily, swearing, making faces as she flashed through the

Still: Hepburn as Jo in Little Women.

processes of scrubbing her face and untangling the mop of recalcitrant red hair' (Baker).

Similarly, in Tildesley's article:

'She sat in the other chair of the tiny interview room, her feet tucked up under her, looking like a tall schoolgirl.

'Her sandy hair was tucked carelessly up under a blue-knitted cap. The cap preserved her reputation for funny hats; it had evidently started out to be a skating cap such as children used to wear. . .

'Her eyes are blue and widely spaced, and her face is a mass of freckles, delightful freckles that enhance that schoolgirl look. She seems very young – but not "ga-ga".'

In his book on *Stars* (British Film Institute, 1979), Richard Dyer has drawn attention to the dialectic of 'specialness/ordinariness' so characteristic of the star phenomenon: if the poetry placed Hepburn at an exalted, mythic distance, the intention here, registered in the fascination with physical presence and appearance, is to reinstate her as a striking instance of a normal, recognisable, everyday

human type. Indeed, the extract from the Baker piece explicitly enacts the transformation, and the extraordinary person with connotations of upper-classness ('graceful gown of pale grey velvet') becomes the bright, unaffected all-American girl (from a 'not too fashionable' dormitory) before our very eyes.

A brisk, frank, spontaneous artlessness, in which a hint of eccentricity ('her reputation for funny hats') is counterbalanced by a healthy democratic contempt for airs and graces, is fundamental to the schoolgirl image.

'The manner in which she received the handsome British actor [Colin Clive] whose presence is usually conducive to female heart palpitation was characteristically unselfconscious. "Hey there," she shouted and began scrubbing her teeth vigorously. Her utter lack of affectation, I observed, was another facet of Hepburn's disarming charm' (Baker).

At the same time, 'spontaneity' can be redescribed as at once 'artistic temperament' and 'natural force', and becomes extraordinary again.

'I saw another side of her mercurial temperament, which changed as swiftly as the patterns of light and shadow cast by the glow of the flames' (Baker).

There is a latent contradiction here which, as we shall see, is later brought to the fore by other elements in the Hepburn persona: is her youthfulness romantically 'other', classy and eccentric, or accessible and American?

Tomboyishness

The image of youthfulness is further complicated by its sexual indeterminacy. This is made explicit at the end of the Baker article, which describes Hepburn, 'looking like a small child caught in the jam cupboard,' confessing to her voice teacher that her hoarseness has been caused by the fact that she 'did a lot of yelling with [her] kid brothers' during a recent visit with her family (Baker); but it is implicit as an undertone throughout in the emphasis on a certain kind of rude, robust energy which is neither 'ladylike' nor 'girlish'. The writer actually registers her amazement:

'Her meal was surprisingly substantial – a juicy beefsteak, potatoes, the inevitable spinach, a custard and after-dinner coffee. "Don't look astounded," she laughed, "that" – pointing to the tray – "represents my last act. I burn up energy so fast that if I didn't fortify myself, by 10.30 I'll be hollow, and I'd act hollow, too".'

The persistence of this note renders even the most inoffensively 'feminine' occupations distinctly off-key:

' "Do you mind coming up to my room?" she yelled over the banisters. "I have to put oil in my hair before my shampoo" ' (Baker).

The 'unaffectedness' which dissociates Hepburn's class characteristics from any suspicion of the snooty or stuck-up also provides the condition for a blurring of 'girlishness' into 'boyishness': here, the glamorous mysteries of the star's toilette are equally defeminised and desanctified by being stridently broadcast over the

Photograph: a publicity shot for Sylvia Scarlett.

Still: Laurie (Douglass Montgomery) and Jo in Little Women.

banisters. The 'tomboy' image is crucial to early Hepburn, and its significance will be discussed later. It is sufficient to note for the present, that while Hepburn's appetite is to be found 'astounding', 'boyishness' is offered at this stage as an emanation of unconventional high spirits – an agreeable tension within, rather than a disturbing negation of, 'femininity' – which coincides, moreover, with the projects of democratising the aristocrat and familiarising glamour, all of which will subsequently disintegrate together. The extent to which the tone is positive can be gauged from the fact that Hepburn's failure to succumb to 'female heart palpitation' in the presence of Colin Clive can be used to support the 'utter-lack-of-affectation' motif and not to suggest aberration.

Hepburn's 'tomboy' image is continually correlated with her red-headedness:

'Few stars have had a quicker rise to fame than this red-headed tomboy.'

' . . . this red-haired vivacious tomboy leapt to stardom after her first screen appearance . . .'

These quotes come from two cigarette-card series: Gallaher's 'Portraits of Famous Stars' (no.16, 1935) and Godfrey Phillips's 'Stars of the Screen' (no.15, 1936), respectively. In an article entitled 'The Screen's Real Mystery Woman' (*Picturegoer*, 20th November 1937), 'red-headedness' is clearly almost synonymous with 'difficulty':

'What is the mysterious power which this tall, angular, red-headed woman wields, which forces Hollywood to put up with her gaucheries? . . . Why should red-headed Katie be allowed to be the sole black sheep of the flock without being baa-barred?'

In *The Philadelphia Story*, which is singlemindedly dedicated to chastising the 'gaucheries' and removing 'the mysterious power', the nickname given by Dexter (Cary Grant) to Tracy (Hepburn) is 'Red'. The tempestuous, hot-blooded red-head – like the tomboy (or even, though more problematically, the lesbian) – remains an attractive image of female intransigence so long as it implies an incitement to imperial ambitions whose success is ultimately guaranteed. *The Philadelphia Story* makes the point explicitly:

Dexter: I suppose you'd still be attractive to any man of spirit, though. There's something engaging about it, this virgin goddess business, something more challenging to the male than the more obvious charms.
Tracy: Really ?
Dexter: Oh, yes! We're very vain, you know – 'This citadel can and shall be taken' – and I'm just the boy to do it.

If the citadel withstands the assault, the red-head/tomboy becomes 'the bitch', 'the shrew', 'the castrator', and hot blood turns to ice. The treatment of Maureen O'Hara in a number of Ford movies speaks for itself, since it provides the paradigm of 'the taming of the red-head' and the process by which, in the quotations above, red-headedness changes from a signifier of 'vivacity' into a challenge

Still: Tracy (Hepburn) and Mike (James Stewart) in The Philadelphia Story.

to invasion. Significantly, RKO used a remake of *A Bill of Divorcement* to launch O'Hara's career in 1940 after Hepburn had moved to MGM. As early as *Little Women* (1933), in which the tomboy image is fully consolidated, a crucial stage in the domestication of Jo (Hepburn) is marked, in a fascinating inversion of the Samson myth, by the cutting of her hair.

Glamour/'star-ishness'

' "Exit glamour!" Katharine Hepburn crowed into the mirror of her dressing-table as she went about the business of removing her make-up.'

That is the opening paragraph of Gladys Baker's *Picturegoer* article, halfway through which we find this:

'As we left the stage entrance, crowds of people lined the pavements. They'd been standing for a solid hour in the cold rain of midnight to get a glimpse of her. Courteously they made a lane for her to pass to her car. As she smiled and waved her hand their tired faces lighted with adoration. At least for the moment they were her loyal subjects and the slim young girl their uncrowned Queen of Filmdom.'

She renounces glamour, and yet she is glamorous; she isn't what a star should be, and yet she is a star – in Hepburn's early publicity, the interplay between 'the unique' and 'the ordinary' implicit in stardom is systematically articulated as an explicit ideological project. We can begin to deduce its nature by considering the terms in which so much 'thirties Hepburn material seeks to relate her to Garbo. One review of *A Bill of Divorcement* was headlined: 'Better come back, Garbo – Katharine Hepburn's here!' (earlier in the year, Garbo had departed on a much-publicised holiday to Sweden after the expiry of her contract with MGM); and in a review of *Christopher Strong*, Regina Crewe re-marked: 'She [Hepburn] is a distinct, definite, positive personality – the first since Garbo' (quoted by Dickens, p.44). Alice Tildesley's article in *Picturegoer* begins and ends by insisting on the comparison:

'On the strength of one picture – a picture that was intended to be entirely John Barrymore's – this young stranger is being raised to Garbo's vacated throne. People take sides for and against Katharine Hepburn as violently as they once did for and against the sulky Swede . . . Katharine Hepburn hates to be compared to Greta Garbo. Yet Greta, like Katharine, came to town unheralded and took the country by storm with her first picture; neither girl had the real lead in her film, and neither was expected to score.'

Here, the confidence that Hepburn is like Garbo is so strong that it can actually acknowledge Hepburn's disclaimer. A later *Picturegoer* article, 'Hepburn's Hectic Headline History' by Malcolm Phillips (14th August 1937, pp.12-13), which sum-marises Hepburn's career to date, draws attention to a similar kind of insistence:

'Writers remark on her astuteness as a business woman and point out a further Garbo parallel in her ability to say "I think I go home" . . . [Hepburn] adds . . . that she doesn't think she looks like Garbo and denies that she is "doing a Garbo" in her private life.'

Photograph: a publicity shot for Holiday.

Whatever grounds for the parallel these writers adduce – Hepburn is like Garbo because she is a 'distinct personality'/hates publicity/became a star unexpectedly in her first film or, Hepburn has deposed Garbo – all of them are obsessed with its appropriateness. At the same time, they emphasise qualities in Hepburn which are the very reverse of 'Garboesque': Tildesley's article, as we have seen, is very strong on the 'schoolgirl' image, and even the tactics of Hepburn's

Stills. Above: Louis Easton (Adolphe Menjou) with Eva and Joseph in Morning Glory. *Opposite: Hepburn as Trigger in* Spitfire.

guerilla war with the press are remote from anything implied by the publicity myth of 'I vant to be alone.'

This phenomenon seems to me to have two contradictory significations:

1) Hepburn is constructed as an accessible version of Garbo – a goddess and glamorous movie star who drives in a Rolls Royce and behaves with star-like idiosyncrasy, but who is also the all-American girl, down-to-earth and familiar. This opposition corresponds to the two faces of the 'youthfulness' image, and from this perspective Hepburn's ideological function is to mediate the romantic 'other' and 'American-ness'. Thus *'la divine'* is remoulded as the everyday, the myth of the androgyne as the myth of the red-headed tomboy, self-realisation through romantic passion as fresh-faced modern confidence. The posture, tone and composition of many early Hepburn glamour photographs (half or full profile, head thrown slightly back with a 'lyrical' expression of wistful yearning; the look beyond the frame suggesting idealism or aspiration: connotations both of frailty and resilience) seek to marry the Hepburn ethos of 'immortal youth' and a photographic strategy which clearly derives from publicity stills of Garbo, while interviews, fanzine material and central motifs in some films (*Morning Glory, Little Women*) locate this 'sublime 'in an American present or a privileged mythic image of its past (Louisa May Alcott's New England). Hence the suggestion that Hepburn has succeeded Garbo. Garbo's popularity at the box office plummeted in 1932/33, never recovering its earlier level, and the use of Hepburn

to revise the 'Garboesque' might be compared with Selznick's attempt, in 1939, to offer Ingrid Bergman as a homely, domesticated version of Garbo's remote Scandinavian exoticism, Bergman's first Hollywood film, *Intermezzo* (Gregory Ratoff, 1939), coinciding with MGM's final attempt to solve the problem now presented by Garbo's persona by casting her in comedy.

2) Conversely, the parallel-in-contrast between Garbo and Hepburn appears as an impulse to recuperate Hepburn by assimilating her to available social images which the persona in fact resists. For the films themselves soon make it clear not only that it is extremely difficult to represent Hepburn as 'all-American', but also that the translation of Garbo's romantic self-assertion and ambiguous gender identity into a contemporary presence raises more critical problems than it solves. In other words, a) the project defined in 1) can work only if other elements in the Hepburn persona are contained, and b) the project itself generates contradictions which destabilise it. Of Hepburn's thirteen movies prior to *Bringing Up Baby* (which marks the crucial transition to comedy), only five are set in modern America: of these, two – *Alice Adams* and *Stage Door* – are distinguished by explicit animus against her; a third (*Spitfire*) defines her as a social outcast; and a fourth (*Morning Glory*) channels her self-assertion into

the comparative ideological safety of the theatrical profession. Alistair Cooke, in an article in *The Listener* (7th April 1937), comments adversely on a tendency to 'Garboize' Hepburn:

'But it seems a pity that so sharp and sensitive a person as Katharine Hepburn should have to bear the brunt of being a star . . . "Come, come" – she hears the voice of the studio executives calling to her – "come, you may be Katie to your pals, but you're La Hepburn to us." And so . . . she must wear a long gown and throw back her head at an angle of ninety degrees and let us see tears that come from depths that Shakespeare never knew.'

Cooke's article clearly embodies the familiar discomfort of the urbane middle-brow when confronted by 'Hollywood'; but this comment, taken in conjunction with the tensions induced by casting Hepburn in an American setting, indicate something of the fragility of the 'Garbo project'.

Beauty

' . . . Hepburn manages all these moods with ease, as ferocious in riding-breeches as she is attractive in her flowing white dress in the swimming-pool sequence' (Peter Cowie, 'Katharine Hepburn', *Films and Filming*, vol.9, no.9, June 1963).

If Hepburn is used to reconcile the glamorous and the ordinary, she is also employed to redefine the beautiful:

' "Gosh, I look awful, don't I?" The reflection in the mirror showed a wrinkling of *retroussé* nose with its indiscriminate sprinkling of freckles.

'Yes, judged by traditional standards I saw in that much-publicised face none of the obviously beautiful features which move poets to immortalise the object of their inspiration.

' "You weren't at all pretty as a little girl," I commented. She threw back her head and roared.

' "Pretty! And you don't suppose anyone thinks I'm pretty now! It was because the make-up man who fixed me up for my first screen-test tried to make me pretty that I was delayed in getting to Hollywood. He tried his best to transform me into the candy-box type – you know, rosebud mouth; shy, drooping eyelids; round, dimpled cheeks. Ye Gods! I was ludicrous. The RKO artist had the good sense to accentuate what he saw in my face that gave me individuality. Unless we're to look like we're rolled out of a stamp machine, the face has to retain the natural lines and contours that are put there by our ancestry, our thoughts, our emotional reactions and just by living. Otherwise it's not interesting."

'Yes, that was part of the answer. The face was interesting without being beautiful. But I sought further to discover the secret of Katharine Hepburn's physical appeal which has actually set a new vogue in feminine beauty' (Baker).

There is a radical contradiction here between Hepburn's own assessment of a face in terms of its 'individuality' – its expressiveness of the person – and the writer's model of beauty as that which is desired (and objectified) by men:

Still: Cynthia (Hepburn) and Strong (Colin Clive) in Christopher Strong.

Still: Sydney Fairfield (Hepburn) with her mother, Margaret (Billie Burke), in A Bill of Divorcement.

Hepburn's remarks both denigrate this model, and define it as a social convention, perpetuated by the cinema, which she rejects. It is this contradiction which produces the writer's evident difficulty in assessing what Hepburn says, and it is significant that the exploration of 'the secret' should proceed at once to poetry – that very paradigm of the male construction and possession of the woman's image from which, at the beginning of the passage, Hepburn's face has been said to deviate.

It is possible, therefore, to read the passage in two different ways. Inasmuch as it does not explicitly contradict Hepburn's position, it can be seen to appropriate it, in line with the 'glamour' argument, to produce the meaning: 'you, too, can be attractive, even if you have freckles and a *retroussé* nose'. At the same time, Baker feels the need to make Hepburn correspond to the violated model, and the lines of poetry which, she tells us, 'flashed through [her] mind,' allow her to assert that while Hepburn's isn't the kind of face which inspires poets, nevertheless a poet *has* been inspired by it. Crucially, both these meanings seek to repress, or recuperate, what Hepburn actually says, and to insist that the satisfaction of the male gaze is indeed the criterion by which a woman's face should be judged.

While Baker is able, here, to effect a neat ideological compromise – 'the ordinary can be beautiful' (Hepburn as democratic schoolgirl), but also 'she is traditionally beautiful anyway' (Hepburn as star/muse) – Hepburn's incorporation in a concept of beauty as 'what is socially considered desirable by men' is only achieved at the cost of much strain: and it is hardly surprising that the extent to which, at any point, Hepburn is considered 'beautiful' is correlated with shifting attitudes to the values she embodies.

Early reviewers seek to emphasise both 'beauty' and 'oddness':

'She fascinates by her strange beauty and inescapable magnetism, by her verve, her harshness and her tenderness . . . '

'That troubled, mask-like face, the high, strident, raucous, rasping voice, the straight, broad-shouldered boyish figure – perhaps they may all grate upon you, but they compel attention and they fascinate an audience.'

'Miss Hepburn is thorough and believable, and sometimes fascinatingly beautiful . . . '

'A slim, gaunt-featured nymph, this actress, with her sharp, pleasantly unpleasant voice, and a penchant for the bizarre in outfits.'

'Miss Hepburn, gauntly handsome and spirited . . . ' (Quotations from HomerDickens, *The Films of Katharine Hepburn*, pp.43-44, 60).

The insistence of the vocabulary is unmistakable: the fascination is reluctant, capture is offset by resistance, and this interplay of attraction and disturbance is focused on Hepburn's unsatisfactoriness as a *feminine* object.

Garbo, once more, provides the requisite comparison, her physical presence – the heavy, angular stride, concave chest and 'prizefighter shoulders' (the phrase is Anne Sharpley's) – being, in many ways, equally troubling. The function of the Garbo close-up is not to rectify, but to contain these anomalies by constructing 'the face' – our first glimpse of which, in the films, is itself repeatedly dramatised – as an object of ecstatic contemplation. At one point in *Queen Christina* (Rouben Mamoulian, 1933), Christina (Garbo) goes to the window of her room, gazes out over the landscape (which we never see), and remarks – 'The snow is like a white sea. One could go out and get lost in it, and forget the world and oneself.' The accompanying close-up seeks to make the spectator's experience of Garbo's face the analogue of Christina's experience of the landscape: it appeals for rapt immersion and intoxicated self-surrender before an object which is at once a real face and an absolute, and the appeal is reinforced by Garbo's incomparable delivery of the line, which transforms it into something between a mystic incantation and a lullaby. While I would certainly argue that other elements in Garbo's acting style – for instance, her irony – contest such strategies, thus imparting to her performances their remarkable internal tension, there can be no question of the nature of the strategies themselves, the significance of which is given in the course of the lovers' conversation in the inn sequence of *Queen Christina*:

Antonio: There's a mystery in you.
Christina: Is there not in every human being?

The close-up's removal of all possible obstacles to the appropriation of the woman's mysterious face as object becomes a medium through which we commune with our own profound mysteriousness.

I have already argued that one of the ideological functions of the early Hepburn is to familiarise the Garboesque; and while this function, in order to work, requires the preservation of certain 'Garbo' signs – as in the 'glamour' stills – there is a latent contradiction between the Garbo close-up, which constructs enigma, and the Hepburn persona. That use of the close-up is, by definition, not easily available here. This, together with the fact that Hepburn, as she herself points out, is in no sense 'pretty', generates the reluctant fascination with Hepburn's face noted by so many reviewers. It isn't 'candy-box', and the very strategy of making glamour ordinary and American pre-empts its construction as 'mysterious'. It diverges from the two available norms of beauty, and thus appears odd. The physical strangeness ('non-femininity'), which, in Garbo, the face recoups, re-emerges in Hepburn's face as a disturbing impediment to complete possession of the image.

We have observed, in Gladys Baker's article, the conflict between Hepburn's assertion that a woman's appearance should be an expression of herself and the writer's feeling – which is, of course, the social norm – that a woman's appearance is for men. While the discussion is about types of physical beauty, this can never be separated, where women are concerned, from the way in which they dress. Male beauty is by no means dependent on being 'well-turned-out' – the sexual promise of the 'stud' image is actually enhanced, we all know, by a certain sartorial inelegance, and too scrupulous an attention to dress in men is widely regarded, significantly, as a symptom of 'effeminacy'. A woman's beauty, on the contrary, is always a relationship between an approved physical type and fashions in *couture*. (Obviously, I am disregarding nudes and pornographic images in both cases.) If the contradiction in Baker's article was partially recuperated by the glamour project, the note of irritation and resentment which emerges with increasing regularity in Hepburn's 'thirties publicity proceeds from the fact that everything implied by, and validated as, 'Exit glamour!' can be affirmed only up to a certain point – the point at which the woman's appearance ceases to be 'for men' at all. Thereafter, all the submerged sexual and class anxieties about Hepburn are released. They are already implicit in Baker's article:

'I observed the exquisite Tanagra-like figure wrapped in a beautifully-tailored grey suit. "Oh, I'm glad you like it!", she exclaimed when I expressed my admiration. "I can't bear poring over clothes, so if this is becoming, I'll probably wear it morning, noon and night."

'She has been criticised for going about Hollywood in overalls and slacks. Her designer, Howard Greer, trailed her all the way across the continent to design for her the three costumes she wears in *The Lake*. He bemoans the fact of her indifference to clothes, but admits that once a costume is finished, she transfigures whatever she is wearing.'

Again, the difficulty is contained: the indifference to clothes is deplorable, but at least she *will* wear them and can present herself to the observing gaze, in

Photograph: Hepburn as Jo in Little Women.

certain circumstances, as 'exquisite'. Subsequently, the indifference is defined either as exhibitionism or as an affront to 'femininity'. Malcolm Phillips's résumé of 'Hepburn's Hectic Headline History' notes, for January 1933:

'Hepburn returns to Hollywood and sets out to startle the rustics. Eccentricities of the new star become the talk of the town. Arrives at studio one day in luxury car and wearing patched dungarees. Later seen driving in battered truck and wearing expensive fur coat over dungarees.'

This suggests very nicely how mediating the glamorous and the ordinary can quickly become scandalous. A later *Picturegoer* article ('Moonshine About Katie' by W.H. Mooring, 9th July 1949, p.11) takes a similar line:

'She aims to be different, look different, so that reaction to the one star among the many will also be different.
    'That slack suit paid for itself several times over – for Katharine Hepburn got special mention in hundreds of different publications.
    'If she'd worn a dress her name would merely have been listed among the fifty-five other top stars who sat down at three long tables facing the Press of the World.
    'Without disrespect to Miss Hepburn, she is an actress, and an actress, like an elephant, never forgets.'

The tone of Romano Tozzi's article on Hepburn (*Films in Review*, vol.8, no.10, December 1957, p.484) is less glibly knowing than hysterical:

'She allowed herself to be photographed without make-up in all her freckles, and, even worse, dressed hideously in mannish garb – sloppy slacks, sweaters, and men's trousers and suits.'

It is assumed that Hepburn is *simply* drawing attention to herself, and that drawing attention to oneself is *simply* bad. The real trouble, of course, is that she is creating herself as the wrong kind of spectacle: had she 'got special mention in hundreds of different publications' by virtue of an extraordinarily striking gown, no problem would have arisen. Individuality has become deviance, and the writers rationalise their offended sense of propriety as Hepburn's self-indulgence. The possibility that drawing attention to certain things about oneself – that one is gay, or, in Hepburn's case, her refusal of the expectation that women should radiate 'attractiveness' – might be a *political* gesture cannot be countenanced. The quote from Tozzi illustrates the intimate connection between Hepburn's being found not 'beautiful', her transgression of 'femininity' and her failure to dress appropriately.

The post-'thirties Hepburn films adopt two lines on her physical appearance: they are mutually contradictory, though they address similar ideological problems in the persona, and they succeed one another chronologically. The first may be exemplified in the remonstration of Tracy Lord (Hepburn) by her father (John Halliday) in *The Philadelphia Story*:

'You have a good mind, a pretty face and a disciplined body that does what you tell it . . . In fact, you have everything it takes to make a lovely woman except the one essential – an understanding heart. Without it you might just as well be made of bronze.'

Still: Lucy (Marjorie Main) and Ann (Hepburn) in Undercurrent.

The Philadelphia Story is quite obsessed, on the one hand, with Tracy's 'loveliness' ('You're the golden girl, Tracy!'), and, on the other, with her impenetrability – she is 'a perennial spinster', a 'Married Maiden', a 'Virgin goddess'. Such beauty and such intransigence are incompatible with each other, the latter, without removing the allure of the former, turning it into a threat, and the narrative is therefore devoted to making the beauty accessible to male control. The film's curious, but representative, misogyny consists in the fact that it demands that women be lovely while bitterly resenting their loveliness because it commands male desire – the impulse to punish Tracy is the corollary of the impulse to exalt her, and the film oscillates, with neurotic intensity, between the two, continually demanding recompense for the deification on which it has itself insisted.

Conversely, Hepburn's 'spinster' roles assert – or, characteristically, require the Hepburn character to assert – that she is plain, dowdy and unattractive, and that no man could possibly give her a second glance, before allowing her to discover, through a man, that she can be attractive after all. While *The Philadelphia Story* seeks to vanquish a too-militant beauty whose confidence precisely isn't contingent on male approval, the 'spinster' films insist that the confidence really masks a gnawing sense of being undesirable, and chart the development towards true confidence through a man's recognition. This motif long precedes the inauguration of the 'spinster' cycle proper with *The African Queen* (1951): as early as *Spitfire* (1934), Hepburn's fifth film, we find Trigger (Hepburn) replying to the proposition by Stafford (Robert Young) that 'one look at you's enough to drive a man crazy' with 'I guess I'm going to have to pray for your eyesight', and at the beginning of *Undercurrent* (1946), Ann (Hepburn) responds to the request by Lucy (Marjorie Main) that she 'do something to herself' before meeting Garroway (Robert Taylor) by affirming her unattractiveness, reiterating the claim later to her father (Edmund Gwenn) – 'You're my father, you love me – I probably look fine to you.' Such moments are ritual features of the 'fifties films, and recur sporadically thereafter – consider, for example, the moment in *The Lion in Winter* when Eleanor (Hepburn) gazes into a mirror and cries, in a tone compounded of irony and despair, 'My, what a lovely girl! How *could* her king have left her?'

In *Spitfire* and *Undercurrent*, the norm of attractiveness involved, and the character's internalisation of it, are critically placed in ways which illuminate the projects of later Hepburn films that lack such a critical dimension: in both cases, the man's finding – or constructing, Pygmalion-like – the woman's beauty is associated with an attempt to gain power over her, and the woman's anxiety about her appearance is associated with a transgression of female roles to which the films are extensively (if with inevitable ambiguity) sympathetic. In both cases, the man in question is discredited, and the norm of 'attractiveness' both parodied and located as an oppressive social convention. While the determinants of this critical tendency are very different in the two films – in *Spitfire*, it is produced by enacting the 'revision of the Garboesque' described above, in *Undercurrent* by the thematic concerns of a radically subversive artist (Vincente Minnelli) – each foregrounds the essential preoccupations of the 'spinster' films, in which the contradiction noted at the outset in Baker's article is settled decisively in the writer's favour.

'A woman discovers herself in the male gaze' – that is the message of these films, embodied in *The Rainmaker* in a peculiarly excruciating form in a scene between Lizzie (Hepburn) and Starbuck (Burt Lancaster):

Starbuck: (*letting down Lizzie's hair*) Now, say – 'I'm pretty.'
Lizzie: No, I can't.
Starbuck: Say it! Mean it!
Lizzie: I'm pretty. (*Starbuck kisses her*) Why did you do that?
Starbuck: Because when you said you were pretty, it was true. Look in my eyes – what do you see?
Lizzie: I can't believe what I see! Is it me? – is it *really* me?

We aren't of course to believe that Lizzie really *is* pretty: the film's point is that she becomes pretty when seen as such by a man, and in becoming pretty for him becomes also the authentic self which she never knew existed. Moreover she must imagine herself in a man's eyes for the rest of her days ('I'll try to remember everything you ever said'), or the self will be lost again. A woman's person, and her confident possession of it, are perpetually at the service of her objectification.

If, as I shall argue in more detail later, the 'spinster' films are readable only as a form of ideological revenge – 'the feminist of her early films has become a spinster eager for love', as Tozzi (p.481) puts it – their central motif (Hepburn is plain) can take effect only because the 'fifties mammary fetish, as a norm of beauty – and therefore, necessarily, an expression of value – is as inimical to Hepburn as any norm could be. The strains and contradictions of relating her to Garbo were extreme enough – but to Marilyn Monroe! This norm explains the emphasis, in Hepburn's 'fifties films, on her thinness. Even the oblique

34

Still: Stafford (Robert Young) and Trigger in Spitfire.

compliment from Mike (Spencer Tracy) in *Pat and Mike* ('There may not be much meat on her, but what's there is choice') is expressed in terms of an absence; in *The African Queen*, Rose is a 'crazy, psalm-singing, skinny old maid'; and, in an extraordinary moment in *The Rainmaker*, Lizzie, deploring her lack of femininity ('Can a woman take lessons in being a woman?'), stuffs a cushion into her bodice, adopts a 'little-girl' voice, and mimics a 'fifties dumb blonde. The tone of these things is peculiar and, inasmuch as two of them might seem to be pro-Hepburn, may be misleading. The attitude to women's bodies implicit in the norm also informs the assessment of Hepburn's divergence from it, and manifests itself either as a rather unpleasant kind of knowingness ('Kate' is skinny) or as a parody in which femininity has been reduced to 'tits-and-ass' on the one hand and 'the old maid' on the other, the reduction leaving behind it nothing but the uncertainty as to whether a woman's sexual provocativeness manifests her sexuality more or less threateningly than unsatisfied

Still: Starbuck (Burt Lancaster) and Lizzie (Hepburn) in The Rainmaker.

spinsterish yearning. *The Rainmaker* does not wish to argue that a woman can't take lessons in being a woman, but only that she must never take them from other women; and for a proponent of the thesis that a woman learns about her beauty from men, Monroe and Hepburn can only appear as two intolerable forms of self-celebration. Conceived in the spirit of placing and debasing both of them, the Hepburn parody of Monroe appears as one of those emblematic moments of male nervousness in which different myths of women collide, exposing both their mythic status and the fears imperfectly contained by them. The 'fifties categories of 'Monroe' (bulging with plenitude for the use of men) and 'Hepburn' (spinster withering for the lack of men), astonishingly juxtaposed, cease for a moment to be containers for female desire and become alarming assertions of it.

Nevertheless, it is clear that one is more watertight than the other:

'Probably no other woman star has had so many unflattering adjectives thrown at her by producers, directors and critics as Katharine Hepburn. Marilyn Monroe exasperated her backers and her directors, but at least she had sex appeal with capital letters . . . Hepburn has had to rely solely on her powers of acting and intelligence (she is a Doctor of Psychology) to win an audience's sympathy, for her physical attributes are minute compared with a Loren or a Garbo. With her russet hair, her mouth and prominent teeth, her equine cheekbones, and her poker-straight figure, she inspires a feeling of irritation, and occasional revulsion, in the spectator' (Peter Cowie, 'Katharine Hepburn', *Films and Filming*).

Probably no other woman star makes it so clear that judgements about a woman's physical appearance are statements of value of quite another kind: unlike Monroe's or Garbo's, Hepburn's face has always resisted the successive historical terms of the construction of beauty as a commodity, and definitions of her as, alternately, beautiful (*The Philadelphia Story*) or plain (*The Rainmaker*), have always functioned as part of a strategy of subordination.

Moreover, if Monroe's death and Garbo's retirement have frozen their beauty in a moment of unalloyed perfection, Hepburn's undecorated public ageing has offered a final affront to woman's duty to seduce the eye. Garbo's retirement *means* the withholding of 'the face', just as those incorrigible attempts to photograph it before it disappears in a flurry of raised hands and hat-brims demand its availability, though now on different terms, as if the exaltation of the star's legendary beauty provoked a resentful impulse to expose its 'decay'. A woman *must* be beautiful, but she must also be punished for the superiority which her beauty is deemed to create. Hepburn has refused either to hide or 'to do something about herself' and this in itself has become mythic, as Hepburn herself points out in a splendid moment in an interview with David Lewin in the *Daily Mail* (20th May 1968):

'Now that I am Saint Katharine, it is fashionable to say that I am a beauty with a well-proportioned face. But when I was beginning they thought I was a freak with all those freckles. It never really bothered me all that much, because I thought the stuff I had to work with wasn't all that bad, and painters seemed to like it.'

Having pre-empted the possibility of humiliation by keeping her face, unlifted, before the camera, Hepburn can now be found beautiful again, and few more recent articles neglect the obligatory rhapsody to 'the incredible face with its copy-righted angles' (*New York*, 16th February 1976, p.35). But it is also true that since the revival of the Women's Movement, it has been possible to acknowledge and affirm the *politics* of Hepburn's appearance for the first time. Citing Hepburn as '*McCall's* first Woman of the Year', the editors are able to assert that Hepburn's beauty consists precisely in the fact that she is a woman 'without creams or formulas, a woman un-made-up' (*McCalls*, February 1970, p.57).

'Eccentricity'/privacy

In a 1981 issue of the *Daily Mirror*, the following was served up beneath the rubric 'They jog to be alone':

'Eccentric actress Katharine Hepburn, who has a habit of taking her own picnics to restaurants to save money, has started jogging at 71, despite suffering from both arthritis and Parkinson's Disease.

'She is a firm believer in keeping fit, along with her even dottier friend, Greta Garbo, 76, and the two have recently been out running together – not in the nearby Central Park, but in the countryside miles from their New York homes.

'To protect their privacy from the swarms of fans they are certain would dog their footsteps, the former Hollywood greats hire separate cars, then meet at upstate Newburgh – where they huff and puff for a few hundred yards once or twice a week.'

The curious paradox of this nasty little piece is that while it is only on offer to the readers of the *Daily Mirror,* because it is about Katharine Hepburn and Greta Garbo the writer can scarcely contain his resentment of the fact that they are still 'news' in any other context than an obituary notice. Not only are they not dead – they are not even decently incapacitated; and what is worse – the cardinal media sin – they 'protect their privacy', even in circumstances (stories in the *Daily Mirror* notwithstanding) where it is no longer necessary to do so. They do the kind of thing which the readers of the *Daily Mirror* do not do (even without incapacitating diseases) and they do them *in private.*

There are two forms of 'eccentricity' – the striking embodiment of a category which is itself 'eccentric', and 'inappropriate behaviour'. The first type, which confirms a pre-existing social value-judgement, is not necessarily threatening: Quentin Crisp, for example, is an 'eccentric' in this sense. He is odd not because he does not conform, but because he *does* – to an odd convention which he recreates. The second type of 'eccentric' behaves oddly for the type that he or she is, or for the norms of a situation. If we go to a restaurant, we consent to pay through the nose, if we are old ladies with Parkinson's Disease, we do not go jogging in upstate Newburgh; if we are 'former Hollywood greats', we die, or at least give interviews. This type will become threatening in proportion to the seriousness and substance both of the norm and of their challenge to it.

In the early days, Hepburn's 'eccentricities' were successfully accommodated to the 'ordinary'/'extraordinary' dialectic of stardom: she has a 'reputation for funny hats', but she also has 'that schoolgirl look'. Later, however, this ideological equilibrium breaks down, along with all the others:

'Interviewers complain of rudeness of new star, who meanwhile has added a monkey and trick of sitting down in the middle of studio streets to read her fan mail to her repertoire of off-screen pranks. Creates further sensation by grabbing waiter's apron and taking other stellar diners' orders in Radio lunchroom' (entry for May 1933 in 'Hepburn's Hectic Headline History').

This represents a mixture of the two types of 'eccentricity'. It is, on the one hand, how we expect spoiled, smart-ass, upper-class girls to behave – it confirms a negative value-judgement: it is not, on the other, how we expect stars to behave (in the 1930s, anyway). The interview has always been one of the principal guarantors of the star's ordinariness and availability, and thus a mechanism for controlling resentment of their special status: through the interview, the star becomes just an ordinary person talking to the reader as anyone else would do, *and* gives the reader access to their extraordinary lives. The intimacy of the relation mediates the star's otherness: both the mode of address and, as Richard Dyer has suggested, the fact that some aspects of the 'private life' may appear as a paradigm of the reader's experience or aspirations, serve to bind star and audience together. Without the interview, the star will tend to appear simply as special, and possessed, it may be assumed, of a snobbish, superior consciousness of *being* special.

Given Hepburn's 'upper-classness', this interpretation of her hostility to the press has always been readily available: indeed, it is worked into the fabric of *The Philadelphia Story* (which was written expressly for her), where Tracy's insistence on her privacy is one of the symptoms of aristocracy which needs to be democratised:

'Who the hell do they think they are, barging in on peaceful people – watching every little mannerism – jotting down notes on how we sit, and stand, and talk, and eat and move . . . And all in that horrible, snide corkscrew English . . . '

The animus which this attitude has generated can be illustrated from an article, framed as an open letter, called 'The Customer Wants to Know You: Don't be Too Hard-To-Get, Miss Hepburn' by Moore Raymond (*Sunday Dispatch*, 7th February 1954).

'I don't suggest that you put a notice on your door saying: "Interviews granted; 24-hour service". I don't want you to address a mass meeting of your fans in Trafalgar Square.

'But I should very much like you to give me 15 or 20 minutes of your time whenever you come to Britain . . . May I remind you, Miss Hepburn, that there is a certain – well, I shan't use as strong a word as "duty" – so let's say that there's a certain obligation required of people whose fame and fortune have been made by the public.

'And that, of course, is the obligation to satisfy at least some of their natural curiosity about the offscreen or off-stage life of a star.'

Whereas Hepburn's 'success' was once attributed to her 'genius' and her (representative) 'flaming individualism', it is now attributed to 'the public'. Her refusal to give interviews has revealed the contradiction latent in the nature of star status, and one could have no clearer indication of the role of the interview in reconciling the conspicuous evidence of social privilege with 'democratic' feeling.

The ascription of 'eccentricity' to Hepburn, and to Garbo (whose association in the *Daily Mirror* piece has a logic beyond that of their being friends who go jogging together), arises from an encounter between this concern for privacy and other kinds of behaviour which are both 'un-star-like', 'un-woman-like' and, more generally, idiosyncratic. The categories, of course, overlap: thus Hepburn's restaurant picnics and spartan regime ('I'm a believer in ice baths'), and Garbo's virtually unfurnished apartment, are both 'weird' in themselves and aberrant in relation to the idea of a star (the fact that an affluent and extravagant lifestyle is widely felt, without animus, to be *de rigeur* for stardom suggests the importance of the myth of success in the star phenomenon). Similarly, a *Picturegoer* article, written in celebration of Hepburn's 'mellowing' during the filming of *The Philadelphia Story* ('The Return of a Rebel', 31st August 1940), interrelates her attitude to the press, anti-democracy ('Can this be the star who for six years almost literally thumbed her nose at Press and public?'), lack of 'femininity' (the caption of an accompanying photograph deplores 'the Hepburn of the old

Still: Hepburn with Giulietta Masina, Edith Evans and Margaret Leighton in The Madwoman of Chaillot.

days, sprawled in an inelegant attitude and wearing slacks') and an exhibitionism ('the *enfant terrible* act') which, 'as in so many cases', can be referred to 'an inferiority complex'. The article corresponds point for point to the film itself, which duly administers the punishment for which the article appeals ('one long[ed] to apply a corrective to that portion of her anatomy on which she was wont to seat herself conspicuously in the studio streets to read her mail'). The connection between the article's pleasure in Hepburn's at last behaving like a star (cooperating with the publicity department, giving interviews) *and* like a woman is implied at the outset:

'When it was learned that a Katharine Hepburn, refreshed and reinforced for the fray by the prestige of one of the greatest stage triumphs achieved by an American actress in recent years, had returned [to Hollywood] on her own terms . . . grievously wounded local sob sisters started laying in a supply of armour-plated panties, and mere male members of the profession just dived down the nearest manholes.'

It is also no doubt true, in Garbo's case as in Hepburn's, that the link between 'privacy' and 'eccentricity' has been reinforced by a further link between their 'independent' images, the withholding of their private lives and the fact that they are women living alone (which is, of course, eccentric in itself). The MGM publicity department's desperate attempts to build up 'romances' for Garbo in the 'thirties, to mitigate the 'I vant to be alone' image which it had previously nourished with an equivalent of the early Garbo's much-publicised affair with John Gilbert; the press's insatiable attempts, in 1932-33, to find out whether or not Hepburn was married, then 'to link her name with those of the eligible Hollywood bachelors' (*Picturegoer*, 14th August 1937), and latterly to get the 'inside story' on her relationship with Spencer Tracy – these things indicate the need to construct the female star's publicity in relation to a man, and avoidance of the press (Garbo), or more or less aggressive hostility to it (Hepburn), not only impede this project but combine with the stars' images to generate another one. It is obviously significant in this context that many of Hepburn's recent film roles have presented her either as a devouring mother or a batty old lady living either on her own or, in *The Madwoman of Chaillot*, in the eccentric company of other batty old ladies. The 'eccentric' is a readily available category for an ageing woman who is not defined by the company of men, especially if she has her own 'idea of a great routine' which includes icebaths, 'go[ing] to bed about 7, then get[ting] up at 4a.m.' and 'lots of exercise' (Rex Reed).

Apropos of 'eccentricity', it is interesting to note that Hepburn remarks, in the same interview, that she and Greta Garbo don't go jogging in Central Park anymore 'because there are so many *nuts* on the streets, they knock you down and never look back'.

Class and upbringing

For the present purpose, two aspects of Hepburn's background are crucially significant – her class origins, and her parents' active involvement in suffragist and Fabian politics.

Hepburn's mother, Katharine Houghton, was a member of an aristocratic Boston family – one of her cousins was the American Ambassador to the Court of St James – and was educated at Bryn Mawr and Radcliffe. She was a friend of Emmeline Pankhurst, Emma Goldman and Charlotte Perkins Gilman, took part in the suffragist picket of the White House during the Wilson presidency, and campaigned for contraception rights: Hepburn has recalled, in interviews, taking part in suffragist demonstrations with her mother, and distributing feminist literature outside factories and in the streets. Her father, Dr Thomas Norval Hepburn, was head urologist at Hartford Hospital in Connecticut, and a distinguished and controversial representative of the feminist/libertarian current within a notoriously reactionary medical profession. He was particularly involved in campaigns to disseminate knowledge of, and combat the stigma attached to, venereal disease, and co-founded the Connecticut Social Hygiene Association. He became a friend of George Bernard Shaw after distributing, through the Association, a translation by Shaw's wife of a Eugène Brieux play about syphilis, and both he and Katharine Houghton were leading American Fabians and proponents of a feminist gynaecology.

One should add here, perhaps, that Hepburn was later an outspoken opponent of Senator Joseph McCarthy. In May 1947, she made a speech at the Gilmore stadium, before an audience of 28,000, on behalf of the presidential candidate Henry Wallace, who had been refused permission to use the Hollywood Bowl for a campaign address. Wallace was the founder of a short-lived Progressive Party which denounced both Republicans and Democrats as warmongers, opposed the increasingly virulent anticommunism of the Truman administration, and campaigned for the revival of the war-time alliance with the Soviet Union. The Progressive Party represented the last stand of left liberalism in America for well over a decade, and with its collapse Wallace himself became a supporter of Eisenhower in the 'fifties.

Hepburn's speech was noted by the House UnAmerican Activities Committee, and Dickens suggests that it accounts for the period of unemployment after *Song of Love*, released in the autumn of 1947 (Dickens, p.20): indeed, she was only cast in her next film, Frank Capra's extraordinary *State of the Union* (which is more or less explicitly about the necessary corruption of the American presidency) at the last minute, at Spencer Tracy's suggestion, after Claudette Colbert had withdrawn from the project. During the filming, Hepburn issued a further public statement attacking HUAC in the name of freedom of speech and artistic expression, and Capra notes in his autobiography *(The Name Above the Title*, Macmillan, New York, 1971) that filming was continually troubled by friction between Hepburn and Adolphe Menjou, an extreme right-wing Republican and McCarthyist. Capra quotes Menjou as saying 'Scratch a do-gooder like Hepburn and she'll yell *Pravda!*'

Clearly enough, these involvements – quite apart from the films themselves – constitute an impressive political record. Nothing about her background invites celebration as 'all-American', but Hepburn's early publicity strives gallantly to negotiate it. Thus, for example, in discussing, in his analysis of 'What her Birth Date means to Katharine Hepburn', the way in which Hepburn's 'temper and temperament' caused her to be fired from parts in *Death Takes a Holiday* and *The Big Pond* on the stage, the editor of *Picturegoer* writes:

'If Katharine Hepburn had had to worry about where the next meal was coming from, she might have remained in these plays longer, but she had been brought up to tell the truth and not to mince words. It sickened her not to say what she thought.'

Similarly, in Gladys Baker's article:

'She spoke then of her family. Her own people are very dear to her, and she is notoriously loyal. Every Sunday during her stay in the East, she journeys up to Hartford to be with them, and if ever she is ill, heads straight for "Daddy" – one of the best physicians in Connecticut. Both parents are blessed with superior wisdom, for they permitted their children to be the individuals they were destined to be.'

While the tone of the first passage is *potentially* hostile, both writers wish, on the one hand, to present Hepburn's background in positive terms, and, on the other, to make it seem as little unlike the reader's as possible. The significance of privilege here is that it is conducive to honesty and the free development of individuality, and the status these qualities are to have for us is implied by the tacit reference to Washington: like the first President, Hepburn could not tell a lie, and suffered for it. If Hepburn's parents are in any way 'superior', it is only by virtue of representing the ideal norm of American parenthood – all democratic parents should be like this. It follows that what makes Hepburn extraordinary also constitutes her ideal typicality: the fact that she is privileged has allowed her to become that archetype of American individuality which presupposes the abolition of privilege.

The argument is fraught with difficulty, in that it might tend dangerously to suggest that one can only become an individual if one has the material wherewithal. Various rhetorical devices are invoked to subdue this potential meaning.

1) Fundamentally, there is the ideological potency of the concept of 'individuality' itself, interacting here with the 'specialness/ordinariness' dyad of the star phenomenon. While the individual, in bourgeois language, is irreducibly unique, everyone is an individual. Thus while Hepburn's background figures as what is 'special' about her, and as a determinant of her 'special' individuality, this individuality is in fact an emblematic representation of the 'individualness' common to us all. The fact that Hepburn is an extraordinary individual means that we are (or are 'destined to be') extraordinary, too: her remarkable difference signifies *ours*. At this level, Hepburn is being used to underwrite the category of 'the individual'.

2) The writers balance the social and economic privileges of Hepburn's background against the proposition that both it and its effects on her can be defined in terms of certain moral and spiritual qualities which are by no means contingent on privilege: on the contrary, one can aspire to and identify with them. This project is strikingly apparent in the very form of the first article – an analysis of Hepburn's character as a paradigm of her birth sign, which both redescribes the social determinants of her extraordinariness as innate, existential properties and provides a further link between the special star and our ordinary/remarkable selves.

'She was born on November 9, 1909, and her solar symbol is Scorpio . . . According to general astrological principles, she should be strongly individual, very uncompromising, critical and judicial in a clear, decisive fashion and possessed of much dramatic ability. Perseverance and determination towards higher attainments should also be well in evidence. She will be full of her own personality and will dispute with superiors.'

For those of us not fortunate enough to be Scorpios, 'the amazing Picturegoer Wheel of Fortune', ('absolutely FREE' in next week's issue), will allow us, too, to 'plan with the planets, shape [our] own destiny, and become master of [our] own fate.'

This kind of language suggests at once the particular historical pertinence of the writer's project: at the height of the Depression, Hepburn is constructed as the embodiment and guarantee of the reality and efficacy of individual self-assertion. In the early films (from *A Bill of Divorcement* to *Morning Glory*), as I shall argue later, she becomes an emblem of its pathos: individual self-assertion is real and possible, but it is 'tragically' doomed. The later films continually demonstrate that its defeat actually provides the sole condition on which Hepburn's assertiveness can be affirmed at all.

3) Baker's article reinforces the bond between Hepburn and the reader through an emphasis on family feeling: 'Daddy' may be 'one of the best physicians in

Stills. Above: as Phoebe Throssel in Quality Street, *with Fay Bainter as Susan Throssel. Opposite: as Alice in* Alice Adams, *with Fred MacMurray as Arthur.*

Connecticut', but Baker stresses the 'family-ness' of the family rather than its 'class-ness', and suppresses any hint of its feminist/liberal affiliations. Later in the article, the same ethos of 'family' is used to soften the class connotations of the mistress/servant relationship when the interview moves from Hepburn's dressing-room to her house in New York.

The recuperation of class in these early articles may also be taken to imply the irrelevance or supersession of class and class conflict – an implication whose significance, in the midst of the most radical crisis in the history of capitalism, hardly needs elaboration. The insistence on Hepburn's embodiment of the category 'individual' signifies the transcendence of the category 'class': her function, as at once daughter of the privileged upper classes and democratic schoolgirl, is to enact the disappearance of class.

The point is massively substantiated by the early films, which can be divided into two groups having in common the casting of Hepburn as a woman whose individualism puts her at odds with the values and aspirations of herclass. What distinguishes the two groups, and at the same time demonstrates the crucial interrelation between class and sexual transgression, is their endings.

In one group, which includes *Little Women, The Little Minister, Alice Adams, Sylvia Scarlett, A Woman Rebels, Quality Street* and *Holiday*, there is a happy ending in which class transgression is resolved by locating Hepburn in the petit bourgeoisie, and sexual transgression by having her marry.

45

Still: Alice and Arthur with Alice's parents (Ann Shoemaker and Fred Stone) and Malina (Hattie McDaniel) in Alice Adams.

It is, perhaps, effectively tautological to adduce the 'happy ending' as a separate fact, for this denouement, endemic in bourgeois fiction, is what the 'happy ending' means. The work of Charles Dickens and D.W. Griffith exemplifies its function in melodrama: consider, for example, Griffith's *Orphans of the Storm*. The opening titles inform us that feudal tyranny and the 'excesses' of Jacobinism (the latter explicitly identified – the film was made in 1921 – with those of Bolshevism) are inverted mirror-images of each other: complementary manifestations of 'intolerance'. Each is associated with a series of evil, repressive father figures (De Vaudrey père, De Praille, Louis XVI on the one hand, Robespierre on the other), who embody a sexual threat to the heroines, and each precipitates an eruption of monstrous, destructive sexual energy (De Praille's revels, the Jacobin bacchanal after the fall of the Bastille). Between them stands the good father, Danton, identified by the film with Lincoln and Franklin, who, at a crucial moment in the narrative, checks his desire for one of the heroines, and presides, at the end, over the containment of sexuality and the resolution of class conflict: the two heroines are married to the good aristocrat and the good proletarian respectively, their 'goodness' consisting in the fact that they have previously broken with their class and with the grotesque, oppressive and sexually 'disordered' family which embodies it.

The rectitude of Griffith's ending is not undisturbed: the film's emotional intensity has been generated by the relationship between the heroines, and the double wedding appears, at one level, as a means of legitimising the celebration of *their* reunion (in the final shot, astonishingly, they kiss – each other rather than their husbands). Nevertheless, the dominant ideological impulse is clear: the film sets out to construct a set of relationships in which the effects of class and sexuality, insistently correlated as agents of disruption, have been mitigated. Just as marriage does not appear as erotic, the petit bourgeoisie does not appear as a class, for sexuality and class are precisely the disorder which has been reduced to coherence.

While we are dealing with a narrative itinerary which recurs in any number of bourgeois fictions, what is remarkable in Hepburn's case is the attempt to dramatise it at a historical moment in which class struggle had been profoundly exacerbated, through a star figure. *The Little Minister* (1934) sets out this function of the persona with remarkable clarity and explicitness by casting Hepburn as a 'double' – Babbie is the ward of a Scottish laird who periodically disguises herself as a gypsy and involves herself in the struggle of the weavers of a village on her guardian's estate against the Glasgow capitalists who are exploiting their labour. The first forty minutes – surely one of the most extraordinary opening movements in the classical American cinema – aligns Babbie against the norms of the petit-bourgeois community, embodied in its new minister, Gavin Dyshart (John Beal). She is introduced as a voice-off, 'desecrating the Sabbath Day' by singing, immediately after Dyshart's first sermon – an outpouring of hellfire rhetoric about original sin and the scriptural promise of redemption in the course of which Dyshart has arraigned, and successfully quelled, another disruptive and dissident voice, that of the village drunkard ('Sit here on the stair and attend to me, or I'll run you out of the house of God!'). Enraged, Dyshart goes in search of the singer and, finding her in the woods near the church, accuses her of crimes against not only religion, but also property ('Don't you know it's unlawful for an Egyptian to be in these parts?'). Babbie does not reply, continues to sing, and runs off, unbeknownst to Dyshart, while he is absorbed in reading to her a notice forbidding trespass which has been nailed to one of the trees.

The introduction, then, cogently defines the nature and function of Dyshart's religion as a repressive ideological discipline which acts in support of bourgeois property relations, and just before Babbie's appearance, Dyshart's concern to re-establish the sanctity of the house of God has been paralleled by his response to the news that local weavers are beginning to turn against the city manufacturers ('And no one has been punished?'). His second encounter with Babbie both refines these themes and elaborates on the significance of Babbie's relation to them. The discussion of the growing class conflict in the village draws up the class lines:

Dyshart: I'm against fighting.
Babbie: Even when they're in the right?
Dyshart: Fighting and bloodshed won't help them.

Dyshart's Christian pacifism, like his regulation of 'sin', transposes the defence of the status quo into the language of moral absolutism. Babbie responds by tricking Dyshart into giving the signal (a series of calls on a hunting horn) which will announce the beginning of a proletarian uprising in the village. Pretending that the real purpose of the signal is to advise her father of her whereabouts, she effects Dyshart's complicity by becoming fragile and tremulous and appealing to his superior masculine potency ('It takes a strong man to blow a lusty blast.' 'I *am* a strong man!').

The scene is played as a variation on Eve's temptation of Adam, and inter-links Babbie's allegiance to the proletariat with her use of her sexuality to capture and displace the patriarch: the real import of the gesture which Dyshart is only too ready to understand as an assertion of his virility is given for us, with beautifully understated wit, in Babbie's appropriation of his walking stick as he applies both hands to the hunting horn. The sexual/political contest is played out again in the scene immediately following, in which Dyshart and Babbie address the crowd of armed workers in the town, where Dyshart's attempt to maintain 'law and order' through an appeal to Christian/patriarchal ideology ('This abandoned woman is inciting you to riot! . . . The truth is not in this wicked woman!') is challenged and overcome by Babbie's to class solidarity ('If you keep together, you can force your way into the country'). The revolutionary outbreak which follows is thus defined as feminist as well as proletarian: it is mobilised and led by a woman, and implies the rejection of ideological disciplines which have at once a class and a patriarchal (indeed, misogynist) character.

Throughout the rebellion and its aftermath (it is successfully contained by troops summoned by Babbie's guardian), the film emphasises Dyshart's helpless

Still: Babbie (Hepburn), Gavin Dyshart (John Beal) and the hunting horn in The Little Minister.

subservience to Babbie. Despite himself, he responds instantaneously to Babbie's command ('Hit him!') to throw a stone at a mounted policeman, and then finds himself acquiescing in her masquerade as his wife when she is escaping from the victorious British army – a masquerade in which she also adopts the colours of the bourgeois lady bountiful ('I thought I might be able to help these unfortunate people, but I can do so little – sadly little'). Thematically, this part of the film is strikingly analogous to *Bringing Up Baby* – the Hepburn character's assertion of her identity is accompanied by the disintegration of the hero's, whose professional integrity, class allegiances, gender role and control of narrative functions all give way together. This fracturing of the hero's coherence is all the more striking for the fact that Babbie's identity (and Susan's in Hawks's film) is both stable *and* polymorphous: both Babbie and Susan catalyse contradictions in the male which entail his fragmentation, but appear themselves as a unity which is expressed through, rather than undermined by, a bewildering succession of permanently renewable, apparently contradictory, incarnations.

The rest of *The Little Minister* is singlemindedly concerned with recuperation (the fact, of course, which distinguishes it from *Bringing Up Baby)*. The *politics* of Babbie's masquerade are progressively redefined as an expression of the 'natural', irrepressible spontaneity which, as an aristocratic lady, she must deny, but which can find an outlet, as the gypsy, in anarchic lawlessness: she later refers to herself, in a letter to Dyshart, as 'that irresponsible, light-hearted gypsy'. Babbie's first appearance, emerging as if magically from the forest into which, a moment later, she will disappear, already intimates the potential availability of the 'nature sprite' motif which we have noted in Hepburn's publicity, and subsequently the film makes full use of it, as in Babbie's appeal for Dyshart's forgiveness ('You don't blame the birds when their songs come for a moment between you and your work; you smile, and forgive them. Let it be that way with me'). The feminist-proletarian revolutionary is transmuted into an artless child of nature whose merry woodnotes wild have disturbed male concentration.

This attempt to reassess the status of Babbie's agency in the first third of the film is accompanied, and partially contradicted, by another line of argument which is in itself incoherent, and which is first announced in Babbie's extraordinary outburst, with interpellations by Dyshart, during one of their rendezvous in the forest.

Babbie: If I were a man I'd choose to be everything I'm not and nothing I am! I would scorn to be a liar – I would try to fight the world honestly. But I'm only a woman, so – well, that's the kind of man I'd like to marry!

Dyshart: A minister can do all these things!

Babbie: The man I love must not spend his days in idleness like the men I know do. He must be brave – a leader of men. He must take the side of the weak against the strong even when the strong are in the right. He must be a man with a mind of his own, and once he's made it up, he must stand by it in defiance of –

Dyshart: His congregation!

Babbie: The world! He must understand me –

Dyshart: I do!

Babbie: – and compel me to do his bidding, even thrash me –
Dyshart: – if you don't listen to reason.
Babbie: He must rule me and be my master!
Dyshart: Your lord and master! Babbie – *I* am that man!

Part of the function of this exchange, clearly enough, is to continue the re-construction of the significance of Babbie's actions, and to deny their positive connotations. Thus, on the one hand, her previous allegiance to the working class because 'they're in the right' becomes an innocuous commitment to 'the weak' even when they're in the wrong; and on the other, she has been driven to her transgression in the first place because of the weakness and effeminacy of upper-class men. A radical political intervention by a woman degenerates into a vague, depoliticised 'heroic individualism' which is itself attributable to her lack of a man with the requisite virtues. The nature of Babbie's rejection of the patriarchal ruling class is obscured and mystified, and the film is now ready to assert that the ruling class and the proletariat represent equally undesirable alter-natives for Babbie, in that the one (construed as male 'effeteness') has imposed on her the 'unnatural' sexual/class identity embodied by the other. Whereas in the first third of the film Babbie was dramatised as a woman who commits herself to the class oppressed by her own and in so doing affronts the ideologies (sexual, racial, religious) which support that class, she now appears as a woman who has been placed in the unfortunate position of having to adopt, aberrantly, a 'male' role. Dyshart's '*I* am that man' is presented quite without irony, and seeks, as far as intention goes, to neutralise the ironic charge generated by '*I am* a strong man' earlier in the narrative. Marriage to the petit-bourgeois male rectifies Babbie's sexual transgression and, since the petit bourgeoisie figures not as a class (let alone as a class which supports the ruling class) but as the location of amorphous moral absolutes, removes her – and us – from the unhealthy atmos-phere of class struggle.

While this seems to account for the film's intention, two facts count heavily against it. The first is a simple question of narrative data: Babbie has very ob-viously been the kind of person which she is required to say, here, she *cannot* be because she is a woman. The film may wish to assert that it doesn't want a woman to be like that, but it is unable to disguise the incoherence involved in denying its possibility. The second is a matter of realisation – the almost hysterical intensity with which Hepburn delivers the lines has the curious effect of transforming them into a passionate protest against the restrictions which compel women to act out their aspirations through men. Hepburn's acting foregrounds that first contradiction between what the dialogue asserts and the narrative-role which Babbie has actually played, and makes the scene less a celebration of, than an assertive expression of resentment at, the man she describes.

If class and sexual themes are so closely correlated in these films, it is because the Hepburn character's class transgression is also invariably a rejection of the father (or, as in *The Little Minister,* his surrogate); and it follows, equally, that the resolution of the class theme is inseparable from a satisfactory Oedipal transaction whereby 'father' is replaced by a husband who inherits his function. One might say that the films have an awareness of the imbrication of class and patriarchy which is at once intense and vague. The hegemony of the bourgeoisie

Still: Babbie and Dyshart in The Little Minister.

at the end of *Orphans of the Storm* also means the reconstitution of the monogamous patriarchal couple, but the hegemony of other classes is defined in terms of the negation of patriarchal sexuality – bad fathers, rampant libido, inversion of gender. The film knows, in other words, what the sexual/class ideal is, but its knowledge of it is not historical, and divergences from it are necessarily construed in an absolute and negative way as forms of pathology. *The Little Minister* recognises the logic of making the proletarian revolution feminist and antipatriarchal, and is able, in the first forty minutes, to give it a positive weight radically unlike anything in Griffith's film by adopting what is in effect the mode of Hawksian comedy. It must settle finally, nevertheless, for the reformist solution – the petit bourgeoisie ameliorates the bad features of the aristocracy through identical institutions. While from Babbie's point of view this means that marriage to an aristocrat is *not* acceptable, but marriage to a middle-class clergyman *is*, the film is never able to recover from the extremity of its own narrative premise, nor from the dislocation of Babbie's character which the denouement requires.

In the 'thirties films in which the class, and the father, rejected by the Hepburn character are aristocratic or haut-bourgeois (*The Little Minister, A Woman Rebels, Stage Door, Holiday*), the rebellion is unambiguously endorsed: the patriarch, and the class values he embodies, are discredited and (in all but *Stage Door*, a special case which will be considered later) reconstructed by the happy ending.

In *Little Women* and *Alice Adams*, the matter is complicated by the fact that Jo and Alice are chafing against the petit bourgeoisie itself (I shall leave aside for the moment the lesbian theme which links *Little Women* to *Stage Door* and makes of Jo's challenge to social expectations of a woman of her class so much more than a demand for professional autonomy). Cukor's film seeks both to honour Jo's aspirations while also concluding, at the cost of much strain, that they can be focused and realised through marriage to a man who shares them, the function of Professor Bhaer (Paul Lukas) being to contain Jo within the American petit bourgeoisie while appearing to propose – as a sensitive, intellectual European – an alternative to it. In *Alice Adams*, on the contrary, the film's response to Alice's dissatisfaction with middle-class middle America is to parody Hepburn as a monster of arch, pretentious conceit whose demands both corrupt male integrity and affront a populist vision, unproblematically affirmed, of the 'democratic' status quo. This development, precipitated by locating Hepburn in a contemporary, petit-bourgeois American community, coincides with the striking change of emphasis in her late 'thirties publicity which I will examine in a moment.

In a second group of 'thirties movies including *A Bill of Divorcement*, *Christopher Strong*, *Morning Glory* and *Mary of Scotland*, transgression issues in a 'tragic' ending: *Christopher Strong* and *Mary of Scotland* are the only films in which the Hepburn character dies, and the latter is the last film until *Summertime*, nearly twenty years later, without a 'happy' ending. Three of the four seem, as far as class is concerned, to present no problem: in all but *Morning Glory*, the Hepburn character violates the norms and mores of the British ruling class and is destroyed by it, the films reworking, as melodramas of defeat, the theme of the rejection of the aristocracy or big bourgeoisie characteristic *of* the previous group. In *Morning Glory*, as in *Little Women* and *Alice Adams*, the Hepburn figure aspires beyond the petit bourgeoisie ('They're so bourgeois in Franklin'), and while the film's attempt to construct Hepburn as an icon of the pathos of American 'innocence' leads it to treat Eva's naive self-confidence with indulgent affection rather than subject it, as in *Alice Adams*, to virulent lampoon, its ending bleakly anticipates the inevitability of her defeat and decline.

The fact that three of the four works in this group are also Hepburn's first three films is clearly suggestive: in that they are primarily concerned with the social impediments to individual self-realisation, they also make its efficacy problematic. Two of them – *A Bill of Divorcement* and *Christopher Strong* – are set in England, and the persistency of the strategy, in Hepburn's 'thirties work, of locating her in British settings can be read as a means of dramatising the class/feminist nature of her rebellion whilst also safely distancing it and the conditions which necessitate it or conduce to its failure. We may postulate, however, a more general change of direction after *Morning Glory* whereby Hepburn is to be used as a figure of containment rather than of tragedy or pathos. *Spitfire*, Hepburn's fifth film, represents a curious middle term, in that its ending seeks to counterbalance its own rigorous narrative logic – Trigger (Hepburn) can be accommodated neither to men nor to the American community – by suggesting that the accommodation will take place in the future. The fact that *Spitfire* is quite unable to dramatise this resolution tacitly rehearses the difficulties of the later films which attempt to do so.

I have argued, then, that Hepburn's early publicity seeks both to soften her class background so as to make it simply what is 'special' about her, and to appropriate it in such a way that she appears as an embodiment of classless individualism. I have also argued that in many of the 'thirties films, a representative melodramatic structure comes into play so that class conflict appears as a contest between individualism and a discredited class which is signalled as 'un-American' (usually the aristocracy or big bourgeoisie; in *Spitfire*, the 'backward' peasant community), a contest resolved either in bourgeois domesticity or in a defeat which further discredits the oppressing class. While *Little Women* seeks to affirm that individualism can actually be fulfilled within the class/patriarchal institutions against which it struggled, the film also bears the mark (in the gratuitousness of Professor Bhaer's introduction) of the difficulty of coping with the sexual/class transgression in which 'individualism' manifests itself on any other terms than those of tragic defeat. The problem appears again in *Spitfire's* attempt to forecast the 'happy ending' it cannot represent. The meaning of the problem is set out in the dialogue from *The Little Minister* analysed above. The marriage of 'upper-classness' to 'democratic schoolgirl' to produce 'democratic individualism' at once creates three problems:

i) it places enormous obstacles in the path of an ideologically satisfactory relationship to a man;

ii) it will tend, if the familiar, everyday, democratic component is stressed, to precipitate a conflict between the individualism of the Hepburn figure and the American petit bourgeoisie;

iii) conversely, if the stress falls on 'upper-classness', the ideologically *negative* connotations of aristocracy will reappear.

The inherent instability of the ideological mix in the early Hepburn persona can be gauged by juxtaposing, on the one hand, *Morning Glory* and *Alice Adams* or *Stage Door,* and on the other the 1932/33 *Picturegoer* articles with a piece entitled 'Should this Rebel have been Tamed?' in the issue for 27th March 1937. Mark Vyse's homily, described by the editor as 'provocative', must be quoted at some length:

'Once, at a tea party at Hartford, Connecticut, a small girl with wide mouth and red curls helped herself to cake from a visitor's plate. The child came of a well-to-do American family. She was neither told to leave the room nor later called [sic] over the coals.

'Similarly, if at a gathering of distinguished friends this little lady thought fit to interrupt the conversation, she was unrebuked for doing so. Moreover, should she choose to play truant from school for a day, nothing – at least, at home – was said.

'This anecdote of child upbringing belongs to a time most of us remember. How vividly it illustrates the "new" type of education that came into vogue a few years before the war! Pioneer days, these, of active revolt against the stern parental discipline of the Victorians.

' "Away with inhibitions and repressions", was the cry of mothers and fathers suffering from too strict control in childhood, and afraid to see their offspring suffer in the same way.

'In the nursery, and to a great extent in the schoolroom, were to be as few commands as possible to "do this" and "do that". There were to be no more "Don'ts" and "I forbid you's"; no more rigid hours for study and meals, no more forced attendances at church.

'Instead, children were everywhere encouraged to think for themselves, to act for themselves, to express themselves. All of which theories were to have a terrific bearing on seven-year-old, thin, lithe, impressionable, eager Katharine, who was afterwards to become Katharine Hepburn, film star.

'Mrs Hepburn, wife of a go-ahead surgeon, was, before the war, a keen suffragette and a member of the Women's Peace Party. She believed that children were never naughty. Therefore, if they tore their clothes and books and were rude to their elders, no correction was needed. Above all, there was to be no spanking.

'Now, Mrs Hepburn was undeniably a clever woman, and clever women are apt to push ideas to extremes. But what have we more ordinary, and perhaps more commonsense, mortals to say of Katharine's upbringing. Was it justified?'

All the strategies of the earlier *Picturegoer* articles have been completely reversed.

1) The 'ordinary/extraordinary' dialectic has broken down, and the star's absolute extraordinariness is held up for judgement by the 'more ordinary, and perhaps more commonsense, mortals' who constitute the readership. The article assumes from the start that there is only a difference between the values embodied by the star and the values prized by the reader, and that the former affront the latter.

2) Rather than emphasising the 'family-ness' of Hepburn's family, the writer insists on its 'classness' ('a well-to-do American family'), and instead of applauding the 'superior wisdom' of parents who promote the development of natural individuality, he chastises, in the disciplinarian mode, the eccentricity of highbrow, trendy liberals who spoil their children. Both terms of this reversal – the suppression of class in some cases, an appeal to class envy and resentment in others – are classical features of petit-bourgeois journalism.

3) Whereas the earlier articles withheld the political affiliations of Hepburn's parents, they are offered here as a symptom of the 'otherness' and unsatisfactoriness of her upbringing which is more or less continuous with its 'class-ness': *they* have 'theories', *we* have 'commonsense'. While Dr Hepburn is described as a 'go-ahead surgeon', a particular animus is reserved for Katharine Houghton's feminism, and the article clearly implies that if Hepburn has gone wrong, it is because she was brought up by 'a clever woman'. A suffragist commitment means allowing your children to be 'rude to their elders'; feminism and bad manners are alike the progeny of a crazy over-reaction to (patriarchal) Victorian disciplines which Mr Vyse concludes, had better be reinstated as soon as possible:

'Of all others, Katharine Hepburn surely realises that discipline comes more easily for being inculcated early; that the kindergarten stage is not too soon for a child to learn consideration for others, and that self-expression, if unrestricted, can become a nuisance and a bore'.

While it is never explicitly formulated, the fact that the aberrations of Hepburn's education are attributed to a woman's, typically, 'pushing ideas to extremes', combined with the fact that the writer is a man, encourages us to feel that discipline really means 'amenability to men', and that it is 'inculcated' by the father. It is interesting to note, in this connection, that later in the article the writer applauds Hepburn's performances as characters who are 'something of a tomboy', but laments the absence of the 'touch of sweetness [which] would be permissible, even welcome' in her playing of love scenes.

4) Individuality has become arrogance and conceit:

'In each case [of Hepburn being fired] self-will was the cause. "I can't play it that way because I don't feel it that way. I don't want to do it the accepted way," this child of the individualistic upbringing would cry. Small wonder that harassed authorities turned to someone more amenable.'

The transition from 'individuality' to 'self-will' is determined by the inadequacy of the former as a sound container for the class and sexual contradictions originally assigned to it. Individuality has become the petulant intransigence of an upper-class girl who needs a good spanking, and analogously Vyse does not appeal, like Baker, to the reader as immaculate selfhood, but to the member of a vast and uniform consensus who is 'like' everyone else. Hepburn, in fact, has acted through a drastic ideological contradiction within the bourgeois concept of 'individuality' itself: for while bourgeois rhetoric privileges 'being oneself', it also identifies this, as Marx and Engels point out in *The German Ideology,* with 'being bourgeois' and thus inscribes the conditions under which individuality becomes aberration – namely, when it embodies a class or group interest which is *not* bourgeois. If Hepburn's individuality was affirmed in 1933, this was because it was constructed as an exemplar of the real potency of self-determination, or employed as a means of asserting the ideal value of self-determination while extracting pathos from its tragedy in social circumstances where the possibility of actually living it was not at a premium. If, in *Alice Adams*, which precedes Vyse's article by two years, the individuality of Alice (Hepburn) is registered as outrageous, it is because the inevitable breakdown of that tightrope ideological balance has produced individuality as the expression of an *oppositional* interest, and the film, like the article, seeks to place it by defining it as upper-class pretentiousness. It is not that Alice's ambitions are radical in themselves (on the contrary), but that the film's allegiance to petit-bourgeois free enterprise for men only endows them with a subversiveness all the more apparent for the ridicule heaped upon them.

Alice Adams is important not because it is typical, but because it is an extreme case of one available strategy for dealing with Hepburn (*The Philadelphia Story* also employs it): the redescription of implicitly political demands as aristocratic arrogance or pretentiousness. Some late 'thirties cartoons of Hepburn, the parody of her in Walt Disney's cartoon *Mother Goose Goes Hollywood* (1938) and the way in which the part of Terry in the Edna Ferber/George S. Kaufman play *Stage Door* is rewritten for her all demonstrate the strategy's dominance during this period, just as the tone of some reviews indicates the presence of a market for it:

'The part of a spoiled playgirl [in *Bringing Up Baby*] is perfectly suited to Miss Hepburn's talents . . . ' (*New York Herald Tribune*).

Still: Susan Vance (Hepburn), Constable Slocum (Walter Catlett) and Dr Lehmann (Fritz Feld) in Bringing Up Baby.

The crucial function of this motif in estranging Hepburn's feminism, so that it is assimilated to 'un-American' class values which have to be 'democratised', scarcely requires commentary.

Acting

'They make a great deal out of acting, but I've never found it that complicated. Spencer used to say, when they get too high and mighty about actors, remember who killed Lincoln' (Hepburn, interviewed in the New York *Daily News*, 28th January 1979).

In a review of *The Philadelphia Story*, the film critic of *The Christian Science Monitor* wonders whether one is to 'regard Miss Hepburn as an important actress or just a glamorous lady with a harshly musical voice'. What constitutes an 'important' actor, and how are we to assess the alleged alternative?

An 'important' actor is an actor who plays 'important' parts, and if Hepburn's reputation as an actress now probably stands higher than that of any other Hollywood star, it is almost certainly for the wrong reasons. With very few exceptions (Laurence Olivier, Charles Laughton, Alec Guinness, Ralph Richardson), the most prestigious actors of the British and American stage have appeared in movies only sporadically, and in some cases hardly at all: many of them, indeed, are on record as saying that they don't take film acting at all seriously, regarding it either as a diversion or a peculiarly lucrative form of prostitution, and have usually graced a film set in the kind of production designed for what used to be called 'the carriage trade', as signifiers of kudos. This division of labour has been particularly striking in the case of female actors, for reasons which are no doubt complex. Given that female stars have always had to correspond to, or rearticulate, dominant social norms of beauty and desirability, it may well be that women who wished to be defined in terms of their skills resisted the cinema on principle, or, conversely, on sexist grounds, were resisted by it.

However this may be, it does not alter the ideological terms of the relationship between theatre and movies. 'Real' acting is stage acting, and consists in subordinating oneself to the part. In film acting, on the contrary, the part is subordinated to the personnel. At its most vulgar, in the false-nose-and-funny-walk theory of 'great acting', acting becomes virtually synonymous with the adoption of disguise: Laurence Olivier provides the paradigm of the actor's art because he plays 'important' parts and never looks or sounds the same twice. Cary Grant, however, 'is' (charmingly or not, according to taste) Cary Grant.

This distinction depends on two complementary errors: the conflation, in the case of the star/personality, of the persona and the person; and the repression, in that of the 'actor', of any concept of persona at all. Performance becomes, on the one hand, a display of personal mannerisms and idiosyncrasies – and, on the other, metamorphosis: it doesn't take much to 'be' Cary Grant (provided, naturally, that one *is* Cary Grant), but massive powers are necessary in order to 'become' Othello. The actor/personality opposition is clearly vacuous – Olivier's performances are as distinctively Olivier's as Grant's are Grant's – but it introduces, with associated value judgements, two forms of naturalism: the conventions and ideologies governing performance disappear, and it becomes extremely difficult to assess performance because an automatic criterion of what performance and excellence *in* performance are has been presupposed. As always, naturalism naturalises a preference as much as a technique.

The cultural cachet of theatre in Hollywood has always been enormous, as the Academy's abject deference to Olivier on every possible occasion continually demonstrated, and Hepburn's current status as an actress is very much determined by the fact that she has sustained a long career as a star while authenticating herself as a performer in the classics. During the 'fifties, she appeared in seven Shakespeare plays, four of them produced by the American Shakespeare Festival Theatre in Stratford, Connecticut, and in Shaw's *The Millionairess,* and since 1959 her film and television work has consisted largely of prestige adaptations of plays by more or less illustrious dramatists – Tennessee Williams (*Suddenly, Last Summer* and *The Glass Menagerie*), Eugene O'Neill (*Long Day's Journey into Night*), Jean Giraudoux *(The Madwoman of Chaillot)*, Edward Albee *(A Delicate Balance)*. In 1971, she played Hecuba in Michael Cacoyannis's film of

Still: as Amanda Wingfield in The Glass Menagerie.

The Trojan Women, one of the rare screen versions of Greek tragedy. Her fellow actors in these films, moreover, have included many reputable theatre names – Ralph Richardson in *Long Day's Journey into Night,* Edith Evans and Margaret Leighton in *The Madwoman of Chaillot,* Vanessa Redgrave and Patrick Magee in *The Trojan Women,* Paul Scofield in *A Delicate Balance* – even Lord Olivier himself in *Love Among the Ruins.* These credentials are almost sufficient to constitute greatness in themselves, by osmosis.

The excellence of Hepburn's work in these films is not particularly in question: the point to be made is that this kind of work is easily recognised as 'acting', and as a gauge of acting skill, by spectators who would regard the suggestion that Robert Mitchum, say, is a fine actor (or an actor at all) as cultural bolshevism. The reviewer of *The Christian Science Monitor* would no longer hesitate before deciding that Hepburn was an 'important actress', and elevating her, safely, to the pantheon.

The point is significant not simply as an index of bourgeois snobbery, for to define an actor's importance in *this* way, in an antithesis of which the other term is 'just a glamorous lady', is obviously damagingly to confine our sense of importance. In fact, the assessment of Hepburn's acting ability has always been closely interwoven with judgements about the values she embodies in such a way as to suggest that the acting of glamorous ladies can be felt to be important too.

In 'thirties articles and reviews, apologists for Hepburn's greatness repeatedly assess it in terms of 'genius'. For Regina Crewe in *The New York American,* Hepburn's performance in *Spitfire* is 'a thing of pristine beauty, lyric tenderness, fired with the flame of genius', and Sydney Carroll, in *The Times,* declares, of

Break of *Hearts*, that 'if further proof were needed of Miss Hepburn's genius, here it is' (quoted by Dickens, pp.57, 65). An Ardath cigarette card from 1933 refers to 'this red-haired, tempestuous genius', and even a *Picturegoer* article that is extremely critical of her acting insists that she 'has undoubted talent, perhaps a spark of genius' (27th March 1937, p.28). The ascription of genius is a familiar feature in the celebration of that kind of star actress designated by the French as '*la divine*' – see, for example, the genteel and polite conversation about Sarah Bernhardt described by Tolstoy in 'The Death of Ivan Ilich'. In the twentieth century, '*la divine*', who draws her sustenance from a long tradition of Romantic representations of women culminating in the throbbing intensities of Algernon Swinburne ('Under the Arch of Life' is exemplary), moves from the stage (Bernhardt, Eleanora Duse), to the cinema: Garbo is her supreme embodiment. '*La divine*' is a male muse, and it is not accidental that a passionate relation of 'creature' and 'creator' is inscribed in the legend of many of her avatars (Duse and Gabriele D'Annunzio, Garbo and Mauritz Stiller, Marlene Dietrich and Josef von Sternberg). The nature of the rapport between '*la divine*' and the male spectator is beautifully caught in Kenneth Tynan's famous valedictory to Garbo:

'What, when drunk, one sees in other women, one sees in Garbo sober. She is woman apprehended with all the pulsating clarity of one of Aldous Huxley's

Still: as Constance in Break of Hearts, *with Charles Boyer as Franz.*

mescalin jags. Tranced by the ecstasy of existing, she gives to each onlooker what he needs' (*Curtains!*,Longmans, 1961).

'*La divine*' is also, it will be seen, Keats's nightingale, and given the characteristic sexual ambiguity of the type, one may risk the hypothesis that she induces a similar state. For if anything is remarkable about the subject/object relation in the 'Ode to a Nightingale' or 'To a Skylark', it is the way in which it subserves the male poet's recovery of polymorphous sexuality: the object of inspiration is interpolated, through the apostrophic mode, as object, but the subject's relation to it (dramatised in both poems in extraordinary images of abandonment and penetration) is also passive and receptive. Romantic 'feeling', we may suggest, is not simply a philosophical/epistemological form – an attempt undermined by its subjectivism, to overcome through the proposition 'I feel' the Cartesian dualism of self and object – but also an erotic state in which it is possible to transcend another set of object relations – those predicated by the Oedipus complex. Possessed by inspiration, the male poet recovers the pre-Oedipal state in which his relation to the mother was both active and passive, and achieves an ecstatic renunciation of gender. Shelley's 'blithe spirit', Swinburne's 'Lady Beauty' and Lesbia Brandon, and '*la divine*' are all bearers of this function, and part of Garbo's enormous significance consists in the fact that she represents the last popular articulation of this current in Romanticism.

Hepburn's early publicity, as we have seen, seeks to place her precisely in this tradition: 'genius' is the corollary of 'immortal youth'.

'*Morning Glory* proves most triumphant Hepburn performance to date . . . 149,854 people pay over £20,000 in one week to see film at Radio City Music Hall. Fervent publicity department compares her with Ellen Terry, Duse and Bernhardt' (entry for September 1933, 'Hepburn's Hectic Headline History').

As a concept, 'artistic genius' separates skill and intelligence from their enabling social conditions (Shakespeare, F.R. Leavis points out, did not invent the language he employed) and redefines them as a mystical natural property – an esoteric power with which the artist is magically endowed. In the present context, 'genius' both reinforces Hepburn's 'extraordinariness' and interlocks with the definition of her as the 'genius', in the older sense of 'presiding spirit', of nature which is so strong in Baker's article, in *Spitfire,* and in the opening scenes of *The Little Minister.*

'Watching [Hepburn] you forget the story, its cheap emotionalism and shallow psychology. Her freshness is unimpaired. Her vitality glows . . . She is impulsive and flame-like.'

Though three years separate this review by Sydney Carroll from Baker's article, the language is more or less identical. Hepburn-as-genius is the presence, as muse, of an androgynous nature-sprite. Baker's article, fascinatingly, not only comments on the 'naturalness' of Hepburn's acting, but also insists on its 'greatness' in the face of Hepburn's disclaimers:

' "Do you actually shed tears?"

' "Heavens, yes! You see, I'm not really a good actress – a good actress can control her emotions – but not me. I bawl to beat the band when I'm really touched by a part I'm playing, and the trouble is I can't play the part unless I am touched by it! I've got to feel whatever I'm doing in order to get the audience to feel it."

'It was typical of her lack of conceit to berate herself for one of the qualities of acting found only in the truly great: the quality of being able minutely and faithfully to reproduce within herself the emotional state of the character prototype.'

Hepburn's implicit model of good acting as the presentment of emotion formed and regulated by intelligence – a model fully realised in her finest work – fails to correspond to Baker's, which is, in effect, an instance of the 'great acting' theory – through his/her 'genius', the actor 'becomes' the character, and Baker responds, as she did in the discussion of 'beauty', by appropriating Hepburn's position as incontrovertible evidence of her own. The disagreement is important not only because of Hepburn's insistence that good acting is *not* a matter of 'living', 'experiencing' and 'naturalising' the part, but because, at this stage of Hepburn's career, this writer can offer Hepburn's acting as 'natural' – and therefore 'great' – and expect assent. What this conviction of 'naturalness' really describes, I think, is the persona's ideological potency – it can be recognised as 'natural' because of the social reality of the needs, values and aspirations it addresses. Given the intensity of this experience, the relation between Hepburn and Garbo that I have defined encourages the elevation of Hepburn to '*la divine*'. Hepburn records her resistance to it in another *Picturegoer* article:

' "Katharine Cornell made her first hit as Sydney [in *A Bill of Divorcement*], and so did a girl in England, Meggie Albanesi, when the play came out years ago. Miss Albanesi died two years later. . . yet today people still speak of her as a genius. It wouldn't be possible to be bad in the part.

' "I wish people would wait till I've done another picture or two before they judge me. No one knows yet whether I'm good or bad . . . It puts me in a spot. If I'm not good in my next picture, what shall I do?" ' (*Picturegoer*, 15th April 1933, p.10).

Photograph: a publicity shot for Spitfire.

Stills. Above: Hillary (John Barrymore), Sydney and Margaret in A Bill of Divorcement. *Opposite: Cynthia and Christopher in* Christopher Strong.

Ironically, of course, Hepburn's very protestations can be put to work ideologically, for while the writers' claims that she is 'a genius'/the new Garbo/ '*la divine*' make her 'extraordinary', her own words provide the leaven of the 'ordinary and unexceptional' required for the project of which she is the focus: Hepburn is 'a genius', but 'it wouldn't be possible to be bad in the part'.

While Hepburn retained her defenders and admirers, the emergence of a growing army of detractors who find her acting remarkable for its extreme 'unnaturalness' exactly coincides, as we might expect, with the moment at which the contradictions within the ideological project begin to become disablingly apparent. If the consensus judgement that Hepburn is a 'limited', 'mannered' – even a 'bad' – actress has fallen into abeyance, or at least been qualified, in recent years, since she began to play 'important' parts, its currency is sufficiently demonstrated by the legendary persistence of Dorothy Parker's crack about Hepburn's performance in *The Lake* on Broadway in 1934 ('She ran the gamut of emotion from A to B'), and of George S. Kaufman's acid comment, on being informed that while appearing in the same play Hepburn had ordered sheeting to be hung up in the wings so that she wouldn't be distracted by what was going on offstage – 'She's afraid she might catch acting'. A brief glance through her reviews supplies innumerable examples of similar judgements:

'Miss Hepburn, gauntly handsome and spirited, makes no attempt to become that elusive, charming creature, a Barrie heroine. She is just Miss Hepburn, vivid, varying little, adored by a vast public' (*New York Sun*, 1934).

' . . . outside the narrow range in which she is superb, Katharine Hepburn often acts like a Bryn Mawr senior in a May Day pageant . . .' (*Time*, 1936).

'[Katharine Hepburn's] Phoebe Throssel needs a neurologist far more than a husband. Such flutterings and jitterings and twitchings, such hand-wringings and mouth-quiverings, such runnings about and eye-brow-raisings have not been seen on a screen in many a moon' (*New York Times*, 1937).

' . . . the thespian tricks and stylized mannerisms of Katharine Hepburn . . . ' (*Esquire*, 1947).

'The budding young actress in *Morning Glory* was, of course, a gift of a part, but it let loose from Hepburn the stock of mannerisms that were later to get out of hand' (*Picturegoer*, 1951).

'Hepburn. . . is great, though there may be some viewers who will be stopped short by her remembered mannerisms of voice, laughter and tooth' (*New York Post*, 1962).

The best way to aproach this phenomenon is through a comparison of *Morning Glory* (1933) and *Stage Door* (1937) – the first (for which Hepburn won an Oscar) produced at the height of her brief, early popularity, and the second, conceived systematically as a variation on it, made in the same year that Hepburn was labelled 'box-office poison' by *Variety*. To confirm the fact that Hepburn and

Morning Glory are the reference points for La Cava's film, one need only compare its magnificent script, by Morrie Ryskin and Anthony Veiller (Veiller had previously worked on the scenarios of *Break of Hearts* and *A Woman Rebels*, and later co-scripted Capra's *State of the Union*, the finest of the Hepburn/Tracy dramas), with the Edna Ferber/George S. Kaufman play, which the film less adapts than abandons. The full significance of the relation between the three works is complex, and discussion of it can be pursued more appropriately elsewhere (*see* Chapter Five) I am concerned here only with the motif of acting.

In the central party sequence in *Morning Glory*, Eva Lovelace (Hepburn), drunk on champagne, confides to Easton (Adolphe Menjou) the anxiety she constantly feels about whether or not she is a great actress: she oscillates, she tells him, between moments of ecstatic self-confidence when she 'feels wonderful and [isn't] afraid anymore', and corresponding depressions ('Maybe I'm *not* a genius') – but 'tonight I'm practically convinced I'm a genius again.' As she speaks, the conviction becomes the need to demonstrate and assert her powers ('I know that I'm a great actress, and I'm going to go on getting greater and greater!') and, silencing the room, she transforms it into a stage on which she delivers, first, 'To be or not to be', and then Juliet's speech from the balcony scene of *Romeo and Juliet*. The guests applaud her rapturously, and her mentor, Hedges (C. Aubrey Smith) tells her that she is 'beautiful – childishly beautiful – impossibly beautiful!'

The scene, clearly enough, is conceived as a *tour de force* for Hepburn, and enacts, with emblematic clarity, the ideological projects which, in the first three

Stills: as Eva in Morning Glory, *with (opposite) Adolphe Menjou as Easton.*

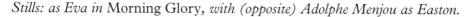

films, the persona subserves. The American girl from the American small-town becomes, as we watch, a genius – the reality and potency of youthful aspiration is embodied there before us. As 'girl', she is 'feminine': the performance over, she kneels to Easton and lays her head on his knees, and it has been preceded by her flatteringly submissive cultivation of his benevolence. Fired by genius she becomes the androgyne, her 'masculinity' enforcing itself in the peremptory, strident force with which she commands the room and its inhabitants, creating objects and persons as objects in her *mise-en-scène*, and in the appropriation of a male character's speech, delivered in a vocal register and with an intensity strikingly different from the tones of the 'girl' who had adopted first Hedges and then Easton as 'the father'. The whole is bound together by the intimations of pathos which acquire such force at the end of the film: the performance is '*impossibly* beautiful'; the discussion of 'genius' has stressed, in the familiar manner, the loneliness and suffering which accompanies it; the conversation with Easton has given expression, through Eva herself, to the 'morning glory' motif of transience and loss ('Drink, for the bird of time has but a little way to fly, and the bird is on the wing'). The scene works to such perfection ideologically because the role of actress, as a medium for female self-assertion, is, and has long been, ideologically innocuous, and because the image of performance assigns the contradictory terms which Hepburn embodies to distinct 'realms' which can be reconciled without strain in the person. We need only compare the film with *The Little Minister*, *Sylvia Scarlett* and *Quality Street* to become aware of the

Still: Stage Door – *Kaye Hamilton (Andrea Leeds), Catherine Luther (Constance Collier) and Terry Randall (Hepburn).*

number of problems *Morning Glory* is able to contain by enclosing the assertive, 'masculine' properties of the Hepburn persona in the category 'professional actress', sub-section '*la divine*': self-realisation (Eva creates herself) and objectification (the performance is for Easton), the discovery of polymorphous sexuality and Oedipal subordination, can be aligned with one another.

The nature of Hepburn's publicity makes it clear that 'Eva as genius' also means 'Hepburn as genius', and that the concept of 'genius', here, works for recuperation: the demands of Eva/Hepburn are the emanation of the 'divine spark' which, moreover, flares up only to die. When we come to *Stage Door*, four years later, we find something very different, though it's no less a matter of an explicit continuity between Hepburn and Terry Randall, the character she plays: the dialogue of the play in which Terry appears is lifted from Hepburn's renowned Broadway flop, *The Lake*. Terry gets to appear in the play not because she is a 'genius', but because her father, unbeknownst to her, has put up the money for it. Her acting, in the rehearsal scene, is defined for us as wooden and unnatural, and its badness is associated with Terry's desire to act with her intelligence ('Do you want me to walk around like a puppet or use my intelligence?') rather than her emotions ('She's about as emotional as a fish'). Terry is also shown, like the young, pre-Hollywood Hepburn, resisting and challenging direction. The intelligence/emotions opposition corresponds to a conventional categorisation of 'masculine' and 'feminine' qualities, and at the end of the film Terry's transformation into a great actress proceeds from her discovery, through

Kaye, of 'emotion' and 'femininity'. On the night of the first performance, Kaye suggests to Terry that, in the opening scene, she should cradle a bouquet of flowers in her arms 'like a child', and the suggestion is based on a model of acting at the reverse pole from Terry's: Kaye adds, 'It's not a play. It really happened – to someone I know.' The 'someone' is, of course, Kaye herself: while we never learn anything about Kaye's life, her own portentous secrecy ('There's no one I can go back to – except somebody I'd never go back to'), together with the reference to the child, clearly imply, through a Hays Code cryptogram, that she has had an illegitimate baby which has died. Acting, for Kaye, is not the 'use of intelligence', but the reliving of her own feelings – the play 'is not a play'. Kaye's advice, driven home by the shock of her death and the guilt it induces – Terry has 'stolen' Kaye's part, as Jean (Ginger Rogers) reminds her in a bitter denunciation of Terry just before the curtain goes up – constitute Terry's spiritual education. A warm flow of spontaneous emotion melts the ice-fields of intelligence ('She hasn't any heart – she's made of ice!'), and Terry *becomes* Kaye ('That wasn't me out there tonight').

In fact, as I shall argue later, *Stage Door* is radically more complex than that: other elements in the film complicate and contradict the pattern I've described, though they don't eliminate it. In order to become a real actress (woman) Terry must be 'feminised', and the cause of her 'feminisation' is also her punishment ('It was Kaye's part and Kaye's life').

Since *Stage Door* goes out of its way to associate Terry with Hepburn herself, we may suggest that the problems which Hepburn's acting have raised for many critics may be discussed in connection with the film's projects. To describe a performance as 'mannered' is to say that performance effects have been calculated, and that one is aware both of the effects and the calculation: acting is present *as* acting, and if 'good acting' means 'losing oneself in the part', the insistent presence of the actor will be objectionable in itself. But in fact, *all* performances are 'calculated', though not all actors get called 'mannered': special circumstances must obtain for calculation to be felt as offensive or inappropriate. These circumstances are usually put down to 'miscasting': the mannerisms contradict the requirements of the part. This explanation explains nothing: the very concept of 'miscasting' may well serve to naturalise the explicit appearance of ideological contradiction rather than its successful elision, just as the sense that the actor is 'ideally cast' may indicate that the critic is underwriting the projects of the film. Thus, for example, contemporary critics of *Alice Adams* concluded unanimously that Hepburn was perfectly cast and that she was very good, and the *Time* critic actually comes out with the thesis that Hepburn's mannerisms have at last found ideal employment: 'Of Hollywood's leading stars, Katharine Hepburn is possibly the least versatile. It is precisely this limitation which made her the ideal choice for the role of Alice.' The critic has got it the wrong way round: the part has been conceived for the actress, in such a way as to place and resolve the problems she embodies.

Conversely, the reviewer of *The Little Minister* who complained that Hepburn 'makes no attempt to become that elusive, charming creature, a Barrie heroine', and remains irreducibly 'Miss Hepburn', really means that the casting of Hepburn foregrounds the contradictions of the persona and the material, as indeed it does. Given the way in which stars function ideally, this is hardly surprising, and with the exception of those cases in which miscasting (or casting against type) is part of the film's strategy (Hitchcock's use of Cary Grant in *Notorious*, for example), we might expect the spectator's sense that the star is 'miscast' to be in proportion to the film's failure to gell ideologically. In Hepburn's case, however, this clearly isn't enough:

'*Bringing Up Baby*'s slapstick is irrational, rough-and-tumble, undignified, obviously devised with the idea that the cinema audience will enjoy (as it does) seeing stagy Actress Hepburn get a proper mussing up' (*Time*, 1938).

'The part of a spoiled playgirl is perfectly suited to Miss Hepburn's talents. . .' (*New York Herald Tribune*, 1938).

'As a lady columnist, she [Hepburn] is just right; as a working reporter, he [Tracy] is practically perfect. For once, strident Katharine Hepburn is properly subdued' (*New York Sun*, 1942).

Here, the sense that Hepburn's manner is appropriate for the part goes with an undisguised dislike of the manner, and the desire to see it 'properly subdued'; and it is broadly true that whether or not she is felt to be 'well cast', a pre-occupation with her mannerisms barely conceals unease with what they represent. Their relation to norms of 'femininity' turns out repeatedly to be the focus of the unease. Take this, for example:

'Douglas Fairbanks, Jnr., who worked with [Hepburn] on *Morning Glory*, did not think she was an actress – in the strict sense of the word. He acknowledged she could play herself, and that she had a good sense of timing. But he was repelled by her preoccupation with self, her masculine mind, and her compulsion to go out of her way to be rude and insulting' (Tozzi).

Whether this was or was not Mr Fairbank's position – Tozzi doesn't adduce a source – it is evidently the writer's, and demonstrates sufficiently clearly the connection between a refusal to see Hepburn as an actress 'in the strict sense of the word' and a certain kind of anxiety.

In all her 'thirties films from *Christopher Strong* to *Quality Street*, Hepburn plays an independent young woman who is required, in the course of the narrative, not merely to fall in love, but to long for and incite a man's attention – a theme revived with a vengeance when she is again cast in melodramas in the 'fifties as a frustrated spinster. Ideologically, this is clear enough – independent women are desperate for men. In the 'thirties films, however, the 'natural' awakening of 'femininity' is disturbingly denaturalised by the way in which Hepburn plays the love scenes; the continual complaints about her 'archness', her artificiality, her 'flutterings and jitterings and twitchings' in the presence of the hero, testify to the fact that Hepburn's acting forces us to become aware of 'femininity' *as* a manner – as a set of conventions which the character adopts, all the more apparent because of their violent collision with the acting style of the 'independent' scenes. Cukor's *Sylvia Scarlett* makes this clash of styles the central principle of the film and, through the theme of the heroine's masquerade as a boy, realises its significance.

Hepburn's acting in these films sends them off course by making their strategies too explicit, and, in so doing, turning them into something else.

Still: as Terry Randall in Stage Door.

Instead of reconciling 'masculinity' and 'femininity', independence and sub-missiveness, self-assertion and self-abnegation, or dramatising a *smooth* transition between them, the playing defines a process of struggle within social roles and conventions, no one of which is sufficient to accommodate the heroine's desire. 'Mannerism' here is more pertinently described as a thorough anti-naturalism: or rather, it is a way of pejoratively dismissing, as the actress's incompetence or limitation, a mode of performance which disturbs the realist illusion and partially foregrounds its determinants. The scene in *Sylvia Scarlett* in which Sylvia resumes female dress and sets out to win Michael Fane (Brian Aherne) by *acting* 'femininity' is exemplary in this respect, and the scandal which the film provoked on its release is no doubt attributable to the fact that its pursuit of the implications of that scene necessitates as radical a disturbance of realism as any the cinema has to show.

We might relate this strategy of playing to Bertolt Brecht's account of the 'alienating style of acting':

'To achieve the A-effect the actor must give up his *complete conversion* into the stage character. He shows the character, he *quotes* his lines, he *repeats* a real-life incident' (*The Messingkauf Dialogues*, translated by John Willett, Eyre Methuen, 1974, p.104).

Hepburn's 'thirties performances continually 'quote' femininity in this sense, presenting it as a social category which the heroine must adopt in order to appear, for men, as a 'woman'. Since Hepburn *is* a woman, this has the effect, conversely, of creating another model of femininity in which conventionally masculine properties are incorporated, and in relation to which the 'feminine' as defined comes to seem grotesque. Our sense of the natural is, as it were, inverted *because Hepburn is playing the part*. At the same time, in that 'masculinity' is socially assigned to men, Hepburn is able to raise, in the way in which she acts, the issue of a heterosexual woman who experiences herself in contradiction. The fulfilment of heterosexual desire, far from seeming synonymous with self-realisation, appears in crucial respects at odds with it: desire for men imposes on the character, in her social situation, forms of behaviour which conflict with those entailed in the fulfilment of other kinds of desire. While all these desires are felt with intensity, and renunciation means loss, there is no style, no role, no position in which the character can reconcile them; and if Hepburn's early publicity is so preoccupied with using her to exemplify the category 'individual', her acting in the 'thirties melodramas does nothing if not demonstrate the struggles and contradictions which the category conceals. There can be no unitary individuality because the social position in which it might be constituted does not exist.

I am not arguing that Hepburn, in her 'thirties work, was consciously a Brechtian actress, but it is clearly significant that, in the Baker interview, she should associate 'good acting' with not 'living' the part.

It is, however, the comedies – in particular, *The Philadelphia Story* – which provide the popular model for Hepburn's mannerisms: they bespeak 'class' and a form of presence and self-confidence which, far from being contingent on men, addresses a challenge to them. The 'Bryn Mawr drawl and tailored walk' and the 'metallic voice' adduced by the critic of *Time*, the 'withering look of the goddess' castigated by Dexter (Cary Grant) in *The Philadelphia Story*, embody at once 'aristocracy' and a vivid, striking female assertiveness and intransigence; and both Cukor's film and *Woman of the Year*, through reciprocal projects of 'feminisation' and 'democratisation', are concerned to present the one as a corollary of the other. Feminism is to appear as a property of spoiled heiresses and highbrow 'lady journalists'. Some variant of this association is common in bourgeois treatments of feminism (Molière, Henry James), and it is not an accident that the two female stars in whose work 'feminist' issues are most clearly and explicitly articulated – Hepburn and Bette Davis – are both 'upper-class' and 'Boston'.

Inasmuch as it works, this strategy is clearly reactionary; yet in *The Philadelphia Story*, it founders on the very hysteria with which the film seeks to enforce it, and in other films it is counterbalanced by the appearance of the Hepburn character in the interests of a revision of a 'democracy' which oppresses women. While this theme cannot be explored beyond a certain point (*see* Chapter Six), its presence is crucial in short-circuiting the connection between 'female strength' and 'upper-classness' to which so many of Hepburn's films have recourse once the early 'abolition of class' project has broken down.

Stage Door, in which what we recognise as the characteristic Hepburn 'manner' is fully consolidated, represents a crucial change of strategy:

1) It mediates Hepburn's transition from melodrama to comedy and while clearly a woman's film, it is also related, through the brilliant repartee of its dialogue, and the presence of an extraordinary array of distinguished female comic actors (Ginger Rogers, Eve Arden, Lucille Ball, Phyllis Kennedy), to 'thirties comedy.

2) It marks the end of the period in which Hepburn is repeatedly cast in British and/or 'period' settings: with two exceptions, all the films between *Stage Door* and *The African Queen* (1951) are set in contemporary America.

3) It is the first film in which Hepburn plays a 'daughter of the American aristocracy', a role sustained through the following five films.

4) With the exception of *Alice Adams*, it is the first film in which the concern of *The Philadelphia Story* to turn the Hepburn character into 'a first-class human being' is significantly present (though this is not a prerequisite of the 'heiress' roles, and figures neither in *Bringing Up Baby* nor in *Holiday*). While this motif relates Hepburn to the convention of the Americanisation of the female socialite, long a staple of 'thirties comedy by the time of *Stage Door* (*It Happened One Night*, Frank Capra, 1934; *My Man Godfrey*, Gregory La Cava, 1936; *Theodora Goes Wild*, Richard Boleslawski, 1936), the Hepburn roles have a number of distinctive inflections. They involve a radical challenge to the male character(s) which extend to a challenge to the terms of male dominance; and the women she plays are exceptionally intelligent (in *Stage Door* and *Woman of the Year*, 'intellectual'). *Bringing Up Baby* preserves the inflections – indeed, takes them to their logical conclusion, and in so doing detaches them from the 'humanisation' project (which really means, of course, patriarchal subordination). *Holiday* restricts the challenge to the male to the father figure, rather than the father *and* the lover/potential husband, with whom Linda is in alliance against the father from the start. It is the only Hepburn film in which the Hepburn figure shares the terms of her rebellion with the leading male character as opposed to discomfiting him by it, a fact which accounts both for its peculiar beauties – it is surely, with Leo McCarey's *The Awful Truth* (1937) the greatest 'thirties comedy – and its peculiar limitations.

If the early melodramas seek to negotiate the Hepburn persona by isolating a woman's rebellion (sexual, political, professional) from modern America, and by installing an opposition between 'masculine' assertiveness and 'feminine' yearning and submissivness which the later melodramas revive, *Stage Door* represents a decision to isolate the ideological negatives ('upper-classness', 'masculinity', confidence, intellection, feminist insistence), define them as a coherent nexus, and confront them head on. Hepburn emerges at this point as a realised identity, as – say – the Cynthia Darrington of *Christopher Strong*, with her strength but without her frailty: we may make the point more exactly by remarking that while the melodramas seek to define the frailty as a latent component of the character, *Stage Door*, *The Philadelphia Story* and *Woman of the Year* thrust it upon her as the upshot of her spiritual education. The ideological disadvantage of this change of tack (which, remarkably, attempts to deal with Hepburn by using her to embody antagonistic and substantially untenable values) is that it creates an image of female strength which can be used for purposes other than that of the films; and *The Philadelphia Story* is largely remarkable because the qualities which, from our perspective, make Tracy so obviously admirable are those which the film expects, and incites, us to detest.

The first three 'heiress' films – *Stage Door, Bringing Up Baby, Holiday* – enact three variations on the role: the snotty, the screwball and the romantic heiress. In the last two, the Hepburn figure, for various reasons, is powerfully affirmed, and the films demonstrate so incomparable a mastery of such a range of comic modes that it becomes necessary to inquire why, in popular memory, the 'manner' of *Stage Door* has come to be definitive of Hepburn. Part of the answer is that this is the manner which the MGM comedies go on to fix, and the rest of it that it gets fixed *because* it is the most threatening. Hepburn's career, it is well known, 'almost ended just before I did *The Philadelphia Story* on stage: I couldn't get a job for peanuts. I had done a lot of bad pictures, and I just couldn't get a job. So I went back to New York and got *The Philadelphia Story* to do. I was to have a marvellous entrance, after five minutes or so of talk, but I said to Phil Barry, "Please don't give me an entrance, I'll die. I'll be standing offstage dying. Write a nice dull scene for me at the beginning where I can be mean to my mother, so that they can see I'm not trying to cotton up to them, that I'm just as horrible as ever, even though I can't get a job, which they all know." So he did. I was rude about a wedding present and then left the stage. Well, Erik Charell was in the audience and came to see me afterwards, and said he had been in fear and trembling because he knew I had a lot at stake. "But you came on and you sat there and you spat right in the audience's face and then left the stage. And I was so happy. I thought – Good old Kate, she's going to be as rude as ever" ' (from 'The Hepburn Years', an interview with David Robinson in *The Times*, 24th November 1973).

While this gives us everything that is of value about the 'manner', it also represents the only condition on which, in 1940, she could continue to be a star. There was now no alternative except not to employ her, or to allow her to be as rebarbative as possible and tame her, institutionalise her as 'Good old Kate (of course she's difficult)'. This strategy can't be paralleled in the case of any other major star, and the fact that it has the effect of opening the stable door and allowing the horse to bolt can be construed from the 'spinster' films and the castrating mother of *Suddenly, Last Summer*.

3. Fathers and Daughters

'With their entry into the phallic phase the differences between the sexes are completely eclipsed by their agreements. We are now obliged to recognise that the little girl is a little man' – Sigmund Freud, *The Complete Introductory Lectures on Psychoanalysis*, Allen and Unwin, 1971, p.582.

'I'll try to be what he [father] loves to call me – a little woman' – Jo (Katharine Hepburn) in *Little Women* (1933).

Freud's account of female sexuality is notoriously problematic and unresolved: he himself acknowledges, with a frankness rarely encountered in his successors, that the answer to the fundamental question 'what does a woman want?' has always eluded psychoanalysis. The nature, and the significance, of the difficulty Freud encountered is nowhere more apparent than in his description of the female Oedipus complex. He argues – and I think we may follow him here – that, as in the boy's case, the girl's first erotic attachment is to her mother, and that it is characterised by 'active as well as passive impulses; if we relate them to the differentiation of the sexes which is to appear later – though we should avoid doing so as far as possible – we may call them masculine and feminine' (*Complete Introductory Letters*, p.584). Thus, women are readier subsequently to acknowledge and give expression to their constitutional bisexuality than most men. Freud also suggests that the replacement, at the Oedipal moment, of the mother by the father as the girl's primary object entails her renunciation of her 'masculinity', and he is even in some sense aware of the cost involved – though not, of course, as his language makes clear, of the extent of his complicity in exacting it:

'A man of about thirty strikes us as a youthful, somewhat unformed individual, whom we expect to make powerful use of the possibilities for development opened up to him by analysis. A woman of the same age, however, often frightens us by her psychical rigidity and unchangeability. Her libido has taken up final positions and seems incapable of exchanging them for others. There are no paths open to further development; it is as though the whole process had already run its course and remains thenceforward unsusceptible to influence – *as though, indeed, the difficult development to femininity had exhausted the possibilities of the person concerned* [my italics]. As therapists we lament this state of things, even if we succeed in putting an end to our patient's ailment by doing away with her neurotic conflict' (*Complete Introductory Lectures*, pp.598-599).

The fact that the irony of the last clause is lost on the writer brings us up at once against the limits within which Freud conceptualises this 'exhaustion of possibilities' in women. In an article on 'The Complementary Oedipus Complex', George Devereux has noted 'the *deliberate* scotoma' in Freud's work, 'probably rooted in the authoritarian atmosphere characteristic of nineteenth-century family life' whereby Freud ignores, 'whenever possible, certain parental attitudes which actually stimulate the infant's Oedipal tendencies' *(International Journal of Psychoanalysis,* vol.34, 1953, p.132). Similarly, in an exemplary critique of Freud's reading of the Schreber case, Morton Schatzman has drawn attention to the tendency, implicit in the Freudian concept of 'object-relations', to theorise the persons who are the objects of an individual's acts or feelings as passive receptacles for spontaneously generated fantasies rather than as *agents* who actively determine the kind of relation that can be formed with them (Schatzman, *Soul Murder: Persecution in the Family,* Allen Lane, 1973, p.93 et.seq.).

The implication of these remarks for an assessment of the Oedipus complex is made clear by Michael Schneider in following through one of Freud's discarded asides in the *Introductory* Lectures:

'Here Freud at least allowed the possibility that the child does not select the parent of the opposite sex as the preferred (Oedipal) love object of its own volition, but "follows some indication from its parents". Oedipal rivalry as a basis for an exclusive claim to the love object of the opposite sex therefore appears to be less a primary action on the part of the child than a secondary reaction to the (Oedipal) preferential treatment of a child of the opposite sex by its parents' (Schneider, *Neurosis and Civilisation: A Marxist/Freudian Synthesis,* Seabury Press, 1975, p.90).

Schneider continues:

'The bourgeois parents themselves have generally interiorised the competition between the different and same sexes to such a degree that they 'automatically' bequeath their 'special love' to the child of the opposite sex. Special and additional competition, of course, also obstructs homosexual eroticism . . . The social ostracism and repression of homosexuality is therefore one of the main reasons for the special turning of the parents towards the child of the opposite sex. In addition, there is the factor that both parents can in this way act out their sex-specific social roles: the father feels more drawn to the daughter than the son because he can better act out this role of "superior man"; the mother prefers the son as an erotic object because she can act out her social 'inferiority' role with respect to him, that is, she places the daughter into a secondary erotic rank equivalent to the latter's secondary social rank.'

Freud's account of the Oedipus complex habitually ignores the fact that it is directly determined by needs, demands and pressures exerted by the parents (themselves, as Schneider stresses, fully constituted social beings): indeed, it is precisely these pressures (which may well be contradictory – a point to which I'll return) which mediate any concrete instance of the Oedipus complex. If, for Freud, the Oedipal structure is a universal invariant of 'human nature', it is because he describes it, predominantly, in terms of fantasies necessarily constructed by the child itself around its perception of human biology (the anatomical distinction between the sexes). The product of a set of dynamic social relationships specific to the patriarchal bourgeois family is attributed to the child's spontaneous mystification of itself and Freud can actually assert that 'the determinants of women's choice of an object are often made unrecognisable by social conditions' (*Complete Introductory Lectures*, p.596). 'Social conditions' are not determinant: they merely obscure the pristine clarity of the real lines of force.

The absurdity of Freud's interpretation can hardly be doubted. The little girl, we are to believe, sees the penis, feels correspondingly mortified, and at once renounces her phallic sexuality under the influence of penis-envy. Her discovery that her mother is 'castrated' too crystallises latent feelings of hostility deposited by the mother's inability to give the little girl enough milk, and exacerbated by jealousy of a second baby; and it follows that she turns to her father in search of the penis she thought her mother possessed and becomes passive. Subsequently, the wish for a penis is replaced by the wish for a baby, and the process is complete.

According to Freud, the little girl inflicts these acts of psychic violence on herself *all on her own*. There is not the slightest sense that massive social forces must be called into play, and massive struggles set in motion, in order to deprive her of her 'masculinity'. And here we come to a point which, while it might seem to contradict the first, in fact completes it. If the Oedipus complex is 'a phenomenon produced by the social interaction of the parents' (Schneider, p.90), should we not conceive both of this interaction and the child's negotiation of it in terms of struggle? If the little girl may indeed turn from her mother to her father in the Oedipal phase, can this not be construed as a rebellion against the model of 'femininity' her mother embodies – as an attempt, that is, to perpetuate her enjoyment of her phallic sexuality rather than an espousal of passivity? The most obvious instance of such a rebellion is the development of a homosexual or bisexual orientation, but it is also implicit in a 'normal' Oedipal development, as Freud himself seems to imply in positing, in *The Ego and the Id*, the essentially dialectical nature of the Oedipus complex: the child identifies with, and takes as object, the parents of *both* sexes. The full radicalism of this concept – and of Freud's most crucial discovery, constitutional bisexuality – can be realised only if we reject the language in which Freud articulates it (such that the Oedipal phase appears as a privatised, imaginary extrapolation from biological givens effected by the child) and redefine it in relation to a conflict of real social forces. Whether 'normal' or 'deviant', the outcome of the Oedipus complex is the product of a struggle in which all the parties are social agents.

Katharine Hepburn's 'thirties movies place her repeatedly in relation to a father figure. In a number of films, the Hepburn character's real father is central to the narrative (*A Bill of Divorcement, Little Women, Alice Adams, Sylvia Scarlett, A Woman Rebels, Stage Door, Holiday, The Philadelphia Story*); in others, he is replaced by a patriarchal figure who fulfils similar dramatic functions (*Christopher Strong, Morning Glory, Spitfire, The Little Minister, Break of Hearts, Quality Street*). I wish to argue:

a) that these films *are* variously concerned with the way in which a girl 'pass[es] from her masculine phase to the feminine one to which she is biologically destined' (*Complete Introductory Lectures*, p.583) – the 'destiny' being, in the films as in Freud's text, an ideological presupposition;

b) that Hepburn's charisma consists precisely in the fact that she is a 'boy-woman', and that the renunciation of masculinity is thus often felt to entail a loss or 'exhaustion of possibilities';

c) that this contradiction tends, on the one hand, to produce the father as a repressive figure and, on the other, to foreground the question of bisexuality;

d) that, consequently, the achievement of 'femininity' can no longer appear unproblematically as 'destiny' but becomes a struggle in which ideological allegiances are called into question;

e) that the precise value attached to Hepburn's 'feminisation' differs remarkably from film to film, in ways which can be correlated with material external to the films (shifts in her popularity, her relation to other stars, the way she is discussed in publicity material).

Hepburn's first film, *A Bill of Divorcement*, was adapted from a play by Clemence Dane which had been an enormous hit in London and on Broadway some ten years previously. The part which Hepburn eventually played had made stars of Katharine Cornell and Meggie Albanesi on the stage, and there was considerable competition for the film role among a number of established stars: Irene Dunne and Anita Louise were tested for it, and Norma Shearer (then, with Garbo, the biggest female star in Hollywood) wanted MGM to loan her to RKO in order to play it. Not only was Hepburn preferred, despite her reputation, as a stage-actress, for being 'troublesome' (she had been fired from four of the seven plays – not counting summer stock – in which she had appeared), but she was hired at an unprecedented salary, for a newcomer, of $1,500 a week – a sum which she had stipulated herself on the hypothesis that the studio would turn it down. She did not, at this stage, want to go to Hollywood (*see* Dickens, pp.6-8).

While an interpretation of the decision to cast Hepburn must remain to some extent a matter of speculation, it is possible, nevertheless, to risk some plausible guesses. Hepburn's most recent performance on the stage had been in *The Warrior's Husband*, an adaptation of *Lysistrata*, in which she had played the Amazon, Antiope; it was on the basis of this performance, indeed, that she was first mentioned to Merian C. Cooper, the executive producer at RKO. Contemporary reviews of the play are much preoccupied both with Hepburn's sexual ambiguity and with the transition to 'femininity' which provides the narrative dynamic of so many later films. Thus, for example, Arthur Ruhl in the *New York Herald Tribune*:

' . . . Miss Katharine Hepburn, as the young Amazon, who finally deserts her band for love of the dashing Theseus – a boyish, steel-spring-like figure, woman in spite of herself, who suggests a somewhat tougher and more dynamic version of Maude Adams' Peter Pan.'

Similarly, the *New York Times* speaks of Hepburn's 'excellent performance . . . as the Amazon who knows when she is beaten by love', and she is described, in *Time* magazine, as 'the volatile but vulnerable warrior' (quoted by Dickens, pp.8 and 208). The consistency is remarkable: Hepburn's androgyny is fascinating, rather than threatening, on the condition that she is ultimately 'really' a woman, and the films continually testify to the extreme difficulty of maintaining this equilibrium.

The 'strangeness' of Hepburn's physical presence, and its relation to her sexual ambiguity, was emphasised in reviews when *A Bill of Divorcement* came

Still: Sydney and Kit (David Manners) in A Bill of Divorcement.

out, but George Cukor's remarks in interviews suggest that it was also a factor in the casting:

'I remember how unslick [her screen test] was. There was a moment when she had to pick up a drink, which was placed very inconveniently on the ground nearby. There was something very poignant in the way she made this difficult movement; her whole body moved me very much' (Gavin Lambert, *On Cukor*, W.H. Allen, 1973, p.120).

He also mentions that 'she was quite unlike anybody I'd ever seen' (p.62). The contrast here between 'unslick' and a 'poignantly' evocative physical grace registers something of the same tension noted by the reviewers of *The Warrior's Husband*.

The action of *A Bill of Divorcement* takes place at Christmas at the home of an upper-class English family, the Fairfields. Margaret Fairfield (Billie Burke), whose ex-husband Hillary (John Barrymore) has been confined for years in a mental hospital, has had the marriage annulled and is about to remarry; her daughter Sydney (Hepburn) has just become engaged. Hillary escapes from hospital, returns home on Christmas morning, and sets out at once to prevent Margaret's remarriage. When Sydney discovers that her father's illness is not, as she had thought, the result of his experiences in the trenches but of 'hereditary insanity' which may have been bequeathed to her, she renounces her lover and agrees to devote herself to Hillary, freeing her mother to go off with her new lover.

Following Helen Foley, Laura Mulvey has noted, in an article on 'Sirk and Melodrama' (*Movie* 25, Winter 1977/78, p.54), that the 'over-valuation of virility under patriarchy causes social and ideological problems which the drama comments on and seeks to correct.' While melodrama is committed overall to the reaffirmation of patriarchal sexual relations, the patriarch himself repeatedly appears as the embodiment of a sexual repressiveness, or sexual licence, which is profoundly disruptive and essentially inimical to social stability. In one of the most profound of melodramas, the Mozart/Da Ponte *Don Giovanni*, each extreme is defined as the other's necessary opposite: the Commendatore entails Don Giovanni, and vice versa.

This disruptiveness is frequently associated with a disrespect for, and lack of, 'femininity'; and in such cases, the problem is recuperated by producing a second, 'feminised' patriarch, whose predecessor is either chastened or disposed of. Thus, for example, in D.W. Griffith's *Way Down East* (1920), F.W. Murnau's *City Girl* (1930), King Vidor's *Duel in the Sun* (1946), Elia Kazan's *East of Eden* (1955) and Vincente Minnelli's *Home from the Hill* (1960), a tyrannical father is replaced by a son who has previously been associated, against the father, with the mother; in the first four cases, the father also undergoes a 'change of heart' which is marked either by the renewal of his relationship with a wife whom he has previously oppressed, or by his acceptance of the son's girlfriend. (This is not to say, of course, that any of these 'resolutions' is unproblematic.) The 'change of heart' may also occur on its own, though it is always linked to the father's 'feminisation' and his reintegration in domesticity. The work of Dickens abounds in both strategies (*Dombey and Son*, *Nicholas Nickleby*, *A Christmas Carol*), as in the device of expiating the 'bad' aspects of a reformed father through a surrogate or complementary figure – Carker, say, in *Dombey and Son*, Sanderson (Lowell Sherman) in *Way Down East*, Lewt (Gregory Peck) in *Duel in the Sun*, Potter (Lionel Barrymore) in Capra's *It's a Wonderful Life*. (The fact that the bad father is so often also a bad capitalist is clearly crucial.) The characteristic structure of the 'Freudian-feminist' melodrama, in which the persecuting husband is either revealed at last to be benign (Hitchcock's *Suspicion*, 1941) or displaced by the heroine's rescuer (Minnelli's *Undercurrent*, 1946, Cukor's *Gaslight*, 1944), represents a crucial variant of this theme. Alternatively, the father's intractability, as in Griffith's *Broken Blossoms* (1919), may enforce a tragic ending, in which the 'feminised' male is destroyed.

While in all these works male authority and male sexuality are seen to generate radical disharmonies, the obligatory reconstitution of patriarchy tends to trap them in a position in which the only viable relationships have been de-sexualised: the modified patriarchy cannot accommodate eroticism at all. This may, of course, be recognised, and become a source of irony, but patriarchy cannot be positively disowned. The difficulty is only foregrounded by Hal Ashby's *Coming Home* (1978), in which the symbolic castration of the 'good' patriarch is festooned with pseudo-feminist trimmings and libertarian rhetoric.

Here, then, the father is a figure of power who is either 'feminised' himself or replaced, and the characteristic emphasis falls on the father-son relationship: where the daughter figures at all (as she does in Dickens and Griffith), it is as a domesticating influence who either effects the change of heart (*Dombey and Son*) or is destroyed by her failure to do so (*Broken Blossoms*). In a number of narratives concerned with the power of the dead father – *Hamlet*, Melville's *Pierre*, Ibsen's *Ghosts* – a 'feminised' son who is closely associated with his mother is destroyed by the father.

A Bill of Divorcement shares with *Hamlet* the theme of a father who rises from the dead to punish errant female sexuality, and with *Ghosts* that of the hereditary taint ('insanity' and syphilis); but in *Divorcement*, fascinatingly, we are concerned with a father/*daughter* relationship, the father's disruptiveness is a fact not of his strength but his weakness (he is shown consistently to be parasitic on *female* strength), and the daughter, far from 'feminising' the father is 'feminised' by him.

A Bill of Divorcement opens on Christmas Eve. I have drawn attention else-where (in an account of *The Reckless Moment* in *Framework* 4, Autumn 1976) to the ironic use of 'Christmas' in melodrama, such that the bourgeois festival of family unity, ratified by an implicit analogy with the Holy Family, becomes an occasion for demonstrating the family's oppressiveness. Here, the regeneration envisioned by Margaret and Sydney Fairfield ('New year, new name, new life') is contingent on the father's absence, and expressed consistently in terms of the triumph, or recovery, of youth and the undoing of time. Margaret remarks to her lover, Gray (Paul Cavanagh), apropos of Sydney and Kit (David Manners), 'Isn't youth glorious?', and adds 'I feel young with you', the following dialogue en-forcing the link between youth, sexual fulfilment ('Life only starts when love comes') and the achievement, for Margaret, of a new freedom ('It's wonderful to be free – you did that'). The theme is generalised through Sydney who, we are told, 'has no sense of time', and who becomes the medium, on Christmas morn-ing, for the explicit rejection of guilt for, or indebtedness to, the past which her father and his sister Hester (Elizabeth Patterson), embody: 'She [Hester] can't expect us to go around with a handkerchief to our eyes all the time. You've got to live'. Crucially, given the significance which will accrue to Hillary, Sydney's refusal to be bound by the constraints of history and the dead father is im-mediately the refusal of Christianity: she won't go to morning-service because 'it's against my principles to kneel down and say I'm a miserable sinner. I'm not miserable and I'm not a sinner.' This is, in tone, weight and implication, dis-tinctively the Hepburn voice.

Even before Hillary's appearance, the film has set up an ironic counterpoint to the women's confidence in the supersession of history. Margaret and Gray's conviction that 'we've time for everything still' is juxtaposed with a sense of the

Stills: A Bill of Divorcement. *Above – Aunt Hester (Elizabeth Patterson) with Sydney and Margaret. Opposite – Sydney and Hillary.*

transience and fragility of the moment ('Oh, let it be Christmas forever!'), and, as in *Meet Me in St Louis* (Vincente Minnelli, 1944), the young couple can only meet (in the one scene in the film which takes place out-of-doors) beyond the walls of a home which, Hester insists, remains the father's province ('Hillary is the master of this house'). Hester, indeed – the woman who has identified herself with the claims of patriarchy – figures throughout the party sequence as Hillary's surrogate, seeking first to get Sydney to dance 'with some of the other young men', and then detaining Kit so that he almost misses his assignation with Sydney in the garden. The relation between the father's power and the repressive regulation of female sexuality has already been clearly intimated.

Hillary himself, of course, is at once the Second Coming and, as the 'undead' ('I was a dead man'), a negative return of the repressed who, like the ghost of Hamlet's father, voices the claims of Oedipal possession in terms of retribution for woman's frailty ('I suppose it *is* a long time – for a woman to be faithful'). The religious imagery, though implied by the film itself, must also be taken to express a self-inflating intention in Hillary. He refers to his sojourn in the hospital as a period in which 'the face of God was turned away', and adds, of his recovered lucidity: 'It only happened today – like a curtain lifting. I was led, like Peter, out of prison.' In a later outburst, the full import of Hillary's appropriation of the role of Christ becomes clear: 'I've been to the war to fight – for her, for all of you, for my country.' Both redeemers exact allegiance in the name of an unpaid debt.

The form repayment is to take is female self-sacrifice, which is inseparably, in the film's terms, the recreation of the present as the past ('Why has Meg moved the clock? We'll have that put back'). The concept of indebtedness to the father forms the connection between the two. Acknowledging to Margaret that 'you've grown right up – away – beyond me, haven't you?', Hillary asserts that he's 'going to catch up – wait for me', and reminds her of her marriage

vows: 'You promised – for better or for worse, in sickness or in health. You can't break your promise . . . you can't drive me out alone like that.' Home must become again the 'vale of peace' demanded by Hillary, and he seeks to place, first Margaret and then Sydney within it in the dual role (the paradox is in fact a corollary) of the redeemed paying the requisite interest on the redeemer's sacrifice *and* of the potential redeemer, guaranteeing Hillary's rebirth through care and devotion ('Give me something! – the bottom of your dress, things you give your servant or your dog!'). The father asks no more of his women than that they should be beholden to him because he is great, and look after him because he is worthless.

The replacement of Margaret by Sydney is anticipated at the moment of Hillary's first appearance. Sydney is alone in the house when he arrives, the others having gone to church: since she has refused to go to the father, the father comes to her. Cukor films her, as she watches Hillary wander round the room, through the railings of the banister, and the sense of her entrapment is reinforced by the enclosing foliage of a vase in the foreground. When Hillary sees her, he mistakes her for Margaret:

Hillary: Meg! Meg! My own darling! *(Recognising his error)* I thought you were another girl. *(Pause)* Who are you?
Sydney: I think I'm your daughter.
Hillary: My wife's not my wife, she's my daughter!

He goes on to tell her that his mother's name was also Sydney.

The marvellous density of this moment, which dramatises the whole range of male demands upon women, alerts us to the force of the decision (the playwright's) to give the father a name which is not gender-specific and the daughter a name which is almost invariably a man's. While Hillary seeks to interpellate Sydney at once as mother/wife/daughter, Sydney has already been compared, by Margaret, to Hillary himself, the occasion for the parallel arising, significantly enough, in the course of Sydney's confident insistence that guilt about Hillary shouldn't impede her mother's remarriage: Margaret blurts out, 'You get so excited, you remind me . . . ', and then breaks off.

The sense that Sydney is 'like' both her father and her mother is again evoked later in the film. In the course of one of his tirades against Margaret, Hillary remarks that he misses 'something you [Margaret] used to have – a kind way with you. The child's got it. She's more you than you are'. A few moments later, he apologises for the fact that he does lose his temper – 'it means nothing'; and Cukor cuts to a two-shot of Margaret and Sydney as Sydney looks up in alarm, remembering (it is suggested) her mother's momentary loss of guard. The point is reinforced at once in Sydney's turning away when Doctor Alliot (Henry Stephenson) speaks of 'the man whose children should never have been born'. By the end of the film, in embracing the necessity of renunciation, Sydney herself advances the contention that 'I'm very like my father' as the essential reason for her staying with him: 'We're in the same boat, father. I need you just as much as you need me.'

Sydney is constantly being told, in other words, that she resembles one or other of her parents. Hillary's insistence that she is her mother, though framed by him as an observation, is clearly dramatised as a demand: Sydney must forego her desire (inseparable, as we have seen it to be, from a challenge to the father's authority) and submit to Oedipal regulation as Hillary's 'little woman' – a 'little woman' who is also, given that Hillary is dependent on, as well as in control of, her, a revival of the first Sydney, Hillary's mother.

The contention that Sydney is 'like' her father is radically different in kind; it is dramatised not as a parental claim, but as a sickness. Through the concept of 'hereditary insanity', the possibility, latent in the social structure of the bourgeois family, of the learning of neurotic behaviour, was redescribed and mystified by nineteenth-century psychiatry as a transmitted somatic flaw ('It's in our blood, isn't it?' Sydney asks), which was, by the same token, private and non-social. (Freud, it may be said, broke with the pathological model of mental illness, but not with its individualism.) The only 'evidence' adduced by the film for the suspicion that Sydney is 'tainted' is that she gets excited and loses her temper when rebelling against paternal authority: her unwillingness to genuflect before patriarchal history becomes the symptom of a disease inherited from the father. The significance of 'insanity' here, therefore, is to imply that Sydney's subordination to the father is, if 'tragic', inevitable and necessary after all.

This line of argument does not displace but, in the strict sense, contradicts the other – both are fully present – and the contradiction is a fact of the insoluble dilemma which the sexuality of Sydney/Hepburn poses for the film. We can approach the nature of the dilemma by noting that if *A Bill of Divorcement* recalls *Ghosts*, it is also close to the various avatars of 'the tuberculosis syndrome' (in practice the specific disease is negotiable – in Edmund Goulding's *Dark Victory*, 1939, it's a brain tumour). The paradigm is, of course, *La Dame aux Camélias*, and the scene in which Sydney renounces Kit is strikingly similar to that in *Camille* (1937, also directed by Cukor), in which Marguerite Gautier (Greta Garbo) renounces Armand (Robert Taylor) at the behest of his father (Lionel Barrymore), both women adopting the tactic of pretending that they are no longer in love, and that the romantic rural idyll promised by the lover (in Canada and Brittany respectively) now bores them.

The ideological project of the syndrome is simple and consistent. At the beginning of the narrative, the heroine's sexuality is in some way aberrant. Typically, she is a prostitute or courtesan (Marguerite Gautier, Violetta in *La Traviata*, Mimi in *La Bohème*); in *A Bill of Divorcement* and *Dark Victory*, she is 'masculine', the masculinity signified, in Goulding's film, by the fact that in the opening scene, before she meets the doctor who will 'diagnose' and seek to 'cure' her, Judith Traherne (Bette Davis) is dressed in jacket, trousers and boots, and insists, in the teeth of male advice, on riding a 'difficult' stallion (she is, naturally, thrown). The heroine's sexuality is then regulated by 'falling in love', and subsequently her punishment for her previous transgression through lingering death from the disease which embodies it is offered as a valedictory for a tragically doomed romance.

Yet in each case, too, the coherence of the project is seriously disturbed. In all but *Dark Victory*, the intervention of a prohibitive, repressive father who explicitly chastises the heroine's sexuality partially foregrounds the narrative's ideological determinants by suggesting that it is indeed a social law, outraged by her transgression, which impedes the romance. Most fundamentally – and here we make a crucial point about the woman's film – the romantic lover himself, ostensible guarantee of the heroine's redemption and of our sense that her intensities have been at last directed to a worthy end, tends obstinately to remain, in conception and performance, the cardboard phallus – a mere ideological mechanism. (David Manners, Kit in *A Bill of Divorcement*, also plays the husband of

Hepburn's conventional, domesticated sister in *A Woman Rebels*.) While this violent discrepancy between lover-as-function and lover-as-realised-presence clearly exerts a reactionary force (by implying that George Brent could ever conceivably be an adequate proposition for Bette Davis in *Dark Victory*), it also serves, by making the heroine's desires at once in excess of, and more dramatically real than, their object, to reinstate the value of the troubling sexual/social presence subjugated by the movement of the narrative.

A Bill of Divorcement departs from this structure in two respects: the heroine's meeting with the lover precedes the opening of the narrative, the prohibitive father is not the lover's but her own, and the film ends not with the heroine's death, but her entrapment – in that astonishing final scene where, having closed the curtains of Hillary's study to shut out Kit, she sits down at the piano with her father as he tries to complete his unfinished sonata – in Hillary's exclusive Oedipal fantasy. Nevertheless, the function of 'the disease' is clearly similar: the insanity theme allows the film to maintain that a) Sydney's challenge to patriarchy is admirable ('You've got to live!'); b) that the disruptiveness of the challenge necessitates a drastic reinforcement of the bond Sydney has sought to break. The pathos generated by the ending obscures, and seeks to anneal, this contradiction and also distracts us from a second problem inextricably bound up with it – the parallel between Hillary and Kit. Sydney's breaking of the rendezvous at the end is in part a recapitulation and in part a reversal of the opening sequence in which Hester tried to prevent the lovers meeting outside the house: Sydney has been co-opted in her own oppression, and interdiction becomes renunciation. Yet, at the same time, that first conversation with Kit has made it clear that he can only offer her essentially the same thing that Hillary does: he gives Sydney his mother's engagement ring, telling her that she'll be 'the bride of the fifth generation to wear it' and that 'I'll have it made to fit your finger if you'll let me.' For Kit as for Hillary, Sydney must be incorporated as a prop in a fantasy scene imposed by the male, and while there is no doubt that the film intends us to judge the value of the lost relationship with Kit by virtue of its difference from that enforced by Hillary, it also demonstrates the continuity between them. Indeed, it is the very existence of this continuity which demonstrates the extent of the difficulty Sydney represents: the film is in some sense aware that mere marriage can't cope with it, and that more stringent remedies are called for. The father cannot simply be replaced; it will be necessary to resurrect him.

A Bill of Divorcement, then, sketches out the nature of 'the Hepburn problem' with admirable clarity: the film certainly wishes to affiliate to her, but the basis for affiliation is also the condition of its impossibility. At this stage, as I hope the discussion above of 'youthfulness' and 'tomboyism' will have made clear, certain mechanisms can be employed to control this contradiction, but the subsequent development of Hepburn's career pays testimony both to their inadequacy and to the anxiety generated by the contradiction. One need only point here to the relation, across twenty-seven years, between Hepburn's first film and *Suddenly, Last Summer,* in which Hepburn is cast as a voracious mother who has not only nourished her son's 'degeneracy' but who also conspires to have a young woman consigned as 'mad' to an asylum in order to conceal it. The extremity of the ideological struggle which Hepburn's presence releases has actually effected an exact reversal of the position in which she first appeared.

4. Gender and Bisexuality

'Psychoanalytic research is most decidedly opposed to any attempt at separating off homosexuals from the rest of mankind as a group of a special character. By studying sexual excitations other than those that are manifestly displayed, it has found that all human beings are capable of making a homosexual object-choice and have in fact made one in their unconscious. Indeed, libidinal attachments to persons of the same sex play no less a part as factors in normal mental life . . . than do similar attachments to the opposite sex. On the contrary, psycho-analysis considers that a choice of an object independently of its sex – freedom to range equally over male and female objects . . . is the original basis from which, as a result of restriction in one direction or the other, both the normal and the inverted types develop. Thus from the point of view of psychoanalysis the exclusive sexual interest felt by men for women is also a problem that needs elucidating and is not a self-evident fact based upon an attraction that is ultimately of a chemical nature' – Sigmund Freud, *Three Essays on the Theory of Sexuality* (Hogarth Press, 1974, pp.11-12).

It has become a critical commonplace to take note of the gender ambiguity of many of the great female stars: Greta Garbo, Marlene Dietrich, Katharine Hepburn, Bette Davis, Joan Crawford and Barbara Stanwyck are obvious cases in point. This is not to say, of course, that the star-as-*person* was gay or bisexual, but that certain dominant traits of the *persona* are strikingly out of true with dominant social norms of 'femininity'.

While there seems to be something like agreement on this point, it has proved to be more difficult to account for it, and none of the accounts of which I'm aware is halfway adequate. In *Stars*, Richard Dyer quotes Caroline Sheldon and Janet Meyer, who 'see these stars as an oblique expression of lesbianism':

'The qualities they projected of being inscrutable to the men in the films and aloof, passionate, direct, could not be missed. They are all strong, tough and yet genuinely tender. In short, though rarely permitted to hint it, they are lesbians' (Janet Meyer, quoted in *Stars*, p.67).

It is certainly true and important that these stars can be appropriated by particular spectators for the *discovery* of lesbian sexuality. In his monograph on Garbo, Raymond Durgnat refers us to *Movies and Conduct*, published in 1933 in apology for the Hays Code, in which one Herbert Blumer collates shocking testimonies of the effect of an unregulated cinema on the morals of the young:

'Female, 17, white, high school senior: "I imagined myself caressing the heroes with great passion and kissing them so they would stay osculated forever . . . practised love scenes either with myself or with a girl-friend. We sometimes think we could beat Greta Garbo, but I doubt it" ' (quoted in Durgnat, *Greta Garbo*, Studio Vista, 1965, p.59).

If Garbo has this effect on white high-school seniors, who is to say what is going on amongst the lower orders? We have here a perfect example of the potentially radical function which a star like Garbo can fulfil: these young women are using her to gain access to possibilities of female sexuality (masturbation, lesbianism) that are not defined in relation to men. But it is also apparent that they are able to do so only by thinking of what they are doing as in some sense a rehearsal, or dummy run, for a relationship with a man: the unguarded frankness of the remark can hardly be construed in any other way. The speaker and her friend have taken the connotations of Garbo's sexuality, but the fact that her films always direct it towards a 'hero' (however perfunctorily realised) has reinforced the traditional circumscription of female desire, and the women 'imagine' their activity through a heterosexual fiction.

While this interplay between the radical and the conservative is probably exemplary for an analysis of the kind of identification which, at the most, Garbo's films make available, it is important to be clear about what one means by 'conservative'. I am not arguing, that is, that Mr Blumer's scandalous interviewee is 'really a lesbian', but that she is having to think of her lesbian drives as 'really' heterosexual. The distinction is an important one, as the epigraph from Freud's *Three Essays* is intended to suggest: what is at issue here, whatever the dominant gender orientation of the speaker, is the social restriction 'in one direction or the other' of constitutional bisexuality.

This is one of the grounds on which I take issue with Janet Meyer's formulation, which, as a hypothesis, practically defies criticism: her decision to define qualities which are not, or need not be, gender-specific as characteristically 'lesbian' simply turns the categories of bourgeois psychology inside-out. The designation of homosexual desire as aberrant and the construction of the exclusive type 'the homosexual' are two aspects, mutually determining, of a single phenomenon. Janet Meyer, having reinstated the type, assigns it properties; the properties are 'good' rather than 'bad', but they are as arbitrary – as little to do with any particular gender identity – as their derogatory ancestors. At the same time she goes one better than bourgeois psychology, and represses the *eroticism* of both gay and heterosexual desire. While it has been central to the politics of the gay and women's movements to contest the ideologies which define gays and women *exclusively* in terms of their sexuality, the positive corollary of such an emphasis must necessarily be that gay sexuality and 'femininity' are neither what they are valued as being nor the 'property' of gays and women. Unless the critique of the notion that gays and women are purely sexual beings is accompanied by a critique of *gender*, it will tend inevitably towards puritanism on the one hand or, on the other, the reinvention of the very social divisions one should be fighting. The lesbian-feminist position endorsed by Meyer illustrates these dangers admirably: having defined lesbianism as 'woman-identification', it follows that we are unable to see lesbianism as a) a form of sexual desire that is b) potentially available to all women. The only way in which the category 'homosexual' can be superseded is through insisting on, and affirming, its sexuality, while denying that this sexuality is specific to 'homosexuals'.

Conversely, of course, Meyer's remarks fail to honour the specificity of the struggles of woman-identified women who are partly or substantially heterosexual and who wish to formulate the basis for some acceptable sexual relationship with men. Such women, presumably, can't be woman-identified, and the implication appears to be that they can't acknowledge their lesbianism without repressing their heterosexuality. In taking over the categories of bourgeois thought, Meyer also inherits their oppressiveness.

These thoughts lead me to another – quite apart from the fact that Meyer seems not to know whether she is talking about the person, the persona or the part (or even to be aware of the necessary distinctions), what she says leads to a confusion between what these stars can be used for and what the films actually do with them. She also shares with a number of other critics the tendency to assume that the perception that, say, Garbo, Dietrich and Hepburn are all 'sexually ambiguous' is enough, whereas in fact the different meanings and functions of this ambiguity are among the most interesting things about them. One can say, however, that all of them, whether one approaches the matter from the point of view of their appeal (to women *and* men) or from that of the themes that are articulated through them – two ways, perhaps, of posing the same question – address the fact of bisexuality.

In a strategy of which there are, regrettably, too many examples in his book, Richard Dyer remarks that Meyer's position 'will not be acceptable to many (including many feminists),' defines it, agnostically, as a 'useful corrective' to another (Molly Haskell's) which he does find unacceptable, and then juxtaposes it, unevaluated, with a third position – his own and Jack Babuscio's:

'Camp, by focusing on the outward appearances of role, implies that roles and, in particular, sex roles are superficial – a matter of style . . . Finding stars camp is not to mock them . . . It is more a way of poking fun at the whole cosmology of restrictive sex roles and sexual identifications which our society uses to oppress its women and repress its men – including those on screen' (Babuscio, *Gays and Film*, quoted in Dyer, *Stars*, pp.67-68).

Dyer adds: 'In this respect, then, independent-woman stars make explicit the life-as-theatre metaphor which underpins the star phenomenon.'

This passage gives us as clear a case as could be desired of the dilemma in which all apologists for camp eventually find themselves: is camp an attribute of something or is it attributed to something? Babuscio, here, seems to subscribe to the latter position ('Finding stars camp is not to mock them . . . '), but the fact that Dyer at once goes on to enlist him in support of what looks like the former (these stars 'make *explicit*. . . the fact that sex roles are *only* roles') speaks volumes about the vacancy of the concept itself. Not only can it mean what you want it to mean, one suspects that the attempt to give it either serious theoretical currency or political value is essentially a matter of rationalisation and double-think.

Whether one decides, in any case, that camp (which I have dealt with elsewhere, in '*For* Interpretation – Notes Against Camp', *Gay Left* 7, pp.11-14) is implicit in the object or bestowed upon it, one will arrive at equally undesirable conclusions. Anyone who has ever had the misfortune to endure a conversation with one of the tribe of Bette Davis's camp followers will know that the kind of appropriation of the star's image which Jack Babuscio describes leads to something very different from that exemplified by Herbert Blumer's interviewee: self-recreation as an oppressive stereotype is not to be confused with that young woman's (albeit partial) self-discovery through Garbo. If she went at least some of the way with the radical grain of the star, the infelicitous combination of self-contempt and misogyny which is always latent, and sometimes nastily explicit, in the camp use of Davis (or Judy Garland, who has been the main victim) goes entirely against it, and transforms a body of work which has great significance for feminism (and thus for gay men) into an opportunity for frivolity or self-oppression.

The other alternative is neither more attractive nor more helpful; for what does it mean to say that these stars show us that 'sex roles are *only* roles' and that 'life is theatre'? If that is what they really did, we would surely have to conclude that their films were silly, dangerous and irresponsible, as the life-as-theatre metaphor invariably is (and I'm not clear, either, how it can be said to 'underpin the star phenomenon' – Dyer doesn't offer help on this point). This reading, in fact, seems to be perilously like an apology, or rationale, for its counterpart. Sex roles are clearly not '*only* roles' in any sense of the word 'role' which has a theatrical connotation: they are deeply structured in the individual, and cannot be donned or discarded at will, like a Bette Davis imitation, as a party turn. This is surely the very distinction that *Sylvia Scarlett* is about. Sexual roles obviously aren't 'innate or instinctual', and they embody 'social expectations and requirements' (Dyer's phrases – *Stars*, pp.67-68), as Freud began, however confusedly, to demonstrate; but Freud also demonstrates that they can't be discussed in terms of 'performance' or 'artifice'. Hepburn's 'thirties films are precisely significant in their indication of the struggle – the conflict of drives and impulses – that is concealed by a concept of gender as a 'matter of style'.

We should note, finally, a third alternative, proposed initially in readings, in *Cahiers du Cinéma*, of *Morocco* (a *texte collectif* written by the editorial board, no.225, November/December 1970, pp.5-13) and *Sylvia Scarlett* (by Pascal Kané, no.238/239, May/June 1972, pp.84-90), and later sown broadcast, which defines the cross-dressing so often encountered in the films of this group of female stars in terms of their construction as 'non-male'. Claire Johnston gives a useful precis of this argument in *Notes on Women's Cinema* (*Screen* Pamphlet 2, SEFT/ British Film Institute, 1975, p.26):

'In their analysis of Sternberg's *Morocco*, the critics of *Cahiers du Cinéma* delineate the system which is in operation: in order that the man remain within the centre of the universe in a text which focuses on the image of woman, the *auteur* is forced to repress the idea of woman as a social and sexual being (her Otherness) and to deny the opposition man/woman altogether. The woman as sign, then, becomes the pseudocentre of the filmic discourse. The real opposition posed by the sign is male/non-male, which Sternberg establishes by his use of masculine clothing enveloping the image of Dietrich. This masquerade indicates the absence of man, an absence which is simultaneously negated and recuperated by man. The image of the woman becomes merely the trace of the exclusion and repression of Woman.'

The striking thing about this amazingly perverse construction – a quality it shares with Janet Meyer's remarks, which are, in one sense, its exact opposite –

is its uncritical enslavement to the very categories it imagines itself to be confuting: Sternberg's critique of concepts of 'masculinity' and 'femininity' is read as a denial of the distinction between the sexes and a repression of the irreducible 'Otherness' of 'Woman'. This conclusion would not be out of place in an editorial in the *Daily Telegraph* or a homily from the Viewers' and Listeners' Association, but it leaves much to be desired as an account of Sternberg. I have argued in another context, in the course of some notes on Kristeva, that versions of 'feminism' influenced by Lacan tend to have their upshot in the Eternal Feminine, now discovered leading us onward to a fateful rendezvous in the deep and inscrutable purdah of 'semiotic process' (*see* my article on 'The Ideology of *Screen*', *Movie* 26, Winter 1978/79, p.14), and a surrender to her siren lure is inevitable, given the formalist model of representation which first *Cahiers du Cinéma*, and then *Screen*, derived from Lacan. Like reality itself, she is not given but produced – by a theory in which, while '*the* woman. . . *is* representation', she is also 'the ruin of representation, unrepresentable' (Stephen Heath, 'Difference', *Screen*, Autumn 1978, pp.82, 89). Representation necessarily represents Woman as the presence and threat of a castration which is continually inscribed and continually disavowed, but she erupts in all her glory in – indeed, she *is* – the free play of the signifier. Mr Heath's article, which post-dated the completion of my *Movie* critique, makes a valiant attempt to have the phallus and eat it by at once attacking Lacan for a theory of sexual difference that eternalises castration as a fact of the perception of nature, while also retaining his account of the 'symbolic constitution of the subject', which is its necessary corollary. He fails to see that, within the Lacanian system, the ascription of castration to the experience of nature and its ascription to 'production in the Symbolic' are exactly the same thing: the stability, such as it is, of the entire edifice depends on their identity, and no amount of reformist tinkering can escape the consequences. Having eternalised the objectification of women as castrated, there is little left to do but locate the essential Woman in a perpetual off-stage 'outside the law' (Heath, p.79), where she will doubtless grow old and grey waiting for a cue that never comes, and obtaining the modicum of satisfaction available to her by 'jamming', through the folds of her veil, the language of the actors who are fortunate enough to have been given a part. The oppression of women – their 'castration', their exclusion from history, their objectification in discourse – is entailed in the terms of the theory, and perpetually rediscovered in the objects to which theory addresses itself.

The perversity is most apparent when the object is a text in which these 'universals' are contested. For if the very process of representation is of necessity the inscription and disavowal of castration, then the cafe sequence in *Morocco*, in which Dietrich appears in drag, must define her as 'non-male'. There can be no question of the sequence being *about* the social conventions of gender, still less can it be about a woman affirming her active sexuality not by becoming 'masculine' but through an ironic commentary on a cultural image of male sexual prowess – the performance by Amy (Dietrich) is, amongst other things, a parody of the urbane 'man of the world', La Bessière (Adolphe Menjou) – because a woman wearing male clothing is *by definition* the repression and negation of Woman. We can see at once that theoretical error may lead by the shortest possible route to the most ludicrously reactionary politics, which would

Still: Monkley (Cary Grant) and Sylvia (Hepburn) in Sylvia Scarlett.

be perceived at once for what they are if theory had not been so totally hived off from a real world of action and practice. Instead, it succeeds in reassigning 'femininity' to biological femaleness and reducing Sternberg's characteristic preoccupation with both the possibilities and the drastic limitations involved in a woman's appropriation of 'masculine' roles to just tracing the male's absence.

Lacanianism postulates 'a psychosexual developmental structure which constitutes itself on the material of a previously formed language whose "invariability" cannot be eliminated either by social or class-specific "variables" '

(Schneider) as the basis of a theory of representation and thus asserts a mono-
lithic formalism whose disciples find in all works of art not a historical articulation (more or less critical) of the languages the works employ and the social
space they inhabit, but an inert reflection of the invariables.

That Hepburn's sexuality was felt, from a very early stage, to be problematic
and potentially contradictory can be deduced from the three photographs that
accompany Alice Tildesley's 1933 *Picturegoer* article. The largest of them, given
considerable prominence in the layout (it takes up half a page at the head of the
article), shows Hepburn 'with Joel McCrea on the beach at Santa Monica'. Both
are wearing swimsuits, and Hepburn is leaning back on McCrea's shoulder,
smiling directly into camera. This image of the young, bright, healthy American
couple, in which Hepburn's self-confidence and sexuality (the photograph
stresses her naked legs) are contained by the presence of the male, is juxtaposed, on the opposite page, with images of quite different signification. One
shows Hepburn wearing trousers and a fur coat, arms akimbo, looking into
camera with a challenging, almost aggressive, assertiveness remarkably unlike
the sunny smile of the beach photo, above a caption which adverts to her
'already notorious unconventionality'. The other is an exemplary case of the
'lyrical' style of early Hepburn publicity still which can be related, in ways
defined in chapter two, to the 'Garboesque', and it is so placed in the layout
that Hepburn appears to be looking up, from the foot of the opposite page, at
the picture of herself and Joel McCrea. The repetition of this compositional
strategy in a later *Picturegoer* article, 'The Screen's *Real* Mystery Woman' (20th
November 1937), both alerts us to its significance and suggests that, in the
intervening four years, the tension registered in the illustrations of the earlier
article has been crystallised: beneath two stills, one in the 'lyrical' mode and
one of Hepburn *en travestie*, a caption announces: 'Feminine Katie and her
masculine self of *Sylvia Scarlett* contemplate each other – and don't seem very
much impressed.'

The conflicting images imply not simply that the character of Hepburn's
sexuality is ambiguous, but that the ambiguities remain obstinately unreconciled
and appear as contradictions. This already suggests something of the difference
between the Hepburn and Garbo personae, to which I'll return; but it will be
helpful to begin by considering *Sylvia Scarlett* – exemplary by virtue of the
system and rigour with which it follows through the issues about gender which
Hepburn ordinarily makes present.

In his interview with Gavin Lambert (*On Cukor*, Putnam, New York, 1972,
pp.92-94), Cukor remarks that 'it wasn't the daring part of *Sylvia Scarlett* that
failed, I see that now. It was when we tried to play it safe!' – and he goes on to
cite the prologue in Marseilles as an instance of compromise ('that was put in
later, it was never intended'). Lambert asks, characteristically, whether it was
'tacked on as a sympathy device. Poor girl – her mother died and what else
could she do?' Cukor replies, 'Something like that', and changes the subject.
There could be no clearer demonstration of the truth of Paul Ricoeur's remark
that intention is to be construed from the text, and not from what its producers
say about it: far from there being any observable discrepancy of intention between
the prologue and what follows from it, the prologue crucially establishes the
relation between the film's sexual themes and its extraordinary narrative mode.

The legendary catastrophe of *Sylvia Scarlett* (it was one of the box-office disasters of all time, and the preview occasioned something akin to a riot) is clearly attributable to the imbrication of its analysis of gender with a dismantling of realist narrative as extreme as anything in the cinema.

It is clearly the case that the fabrication of the narrative *donnée* in the opening sequence is, in naturalistic terms, ostentatiously gratuitous; the film goes out of its way to affront our assumption that narrative events should be motivated 'convincingly'. It is partly a question of the hectic speed with which important data are introduced and decisions made, and the blatancy (so extreme as to become alienating) of the invitation to take the prologue as a justification for the action it initiates: in the space of a bare three minutes, we learn of Sylvia (Hepburn) that her mother has just died, that her father, Henry Scarlett (Edmund Gwenn), has been embezzling from his employers and has been found out, that although Sylvia 'has never been out of France' she will be able to get by in England because she is 'half English', and that the obvious solution (spontaneously discovered by Sylvia) to the problem of evading the police during their flight is for Sylvia to masquerade as a boy. This strategy is too consistent with the film's general mode to be accounted for as an aberration or a desperate afterthought. Instead of initiating the action in terms of conventions through which a coherent dramatic world is realised, the film requires the conventions to operate inertly, the inertia appearing as cliché. It is a process with which we are familiar from the ironic happy ending in melodrama, where convention ceases abruptly to function as a significant dramatic medium and is reduced to a set of standard values and devices which are simply and disconcertingly *applied*. In both cases, the communicated sense of a *failure* of realisation is precisely the point: the bald appearance of conventions which have been deprived of any substantial dramatic reality has the effect both of presenting us with our expectations and directing our attention to other kinds of significance.

For the foregrounding of narrative mechanics and conventional artifice isn't, in these cases, *sui generis*; in *Sylvia Scarlett* it is defined, through Hepburn's performance, as a corollary of the film's sexual themes. I have already noted, in discussing Hepburn's acting style in the 'thirties films, the way in which her playing of romantic scenes tends to work against them by making the character's surrender to 'female heart palpitations' in the presence of the male lead too explicit and extreme. When she is required to become frail and tremulous, she becomes very frail and very tremulous, and the excess disturbs the scene's ideological function by adverting us to it. The prologue of *Sylvia Scarlett*, like the ensuing love scenes with Michael Fane (Brian Aherne), deliberately cultivates this manner: everything in the scene is dedicated to the foregrounding of the conventional norms of gender.

Sylvia is discovered, fragile and melancholy, at the window of her father's apartment: her mother has just died and, removing a card announcing 'Madame Snow, Modes and Robes' from the sill, she casts aside her funeral crepe with elaborate grace, tears up the card and puts it in the incinerator, murmuring 'Poor Mama!' If Hepburn's acting insists that we take note of a particular convention of 'femininity' (the yielding delicacy and plangent helplessness of the Victorian heroine), the destruction of the card already anticipates Sylvia's rejection of it, and the conversation with Scarlett that follows at once elaborates

Still: Sylvia and her father, Henry (Edmund Gwenn), in Sylvia Scarlett.

the motif implied by this opening – the contradictions, experienced as a conflict, of Sylvia's attitude to her mother. On the one hand, she seems passionately to consign herself to Oedipal subordination to the father, in terms which refer us to Sydney in *A Bill of Divorcement*: 'I'll work for you just as hard as mother did! . . . I'm not going to get married, I'm going to stay with you.' This impulse to replace the mother and submit to the father is repeatedly interspersed with aggressive criticisms of him, registered by Hepburn in an abrupt change of manner and vocal register: when Scarlett tells her what he has done, she exclaims, 'Father, that's downright stealing!'

Sylvia, that is, at once adopts and resists her mother's position, and she resolves the tension by staying with her father while refusing the feminine relation to him through becoming a boy. The arbitrariness of the prologue as a naturalistic motivation of the action is a function of its status as metaphor: it is there to dramatise Sylvia's attempt to negotiate incompatible drives, and reconcile serving the father as her mother did with refusing to be a woman. The tension which this suggests between an internalised 'femininity', defined by the style of the prologue as a social convention, and desires which transgress it, is one of the film's central themes, the complexity of which can be noted by pointing out that Sylvia thinks of those desires as being the prerogative of men. 'I won't be a girl, weak and silly! I'll be a boy, rough and hard!' Sylvia continues to accept the conventional oppositions even as she confounds them: she demonstrates that girls needn't be 'weak and silly', but the social position of women is such that she associates her strength with her masquerade. By the same token, she *dissociates* it from her heterosexuality: in order to be desired by men, not only does she have to become 'weak and silly' again, but she must also feel her strength as 'unattractiveness'. In a sense, of course, she is right – that kind of self-alienation is entailed in those social norms – and as long as she is primarily related to her father, the latent tension, sexual desire for a man not being in question, can be contained. It is when she 'falls in love' that it appears again with all its disabling force: here, the consequences of her partial and incomplete resolution of gender contradictions become fully apparent.

Consider Sylvia's relationship with Michael Fane, whom she first encounters when the troupe, now known as the Pink Pierrots, stops to give a show at Trebell Cove. Fane is an artist, upper-class and calculatedly Bohemian, and he and his friends are much amused by the show's ingenuousness, continually interrupting it with loud outbursts of laughter. Sylvia/Sylvester is provoked beyond endurance by their disruption of the solo by Maudie (Dennie Moore) and, bringing the performance to a halt, she chastises Fane violently, addressing him as a 'fake artist' – 'If you think you're so much cleverer than we are, why don't you get up here and do a turn yourself?' Momentarily taken aback, Fane at once recovers his cool and proceeds to deliver, with practised ease, an urbane and disarming apology. Sylvia becomes, on the instant, frail and self-abnegating, and virtually concedes Fane's point:

Sylvia: Don't stop and listen to this.
Fane: Why not?
Sylvia: It's horrible!

That we are to associate the disintegration of Sylvia's stridently assertive self-confidence with the onset of 'love' is made clear in the following sequence, where she attempts, for the first time in the film, to say that she isn't a boy, though her confession is interrupted by the arrival of Fane's lover, Lily (Natalie Paley).

After the revels have erupted into violence, Sylvia returns to Fane's house to apologise, immaculately attired in three-piece suit and trilby. Although the trouble has in fact been caused by Lily, Sylvia takes all the blame upon herself: 'Everything was so lovely, and I made it horrible! . . . I'm cheap, I'm loud-mouthed, I can't control myself – I never could!' Sylvia's strengths, since Fane, she feels, can't find them attractive, suddenly appear to her as weaknesses – in that she desires him, she is blameworthy because he blames her, and winning his love means prostrating herself to him. Yet the ensuing dialogue reveals that it is precisely to Sylvia's 'masculinity' that Fane is drawn: he is fascinated by the very things about her which she wishes to repress in order to be a desirable woman. Sylvia and Fane are, in fact, representative complementary figures: Sylvia doesn't want to be 'feminine' and Fane doesn't want to be 'masculine', but both know that they *have to* be if they are to be a 'real' woman and man. The parallel consequences are systematically worked through. For her part, Sylvia is trapped in a position in which she must despise whatever she is. While she assumes automatically that the fulfilment of heterosexual desire necessitates the adoption of 'femininity', the fact that she isn't 'feminine' in that conventional sense leads her to experience the manner and costume she assumes as grotesquely alien and inappropriate: she tells Fane that she keeps 'wanting to put

Still: as Sylvia in Sylvia Scarlett.

[her] hands in [her] trouser pockets', and that her feet 'are squeezed to death in these shoes'. On the other hand, the behaviour which feels natural to her is supposed to be specific to men, and it is 'unnatural' to feel natural in that way: 'I should have stayed a boy – it's all I'm fit for!' Sylvia faces a choice between acting in a way which seems authentic for her and feeling inferior, and acting as women are 'meant' to do and feeling monstrous, and the film makes it pointedly clear that the dilemma is created by the form of patriarchal heterosexual relations. Her desire for men is real enough, but the social conventions which mediate it construct a necessary self-alienation whereby 'masculinity' is retained at the cost of a sense of freakish aberration and heterosexuality at the cost of self-abnegation.

By the same token, her access to her lesbianism is blocked, and the paralleling of the scene between Sylvia and Maudie in the caravan with that between Sylvia and Fane in his bedroom demonstrates remarkably that the terms of the film's analysis extend to the disavowal of homosexual desire. Maudie's interest in Sylvia

Still: Fane (Brian Aherne, at left), Sylvia and Henry in Sylvia Scarlett.

is explicitly lesbian ('Your face is as smooth as a girl's'), but it can only find
physical expression in a kiss after Maudie has endowed the face with a moustache with her eyebrow pencil ('You look like Ronald Colman'). Gay sexuality
can be acknowledged on condition that it is redefined, however tenuously, as
heterosexual, and the scene is all the more significant in this respect because
Maudie still believes at this point that Sylvia is a boy: even though the object,
for all Maudie knows, is authentically male, the bisexual component of her
response cannot be fulfilled until it has been emphatically disavowed by re-
inforcing the 'maleness'. Sylvia responds with delight to the moustache ('Oh, I
say, that's marvellous!') but hastily withdraws from the kiss ('No, I've got a girl
already'), and the double reaction beautifully embodies the contradiction within
Sylvia's masquerade, which allows her to act through her 'masculinity' while
detaching it from what she is *as a woman.*

Fane's response to Sylvia is also gay: he receives her, in pyjamas, in his bedroom ('You are an exceedingly nice boy'), tells her that 'you can bed down here if
you want to', and announces, before saying that he wants to paint her, that 'I
know what it is that gives me a queer feeling when I look at you.' Fane's
handling of the 'queer feeling' is again offered as representative: he remains a
'man' by disavowing it, and at once expresses it in a displaced form (he can
only wish to paint Sylvia's picture) and retreats into misogyny. Discussing Lily
with Sylvia in the bedroom sequence, he remarks, 'Women! Women! They always

96

mess things up!' – and the relation between his repression of his 'femininity' and the contempt for women which accompanies his salvaged maleness is made fully apparent, in the film's most painful and distressing scene, when he discovers that Sylvia is, after all, a girl. He mocks her cruelly both for her lack of 'femininity' ('The way you stick out your legs!') and for what she will become when she acquires it ('You'll soon play the game like all the rest of your sex! You'll lie, you'll tease, pretend indifference! You'll refuse our kisses as before – of course, a little more gracefully'). Because he knows she's a woman, her 'masculinity' is no longer attractive, and she appears either as a 'freak of nature' (a damaged boy) or a potential woman. That Fane wishes to think of himself as heterosexual, but can only desire Sylvia while believing her to be male, is the essential fact about him, and the viciousness which accompanies the revelation of his mistake is that fact's logical corollary.

It is part of the tragedy of the masquerade, from Sylvia's point-of-view, that Fane's charge, in response to her resistance to his diatribe – 'I said the sort of things she's saying herself and she didn't like it' – is true: the irony of the unmasking scene consists in the fact that while Sylvia has obviously transgressed the norms and assumptions which Fane brings against her, she has never actually broken with them. She has earlier been brought to the point of replying to Fane's observation that women 'always mess things up' with 'I hate women too', and while this isn't the case (what she hates is social expectations of women), she is also adopting, even as she says it, the sanctioned passive role by accommodating herself to what Fane wants to hear and caressing the statuette of a naked nymph which stands on his mantelpiece. The masquerade offers Sylvia partial self-realisation, but it is also a trap in which self-realisation is perpetually short-circuited and the opposition between 'activity' and 'femaleness' continually reaffirmed. It hardly needs to be said that Fane's and Sylvia's saying some of the same sorts of thing doesn't in the least affect the film's relative judgement of them. Fane is patently discredited, and even the obligatory happy ending in which he is trumped up as a satisfactory partner for Sylvia works for the film here. Sylvia's final 'I worship you' is available to be read straight but it is entirely consistent with the radical alienation which the film has explored, and it has always been clear that Sylvia's susceptibility to Fane must be referred to the unsatisfactoriness of the masquerade, with its tendency to institutionalise as 'role-play' a violation of gender which is far more radical in its implications.

The inadequacy of the masquerade for Sylvia's purposes is dramatised in the first half, before Fane's appearance, through a brilliant critique of the Augustan picaresque. As a narrative mode, the picaresque is structured by the travels and adventures of a male protagonist, and recounts his spiritual/romantic education, culminating in his achievement of a social and an individual identity – his successful location as bourgeois and as patriarch. Pascal Kané notes the (after all, sufficiently obvious) appropriation of this structure in *Sylvia Scarlett* – by becoming 'Sylvester', Sylvia is able to engage in the quest for self-definition which is traditionally the prerogative of a male hero – and concludes, ineptly, that the film is premised on a denial of the distinction between the sexes.

'In his analysis of Cukor's *Sylvia Scarlett*, Pascal Kané shows [*sic*] how Sylvia must cut off her pigtails in order to become the "hero" . . . suspending the desire

Still: Monkley, Maudie (Dennie Moore), Henry and Sylvia in Sylvia Scarlett.

of the character and excluding [her] from the social order altogether. Woman as a social/sexual being is repressed in the classic text, and if the male does not, as is usually the case, dominate the film at the narrative level, the woman can only become the pseudo-centre of the filmic discourse' (Claire Johnston, 'Femininity and the Masquerade', *Jacques Tourneur,* edited by Claire Johnston and Paul Wille-men, Edinburgh Film Festival, 1975, p.37).

What Kané's analysis 'shows' is that he has succeeded in finding in the text the presuppositions he brought to it: far from 'suspending' the protagonist's desire, *Sylvia Scarlett* uses it to effect a dismissive criticism of the dream of romantic male heroics which Sylvia initially embraces. The dream, it is continually stressed, has been derived from fiction ('We'll be like the Three Musketeers!' 'Why can't we be like Robin Hood?' 'I thought it was like being a highwayman'), and it is certainly part of the point that at the outset Sylvia imagines her invasion of the world of action in terms of re-enacting a prototype of glamorously buccaneering masculinity. At this stage, Monkley (Cary Grant) appears to embody it, and Sylvia has been prepared, precisely because of her inexperience, to embrace even his 'hawks and sparrows' philosophy ('The 'awks passes over the sparrers – that's nature!') in that it seems to offer the promise of free, expansive action – 'I'm out to beat the system! I'm free, I see life!' In the event, Sylvia interprets her actual experience as demonstrating the spuriousness of the romance, and throughout the film she invariably disrupts the performances in which she has collaborated by breaking the fictional world and siding with the sparrows. It is hardly an accident that her first expression of disappointment in 'adventure', in the wake of the disastrous episode in the park, should inspire Monkley to rebuke her with 'You've got no more sense than a girl'; and her reply – 'If I was a girl, I'd see you dead before I got mixed up with you' – implies a distance from her adopted role which is effectively realised in the next 'adventure', where she spoils Monkley's plan to use Maudie for the theft of the jewels. The film could hardly be clearer that this intervention, on behalf of another woman being exploited by men (her father and Monkley), has to do with Sylvia's *being a woman* – with the fact, that is, that she is not the male (or 'non-male') hero – though the climax of the sequence in Buckingham Gate, which has Sylvia, drunk on champagne, reaching out to a mural seascape and crying, 'I want the sea, I want the sea!' is there to suggest her continual expectation that there will eventually be a role adequate to her ideal conception of the world of action. The fact that none of them *are* is, of course, the point: the 'masculine' role which Sylvia has glamorised is as unsatisfactory as its 'feminine' counterpart (the domesticity she rejects), and her refusal to 'suspend her desire' is used by the film to 'place' her male educators.

One of the functions, indeed, of the first part of the film is to demonstrate that Sylvia's desire cannot be contained by either of the authenticated gender identities. The point is beautifully made when, out of sympathy with Maudie, Sylvia confesses that she and her companions are confidence tricksters: shaking her finger at her, Sylvia tells her that she is 'a very silly girl', and then, pointing in turn to Monkley, Scarlett and herself, adds, 'He's a crook, he's a crook – and *he's* a crook. Three *bad* eggs! – and we were all broke this afternoon.' Hepburn, with extraordinary skill, conveys not only the generosity and fellow-feeling which informs the rebuke and makes it so different a thing from what it would have been if voiced by a man, but also the implicit self-criticism involved: Sylvia has previously been taken in herself in exactly the same way, and has become the 'crook' who practises an identical imposture on another. The latent acknowledgement that the masquerade condemns Sylvia to oscillate between two terms which are *both* unacceptable – that the hiving off of her 'masculinity' as the male adventurer can no more be countenanced than being a girl – issues immediately in 'I want the sea'.

The symbolic function of the sea in *Sylvia Scarlett* anticipates that of the swamp, Sulphur Bottom, in *Home from the Hill*: it represents the unknown possibilities of sexual identity which lie beyond patriarchy. The particular force of this significance in Cukor's film can be noted by pointing out that the sea imagery also relates to Shakespearean romance – with the picaresque, the film's main literary referent. If the masquerade itself evokes the tradition supremely exemplified by Shakespeare's middle-period comedies (and Hepburn, it should be recalled, later played Rosalind, Viola and Portia on the stage), the imbrication in *Sylvia Scarlett* of the father/daughter relationship, symbolism of sea, tempest and death and resurrection by water, and Scarlett's ungovernable jealousy (as 'unmotivated' naturalistically as Leontes's) clearly recalls the characteristic imagery of the last plays. Analogously, the rural bacchanal halfway through the film can be related both to the Arden sequences in *As You Like It* and the Bohemian pastoral in *A Winter's Tale*, and the transvestite masquerade recurs in *Cymbeline*.

The reference is, of course, again ironic, and the irony is generated around Shakespeare's theme of the redemption of the patriarch by his daughter. From the outset, Sylvia's transformation into Sylvester is correlated with the 'feminisation' of her father: he tells Monkley that the lace he is smuggling is 'wrapped all round me like a corset', and while, on the boat, Sylvia's sea-sickness inspires him to reassert his former role (he calls her 'poor little girl'), the film is clear that their real relation has been reversed. Scarlett is 'afraid of everybody I see', and Sylvia becomes his guardian and protector ('Don't be nervous, don't be worried'). Part of the significance of the Buckingham Gate episode, from Scarlett's point of view, is the opportunity it provides for the recovery of his patriarchal status through performance – at Maudie's expense. He pretends initially to be an influential theatrical impresario who can get Maudie on the stage, and when they all start dressing up he casts himself as Napoleon ('*Vive l'Empereur!*').

Sylvia's very different interpretation of his costume ('Why, it's Little Lord Fauntleroy!'), and her subsequent exposure of the impresario story, reminds us of the very different nature of her and her father's 'masculinity', dissociating hers from the exercise of exploitative control and defining his in terms of a perilously flimsy self-aggrandisement which is inversely proportionate to what he actually is, and which thus appears as a kind of desperate compensation. However inadequate the masquerade may be as a mould for Sylvia's 'masculinity', she eagerly embraces it, but Scarlett's discovery of his 'femininity' is disabling, and we are to read his descent, first into unformulated anxiety and then into paranoia, as an expression of his inability to countenance it. When, shortly before his death, he sees that Sylvia has resumed female dress, his response is to say – 'You've come out in your own colours! Don't do that! Keep hid! Keep hid!' The remark is deeply ironic in that we have just seen, in Sylvia's conversation with Fane, the grotesque charade which putting on the dress has entailed for Sylvia, but the fact that Scarlett should feel that Sylvia's 'masculinity' is a *disguise* is crucially important for our assessment of his own, which really is, we are to gather, a protective camouflage.

Hence the significance of Scarlett's dying in the sea which has been connoted, through Sylvia, as a metaphor for non-patriarchal sexuality: the image which suggests the possibility of regeneration to his daughter means death for Scarlett. His breakdown, moreover, takes the form of an overwhelming and irrational fear that Maudie will leave him, and the film suggests that his love for her is intimately bound up with an attempt to recoup his maleness: having lost his patriarchal relation to Sylvia, he seeks to reaffirm the identity it implies through Maudie, and the extremity of the jealousy bespeaks both the intensity of the need she answers and the impossibility of anyone's satisfying it. His love is very much a matter of requiring a woman to confirm his 'masculinity'.

Scarlett's death by water is followed at once by Lily's attempt to drown herself and her rescue by Sylvia. The lesbian feeling which potentially unites Sylvia and Lily has already been implied in the 'unmasking' sequence at Fane's house, and the diverse reactions of Lily and Fane to the discovery that Sylvia is a woman are central to the film's meaning. Where Fane retreats from his desire into patronising ridicule and an attempt to disavow Sylvia's sexuality ('She knows nothing of that sort of thing'), Lily is instantly drawn to her. Recalling the slap Sylvia gave her for taunting Scarlett, Lily adds, 'I must give you that back', and

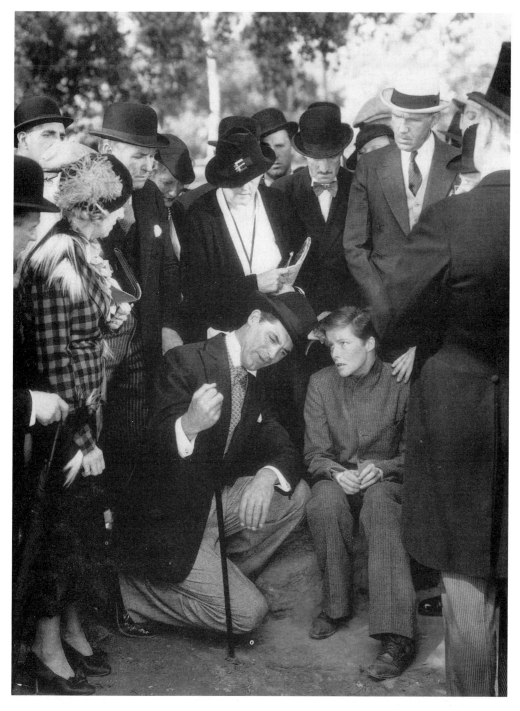

Still: Monkley and Sylvia in Sylvia Scarlett.

kisses her, the dialogue alerting us to the fact that it is precisely Sylvia's violation of gender which attracts her ('Were you a girl dressed as a boy, or a boy dressed as a girl?') The relationship develops in the conversation which follows Fane's departure, and both Lily's suicide attempt and Sylvia's decision to go off with

Monkley after her father's funeral can be read as complementary responses to the perception that, while Fane's presence blocks their friendship with each other, this in its turn affects the nature of their feelings about the man: each renounces him for the other.

The reciprocity of the two extreme forms of self-abnegation which the women adopt is dramatised in the staging of the attempted suicide and rescue. Lily's cries for help intrude on Sylvia just as she is breaking into tears after agreeing, in despair, to Monkley's proposal that they should 'muck along together', and the tacit suggestion that, in rescuing Lily, Sylvia is also symbolically renouncing suicide as a solution for *herself* is followed through after the rescue when Sylvia explicitly identifies herself with Lily ('Well, I suppose it's just her luck, like mine'). But the identification has a further significance: in denying herself Fane, whom she still loves, for Lily's sake, Sylvia condemns herself to live through a reunion with Fane *in fantasy*. She continues to be held within patriarchy, in other words, by a romantic idealism whose consummation will be infinitely postponed, and whose corollary is her hopeless, apathetic surrender to Monkley. It is this which gives point to the fact that Sylvia rescues Lily from the same stretch of water in which her father was drowned, and confirms at the same time the ironic function of the reference to Shakespearean romance, with its theme of women's transformation of patriarchy. Sylvia can refuse to die, or to compete, for a man, but the contradictions of the masquerade are such that she cannot escape an imaginary relation to him.

I suggested earlier that while many of the great female stars are sexually ambiguous, each of them gives a distinctive inflection to the interrogation of gender, and it is appropriate to conclude this chapter with a few brief comparisons.

The recurring love relationships between the Hepburn character and father figures in many early Hepburn movies suggest that her erotic appeal, for heterosexual men, is that of the 'son-daughter'. Given the stringent taboos which regulate the expression of affection and physical intimacy between father and son, the fact that Hepburn is 'really' a woman legitimates her appeal to male bisexuality. Conversely, her yielding devotion flatters the father's status, and confirms his possession of the phallus. The fact that the tomboy is finally a girl both permits the evasion of the prohibition of father/son eroticism and pre-empts the strain and antagonism produced, in the bourgeois family, by the potential sexual/social equality of father and son as men. At once little man and little woman, the tomboy can be a polymorphous sexual object while also providing the narcissistic satisfactions which the father requires of the daughter. *Morning Glory* remains the most systematic and efficient attempt to cast Hepburn's sexuality in this mould because the film's central metaphor, acting and theatre, allows it to assign 'masculinity' and 'femininity' to separate spheres and thus contain both the themes of the struggle within and resistance to the norms of gender which insist on expression in other films. For the tomboy is both an enormously satisfying and an extremely unstable sexual character, in that the tomboy's masculinity may voice itself in claims of parity and equality all the more disturbing for coming from a woman. A figure who promised simultaneously to fulfil the Oedipal offices of a daughter and eliminate the Oedipal tensions and inhibitions implicit in the relationship with a son may suddenly appear as the worst rather than the best of both worlds, refusing the daughter's position and taking up, as a woman, what ought to be the son's.

If Hepburn's early films seek to define her sexually as the 'son/daughter', Garbo movies set out increasingly to construct an image of the good phallic mother. If the Garbo character's relationships with younger women in her later films – Ebba (Elizabeth Young) in *Queen Christina*, Kitty (Maureen O'Sullivan) in *Anna Karenina*, Nichette (Elizabeth Allan) in *Camille* – have lesbian connotations, they retain heterosexual conventions, with Garbo in the 'male' role, and carry overtones of protective, parental tenderness and solicitude. *Queen Christina* is particularly striking in this respect: in all her scenes with Ebba, Christina is dressed as a man, and the dialogue of their first encounter deliberately evokes the convention of overworked 'husband' (public figure) and neglected 'wife' (excluded from her partner's business affairs and pining for his attention). The films, in other words, while 'masculinising' Garbo, are careful to preserve the distinction between the genders and, at the same time, to construct an opposition between eager, impulsive youthful innocence on the one hand and indulgent, generously ironical worldly experience on the other.

The significance of this strategy is that it assimilates 'masculinity' to the maternal, endowing Garbo with a specific set of virtues (a concern and tenderness accompanied by protective strength, a commitment and solicitude all the more intense for a suggestion of knowing serene detachment) which will later, with the onset of romantic passion, become the province of the hero, who is frequently as much son as lover. In *Conquest* (Clarence Brown, 1937), Marie Walewska refers to Napoleon (Charles Boyer) by his mother's pet name for him; in a legendary sequence in *A Woman of Affairs* (Clarence Brown, 1928), Diana Merrick displaces both her grief for her dead child and her yearning for her lover into the cradling embrace of a bouquet of flowers. The point is most clearly made by noting that in *The Single Standard* (John S. Robertson, 1929) and, most extraordinarily, the two versions of *Anna Karenina* (*Love*, Edmund Goulding, 1928; *Anna Karenina*, Clarence Brown, 1935), the Garbo character's desire for her son is created with an amazing erotic intensity, and the child, rather than the husband, becomes the lover's rival. When, in other words, Garbo plays a mother with a male child, her allegiances are divided, maternal love appears as an antagonistic sexual drive, and the lover presents a conflicting claim to her maternity, but when maternal/sexual love is invested in a young woman, the lover supersedes her. Bidding farewell to Ebba at the Swedish border before riding off to join Antonio (John Gilbert), Christina embraces her and adds, 'Goodbye, Sweden': lesbianism and political power make up that world which is well lost for love.

There is, of course, as in Hepburn's case, ample room for contradiction here, of which Garbo's acting takes full advantage: the evidence of a narrative intention does not necessarily entail its unproblematic realisation, nor eliminate the possibility of putting film and performance to other uses. It does seem strikingly the case, however, that Garbo's films seek to code her sexual duality as a perfect wholeness, in which diverse elements bespeak not conflict and tension but ideal unity. As protective phallic mother and little man/little woman respectively, Garbo and Hepburn stand in very different relations to patriarchy, the second of which is fraught with greater dangers than the first. One can be ultimately recouped as androgynous goddess; the other is a potential Prometheus.

5. The Female Community

Before discussing *Stage Door* I wish to consider the significance, in a number of Hepburn's 'thirties films, of relationships between sisters and between mothers and daughters, most obviously, of course, in *Little Women*, but also in *A Bill of Divorcement*, *A Woman Rebels*, *Quality Street* and *Holiday*. The Hollywood cinema provides numerous examples of films about female relatives – sisters, cousins, mother and daughter – bound together in passionate, destructive resentment and animosity: *The Old Maid* (Edmund Goulding, 1939), *The Little Foxes* (William Wyler, 1941), *Mildred Pierce* (Michael Curtiz, 1944), *The Dark Mirror* (Robert Siodmak, 1946), *A Stolen Life* (Curtis Bernhardt, 1946), *What Ever Happened to Baby Jane?* (Robert Aldrich, 1962) are obvious representative cases. The animosity is invariably generated by the women being rivals for a man and/or, as in the twin-doubles films, by their embodiment of the 'good' (wifely, domesticated) and 'bad' (sexual) woman respectively. There are also, conversely, many instances

Stills. Below – Pamela Thistlewaite (Hepburn) in A Woman Rebels. *Opposite: Susan and Phoebe Throssel in* Quality Street.

of female relatives achieving solidarity in the name and interests of the father: *Since You Went Away* (John Cromwell, 1944), in which the absent patriarch is explicitly compared with God, is classical in this respect.

In the Hepburn films we have something radically different. Here, the bond between female blood-relatives creates an oppositional unity in contradiction to that of the patriarchal family which gives it its basis: the Hepburn character is profoundly committed to this 'other family', and it is destroyed by the intervention of men. In each case, too, as we might expect, the commitment to sister or mother or both is inseparable from the challenge to the authority of the father. *Meet Me in St Louis* (Vincente Minnelli, 1944), offers a partial similarity: Tootie (Margaret O'Brien), who orchestrates the destruction of the patriarchal middle-class family and its concomitant gender roles in the Halloween sequence, might well grow up to be Susan Vance *(Bringing Up Baby)* or the feminist Leninist of the first thirty minutes of *The Little Minister*. (One wishes indeed, that Minnelli had been there to direct *Alice Adams* – a work whose latent possibilities are central to his thematic concerns.) But if the female members of the Smith family are profoundly hostile to the father, and the film is bent on demonstrating the *objective* contradiction between their interests as women and the claims of patriarchy, it is predominantly concerned to analyse the social process whereby that contradiction is annealed, and the women's oppositional solidarity actually recouped for patriarchy. (I have argued this case in detail in the *Australian Journal of Screen Theory* 3, reprinted in *CineAction!* 35, 1994.)

The Hepburn films begin to go further than this, though the very fact that they do so necessitates a nervous scurrying towards the emergency exit at the end, which isn't, as it is in Minnelli's movie, offered ironically.

If we compare *Little Women* with two of the other 'sisters' films, *A Woman Rebels* and *Holiday*, we at once become aware of a very striking difference between them. In the first scene in which Jo (Hepburn) appears in *Little Women*, she is told, admonishingly, by Aunt March (Edna May Oliver) that she is 'so much like [her] father', and her reaction indicates that she reads the remark as a criticism not of herself but of *him* – 'I'm very proud of father, and you should be so too!' In the other two films, on the contrary, the Hepburn character is violently at odds with her father. This difference is determined by another: whereas in *Little Women*, the father (Mr March) is absent throughout most of the film (he is away fighting in the Civil War), leaving a family which consists entirely of women, in *A Woman Rebels* and *Holiday* the father is a dominant and repressive presence in the house and the mother is dead.

The distinction is clearly crucial, and the fact that it depends on the presence or absence of the mother and father already indicates its significance. The father's Oedipal admonition is still there in *Little Women*, in the form of the letter from Mr March, read aloud to her daughters by Marmee (Spring Byington), which expresses his confidence that the girls 'will remember all I said to them' and go on to 'conquer themselves beautifully;' but the fact that he is not physically present removes the main obstacle in the path of Jo's preservation of her 'masculinity'. In other words, Jo can only like him because he isn't around, and while she vows to 'try to be what he loves to call me – a little woman', she is able to remain a 'little man', and retain both her lesbian attachment to her sisters and her aspiration to fulfil herself creatively as a professional writer. In the other two films, the father being present, the refusal to renounce these desires and demands enforces open conflict.

Little Women has become emblematic in popular memory of sentimental Victorian girls' fiction. A contemporary reviewer of Cukor's film described it as 'an entertaining romance of heart-throbs and tears, girlish laughter and innocent joy', and another remarked:

'Because *Little Women* is a homely story of family life, of the love of parents for their children, of the close bonds of union that will forever survive in many families as self-sacrificing and mutually co-operative as the March family, and because the joys and sorrows of this little group are of the kind which, in one way or another, come at some time or other to thousands of households, it is of the type which never ceases to hold appeal.'

While the writer is, in one sense, more accurate than he knows, the whimsy is his own gift to the text, and bears no relation to anything provided by either Alcott or Cukor. Alcott was an active feminist, one of the founders, in 1870, of the Massachusetts Woman Suffrage Association; and we may relate Jo March to those 'heroines with the strengths and aptitudes of men as well as the domestic skills and sensitivities of women', which, in her admirable biography of Alice James, Jean Strouse shows to have been characteristic of a number of popular nineteenth-century female novelists. Strouse remarks:

'There were probably as many private reasons for this fictional cross-dressing as there were writers; viewed socially, these heroines probably represented the longings of nineteenth-century women for a world in which roles divided less absolutely along sexual lines – one in which they could become active, whole, fully functioning individuals' (Strouse, *Alice James*, Jonathan Cape, 1981, pp.195-196).

Elsewhere, Strouse quotes a passage from Alcott's diary in which she discusses her decision to volunteer for nursing duty in Washington during the Civil War: 'I *must* let out my pent-up energy in some new way . . . I want new experiences and am sure to get 'em if I go' (Strouse, p.79). This both confirms our sense of the literary tradition from which the Hepburn persona derives and indicates the nature of Alcott's interest in Jo, whose first response to Mr March's Oedipal epistle is a feeling of guilt about wanting to do what Alcott *did*: 'I'll try to do my duty here at home, and not want to go to war and help father.'

The subject of Cukor's film is the contradiction between what Jo wants the family to be and what, as a patriarchal family, it necessarily is: more properly, since the contradiction is never fully available to her, the film is about her attempt to use the family to reconcile a number of things which are incompatible both with it and with each other. The opening scenes dramatise with great economy and lucidity the nature of the potential tension between Jo and the family and the way in which it is contained. She is introduced reading aloud to Aunt March, who has dozed off, from a tract on exemplary female conduct, which enjoins young women to 'crush and blot out pitilessly' the seeds of defiance and impropriety. She tries to slip out quietly, but her aunt wakes up, and when Jo explains that she was 'off to rehearse [her] play' she is reprimanded for her selfishness ('Never a thought about *my* Christmas'). Aunt March lets her go, giving her a dollar each for herself and her sisters as a Christmas present and commanding her to dust the stair-rail before she leaves. As soon as her aunt's back is turned, Jo dusts the banister by sliding down it, and hurries out.

The scene, which turns on Aunt March's observation that Jo is 'so much like [her] father, 'might be compared with the opening scene of *A Woman Rebels,* in which Pamela (Hepburn) is taken to task by her father for the 'violation of every rule of this house' and ordered, as a punishment, to learn by heart selected passages from another primer for women, described by her governess as 'the Bible of English womanhood – every word is a holy command.' The force of the comparison depends on the different ways in which the Hepburn character responds: whereas Pamela is openly intransigent ('I don't believe in the book or anything in it! It's rubbish!'), Jo seeks to negotiate between her opposition and the status quo. She doesn't want to do the housework but her *method* of doing it allows her to combine a rebellious gesture with the fulfilment of her aunt's injunction: she can be seen to have done what she has been told while also expressing her desire not to do it. Her disagreement with the contents of the book issues not in confrontation but (a beautifully significant detail) in an attempt to creep out of the room while still reading, so that Aunt March won't be startled out of her nap by the abrupt cessation of speech. Of Jo's three acts of defiance in the scene, one is surreptitious, another aspires to be, and the third is a *defence* of her father.

And this, of course, is the point. The tone and contents of Mr March's letter indicate clearly enough that, if he were actually there, he would appear, for Jo,

Stills: Amy (Joan Bennett) and Jo in Little Women.

as Judge Thistlewaite (Donald Crisp), the father of *A Woman Rebels*. Because he isn't, Jo is able to channel her opposition to patriarchy into *replacing* the father rather than challenging him; by the same token, she commits herself to a project of seeking to fulfil, through the family, desires and impulses which logically entail breaking with it. If the father's absence allows Jo to hold on to her 'masculinity' in the first place, it also permits her, by pre-empting a clash with him, to believe that her family can remain an appropriate context for it. Because, by the same token, her desire and her father's desire for her have never come into conflict, she is placed in the paradoxical position of really wishing to 'try to be what he loves to call me – a little woman' when in fact everything that she is and does bespeaks resistance to such an invitation. The peculiar situation in which Jo finds herself both makes the reality of her desires partially opaque to her (she *doesn't* actually want to be a 'little woman', though she can at points persuade herself that she thinks she does) and diverts transgressive desire back into the institution it transgresses, where its frustration is inevitable.

The main way in which, in the early stages of the film, Jo tries to resolve her situation is acting (*Little Women* is close to *Sylvia Scarlett* in this respect): theatre provides a medium through which the desires that strain against the confines of the Puritanical middle-class family – Jo's love of pleasure, her 'masculine' sexual drives, her literary creativity – can be accommodated to it. We have already noted how Jo's confession to Aunt March that she was 'off to rehearse [her] play' brought forth an accusation of selfishness, and throughout the film the sisters are constantly enjoined, or placed in a position in which they feel compelled, to make sacrifices. When they are discussing what they should do with Aunt March's dollar, Jo exclaims at once – 'Buy what we want and have a little fun!' At the end of the same sequence, Beth (Jean Parker) – of the four sisters the least like Jo, and the one Jo loves most deeply (a point to which I'll return) – suggests that they should 'get something for Marmee with our dollar'. The suggestion immediately follows the reading of the paternal letter, with its request that the girls should 'conquer themselves beautifully'; and it is, indeed, through Beth that we discover what conquering oneself beautifully ultimately entails – death. The implication, for the discussion of Jo's love for Beth, of the contrast between Jo's spontaneous commitment to personal pleasure and Beth's embodiment of self-sacrifice can be left to one side for a moment: but it is clearly significant that the latter should appear here as self-sacrifice for the mother, and that it should entail not 'spending' but 'saving' (the sexual connotation of the denial or postponement of gratification will turn out to be crucial). We are

told that in the past Jo has tried to make 'saving' pleasurable again by turning it into a game based on *The Pilgrim's Progress*, in which the saving is imagined as Christian's burden, and the image captures perfectly both the contradiction between Jo's desire and the morality enjoined by her family, and her way of coping with it. The reminder of the game evokes the chilling reply, 'You have real burdens now', and the scene ends with the sisters gathered round the piano to sing 'Abide with me' in a group in which Jo stands slightly apart from the rest. On Christmas morning, Marmee appeals to them to make a further sacrifice, their Christmas breakfast (Jo has just exclaimed, 'I can't tell you how hungry I am!'), for a starving and impoverished family living (inevitably) just down the road. In each case, at the behest of Marmee or Beth (the father's wife and the epitome of the beauty of self-conquest), Jo finds herself having to want and enjoy the things she does not.

The game/theatre metaphor is fully elaborated through Jo's play, 'The Witch's Curse'. It has already been associated, in the scene with Aunt March, with Jo's 'selfishness', her infringement of her domestic duties and her indifference to the promptings of the text she is reading, and its rehearsal is interrupted by the arrival of Marmee with her husband's missive. Jo plays both the male parts – the hero, Roderigo, and the villain, Black Hugo; and the scene we are shown, in rehearsal and performance, is that in which Hugo, having captured the heroine played by Amy (Joan Bennett), comes looming towards her 'to carry

Stills: Little Women. *Opposite – Amy, Marmee (Spring Byington), Meg (Frances Dee), Beth (Jean Parker) and Jo. Below – Amy, Jo and Meg.*

out [his] fell design'. Jo is enraged, in rehearsal, by the lifelessness of Amy's acting (she is required to cry 'Roderigo! Roderigo! Save me! Save me!', and swoon), and in order to demonstrate the bravura with which the thing should be done, doubles briefly as the heroine and her assailant.

We should note, to begin with, that Jo's writing is Gothic, and that the Gothic serves her, as it did so many Victorian women writers (the Brontës, Christina Rossetti, Elizabeth Barrett Browning), in providing a mode through which illicit sexual preoccupations, otherwise 'unthinkable' and inexpressible, could be articulated. In Jo's case it allows her to enact the displacement of the father and dramatise her erotic feelings for her sisters. These feelings, in 'The Witch's Curse', are both asserted and denied inasmuch as their medium is that hero/villain convention, germane to Gothic melodrama, in which the hero's sexuality is projected on to his antagonist and imagined as evil. The fact that Jo plays both parts at once makes the 'doppelgänger' motif explicit, and indicates the nature of the process whereby Jo's desire is sublimated into protectiveness (directed here towards Amy, but elaborated most fully in Jo's relationship with Beth).

It also demonstrates, of course, the insolubly problematic nature of Jo's position – the position of a woman who is seeking not to challenge and reject the father's function but to appropriate it, and who inherits with it something of its repressiveness. For the conventions of male sexuality which inform 'The Witch's Curse' are repressive not only in their assimilation of sexuality to wickedness, but in their construction of the heroine as the male's object, to be persecuted by the 'bad' father and rescued by the 'good'.

Stills: Little Women – *Jo with Professor Bhaer (Paul Lukas, above) and Laurie.*

What the curse *is* in Jo's play doesn't appear, but the film is certainly about the way in which Jo's writing embodies all the ambiguities of her relation to patriarchy. On the one hand it is, both as an activity and in its particular content, an affront to norms of 'femininity'. In rejecting the proposal from Laurie (Douglass Montgomery), Jo remarks that 'you don't like my scribbling, and I can't do without it'; and subsequently Professor Bhaer (Paul Lukas), while telling Jo that she has 'talent', and that she should 'sweep the streets before [she is] false to that talent', takes exception nevertheless to the manner in which it expresses itself – he describes her stories, which are again Gothic (one of them is entitled 'The Curse of the Coventrys, or the Secret of a Guilty Heart') as 'artificial', and adds pointedly, 'And those women!' We are invited to feel that, as a prospective partner, Bhaer is to be preferred to Laurie in that he is prepared to acknowledge and affirm Jo's creativity, but the terms in which he rejects what she has done before she had the good fortune to meet him are crucial, and it is implied that she can be true to her talent only by following his advice. 'And those women!' is evidence enough that even as flexible a patriarch as Professor Bhaer cannot unbend far enough to accommodate Jo's Gothic, and the association of 'artifice' with immaturity and lack of 'femininity' ties in interestingly with characteristic motifs of later Hepburn material, within and outside the films.

On the other hand, the writing also carries the connotations of repressiveness and self-oppression which can be divined from the play: Tootie's Gothic obsession in *Meet Me in St Louis*, manifest in her attempt to make up for her oppressed position in the family by creating a surrogate family of dolls over whom she exerts the extreme of patriarchal power, the regulation of life and death ('She has three fatal diseases'), provides an interesting parallel. The story of 'The Curse of the Coventrys', with its telling sub-title, concerns the extravagantly bloody murder of a pair of young lovers, and suggests an imaginary acting-through of Jo's resentment of the courtship of Meg (Frances Dee) and Brooke (John Davis Lodge). The placing of the scene in which part of the story is read out is eloquent in itself: it has been preceded by Jo's discovery, through Laurie, of the romance between Meg and Brooke, and, more immediately, by the scene in which she has cut and sold her long hair (after insisting, near the beginning of the film, that 'I'll leave it down till I'm a hundred') in order to get money for Marmee's trip to visit Mr March in hospital. The juxtaposition captures the paradox – the cycle of oppression and self-oppression – entailed in Jo's commitment to the family: she hates Brooke because his presence threatens to disrupt the female group in which she has invested everything, and yet the cause in which she surrenders her hair speaks directly of female self-sacrifice for the father, and thus of the patriarchal basis on which Jo's 'other family' ultimately rests. The violence of the story arises from this impasse, and its reading is interrupted by the arrival of Beth with the first symptoms of the scarlet fever that will later kill her.

The relations between Jo, Meg and Beth are, indeed, the heart of the film. *Little Women* shares with *A Woman Rebels* and *Holiday* the theme of the conservatism of the Hepburn character's sisters, but it is distinguished by the unique

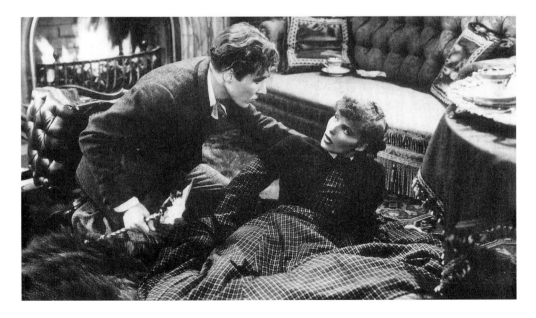

(and, as we feel it, tragic) imbrication of radicalism and conservatism in the Hepburn character herself. The fact that Meg, Beth and Amy are, differently but unshakably, their father's daughters preordains the frustration of Jo's feelings for them, but it is also what Jo's project of replacing the father requires them to be, and the effect of the contradiction is followed through, as a set of variations, with each sister. As exemplary 'little women', Meg and Amy see in Jo a way, not of being a woman, but of being a tomboy and a disgrace. During the rehearsal scene, Amy tells Jo that she is 'unladylike', and that she is 'old enough now to leave off boyish tricks;' as the sisters prepare to leave for Laurie's party, Meg cautions Jo to 'behave nicely' and refrain from 'disgracing us all' with her favourite expression of enthusiasm or surprise, 'Christopher Columbus!' The latent conflict with Meg comes to a head over Brooke: after Jo has succeeded in breaking up their tête-à-tête outside the March house ('Goodbye, Mr Brooke – come along, Meg'), Meg turns on her with, 'When will you stop your childish romping ways?', drawing from Jo the passionate cry – 'Not till I'm old and stiff and have to use a crutch!' As Meg walks away, Jo dissolves into tears.

Meg, who wants nothing for herself but the conventional destiny, notes Jo's divergence from the 'feminine' norm which that destiny entails, and Hepburn powerfully communicates both the distress which Meg's priggish, patronising self-complaisance causes Jo, and the accompanying refusal of Jo to win Meg by compromising herself. But Meg's conservatism guarantees and necessitates both her impatience with Jo and her inability even to begin to conceive of the kind of commitment Jo could have to her and to the community of the sisters. Thus while the failure of reciprocity is built into Jo's love for Meg, which comes up inevitably against rebuttal and asperity, Jo's own attitude is clearly possessive. On learning from Laurie of Brooke's interest in Meg, she accuses Brooke of 'trying to break up people's happiness,' and later says to Meg, 'Do you have to fall in love and spoil all our happy times together?'

The painfulness of this is a matter of our recognition that Jo's situation has conduced to the imagination of radical possibilities while also returning them to a conservatism more extreme than Meg's. Jo can see, as Meg cannot, the possibility of relationships between women which are not mediated by, or predicated on, men, but Jo's assumption of the father's role directs her desire into Oedipal jealousy: she becomes the patriarch who resents his daughter's lover, and is endowed with the sexual repressiveness which that implies ('Romantic? – rubbish!') Because Meg is Mr March's 'little woman' while Jo seeks to replace Mr March, Jo is cast as both oppressor and oppressed – as the patriarch of her own family and the 'disgrace' of Meg's.

Jo's deepest love is reserved for the sister who is the most extremely different from herself and who, as the incarnation of female passivity, embodies everything which Jo's identity affronts. Beth makes the point herself, just before her death, when she compares herself to 'the cricket on the hearth' and tells Jo that she has always 'reminded [her] of a seagull, strong and wild, flying away'. The extent of the difference is the corollary of the extent of the love: in loving Beth, Jo loves exactly what her father does, and what she herself has refused to be. It is in this context that the significance of Beth's scarlet fever is clarified. Discussing the function of tuberculosis in nineteenth-century fiction, Susan Sontag writes:

Still: Little Women – *Meg, Jo, Beth and Amy with, standing, Hannah (Mabel Colcord) and Marmee.*

'Like all really successful metaphors, the metaphor of TB was rich enough to provide for two contradictory applications. It described the death of someone (like a child) thought to be too "good" to be sexual: the assertion of an angelic psychology. It was also a way of describing sexual feelings – while lifting the responsibility for libertinism, which is blamed on a state of objective, physio-logical decadence or deliquescence. It was both a way of describing sensuality and promoting the claims of passion, and a way of describing repression and advertising the claims of sublimation, the disease inducing both a "numbness of spirit" (Robert Louis Stevenson's words) and a suffusion of higher feelings' (Susan Sontag, *Illness as Metaphor,* New York, Farrar, Straus and Giroux, New York, 1978, pp.33-34).

While it should be added that the contradiction noted by Sontag is a dialectical one, in that the 'claims of sublimation' also underlie the 'promotion of the claims of passion' (the passion, which is almost invariably female, must always be *doomed*), her description of the use of the metaphor to 'assert an angelic psy-chology' is clearly correct, and may be extended to cover Beth's scarlet fever.

Beth contracts the disease while nursing the sick child of the family for whom the sisters sacrificed their Christmas meal: the illness is associated with the self-sacrifice to which the girls are generally enjoined, and figures as an embodiment of it. The essence of that sacrifice, which constitutes the 'little woman', is active sexuality, for the removal of which death provides the ultimate guarantee. Jo has refused that sacrifice, and given her preservation of pre-Oedipal desire, and the love for Beth in which it manifests itself, Beth's lingering prostration functions both to elevate Beth to the inner sanctum of womanhood, and to punish (and pre-empt the consummation of) Jo's transgressive desire by removing its object. Beth is taken away by the father *par excellence*, and her death is followed at once by Jo's confession of loneliness ('It means more to me now to be loved than it used to') and her acceptance of Professor Bhaer. In this unique inflection of the illness metaphor, Beth's scarlet fever operates as a means of regulating female desire through *both* parties, and reflects the implicit acknowledgement that it is finally Beth's presence which militates against Jo's attachment to a man: with Beth gone, the heterosexual liaison is swiftly effected.

The reading is confirmed by the way in which the narrative organises Beth's decease. The first bout of scarlet fever occurs halfway through the film, and Beth recovers from it: immediately afterwards, Meg and Brooke get married. The marriage is decisive in Jo's development, for it is during the celebrations after the ceremony that Jo refuses Laurie's proposal and resolves to leave home, an intention she communicates to her mother in the subsequent scene ('I'd like to see and hear new things, and get a lot of new ideas for my stories'). This chain of events is crucially significant: the fact that the Meg/Brooke marriage goes through alerts Jo for the first time to the recognition of the frustration that is entailed for her in the attempt to hold the family together ('Why can't we stay as we are?') on her terms, and precipitates her decision to leave the family. It is at this point that Jo becomes ideologically dangerous, for the loss of Meg isn't accompanied by a turn towards a man: she tells Laurie, in the midst of the nuptial ceremonies which so obviously distress her, that 'I don't think I'll ever marry'. Jo retains her 'masculine' identification, but resolves to move outside the home in which it could only find expression in a re-enactment of the father's role. The film at once introduces Professor Bhaer, but it is necessary for Beth to die before Jo can become fully available to him, and the telegram announcing the fatal recurrence of Beth's illness arrives just as Bhaer is asking Jo for her father's address (he wishes, though Jo doesn't know it, to ask Mr March's permission to court her).

That Bhaer's function is tied to Beth's is made fully explicit in the final scene, when Jo, Meg and Brooke, and Amy and Laurie (who are now engaged) gather together in the March house. As the others celebrate their reunion, Jo moves off on her own and, raising her eyes, whispers, 'Fun, isn't it, Bethy? – now that we're all together again.' The moment corresponds to Jo's prayer earlier in the film: during the crisis of the first bout of Beth's illness, Jo has again isolated herself from the rest of the house and begged God to spare Beth's life – 'Please don't'. He *does*, of course, but the final scene suggests, appallingly, that it doesn't matter: not only is Jo maintaining her relationship with Beth, but she is addressing her in preference to the Father, and appears to be set, in the face of divine interdiction, to recreate the previous disposition of the family. Bhaer turns up at the last minute with a fumbling and inept proposal, delivered on the front porch, and Jo ushers him into the house with the 'Welcome home!' which is the film's last line. Both final alternatives – enclosure within the home through marriage or through an imaginary reconstruction of the lost unity of

Still: Ned Seton (Lew Ayres), Linda Seton (Hepburn) and Johnny Case (Cary Grant) in Holiday.

the sisters – are equally unacceptable in terms of the possibilities Jo has discovered after Meg's marriage, but Jo's logical trajectory – the development of a relationship with another woman outside the home – was, of course, in 1933 and for long thereafter, unfilmable in Hollywood.

In the light of the preoccupations of *Little Women*, it is pleasant to note that the film's enormous contemporary success – it was, with Mae West's first film, *She Done Him Wrong*, the box-office smash of the year – was taken as evidence, by apologists for the Hays Code, that audiences really did want *nice* films as well as smut.

Holiday, like *Little Women*, is structured round the relationship between 'non-conformist' and conventional sisters – here, Linda (Hepburn) and Julia Seton (Doris Nolan). The nature of the opposition between them is beautifully defined in the scene in which Mr Seton (Henry Kolker) discusses with Julia her engagement to Johnny Case (Cary Grant), whose character, background and aspirations are strikingly out of true with Seton's ideal of a son-in-law. In order to indicate the nature of his objections, he draws an analogy with his cigar, the tobacco for which was grown on a plantation owned by him, and which he knows in advance will provide him with familiar and certain pleasures. Julia takes up the point, assuring him that that is exactly what Johnny will be like, and Seton finally gives his consent. Linda knocks on the door to discover the verdict, and on finding that her father has retreated from his previous opposition, embraces him enthusiastically. He withdraws slightly, and tells her to be careful – 'you'll put out my cigar'.

Still: Ned and Linda in Holiday.

The scene has no equivalent in Philip Barry's original play, and the bare description cannot do justice to the tact and delicacy with which the symbolism is realised. The cigar isn't simply a sexual image – the economic connotation (Julia's husband should be a good capital investment) is equally important: indeed, the meaning of the image is a question of the imbrication of the two, and the parallel indifference they describe between Julia's pleasure and her father's. Mr Seton grows the tobacco, reaps the profit and smokes the cigar, and wishes to be assured that Johnny will operate in the same way *for* Julia, who will find her satisfaction in her husband's having a cigar with analogous credentials. In relating Johnny at once to Mr Seton and to Julia, the metaphor dramatises with great succinctness the agreement between father and daughter on the requisite place of women in patriarchal-capitalist relations, and illustrates, correspondingly, the significance of Linda's threat to put out the cigar.

The film's central sequence – the New Year's Eve party at which Julia's engagement is to be announced – takes place largely in the playroom which the Setons used when they were children. As Linda's private home-within-the-home, it corresponds to Jo's family-within-the-family in *Little Women*, but its oppositional status, unlike its predecessor's, is explicit: it contains those possibilities in the children which the patriarchal family has repressed, and which can only be regenerated in defiance of it. During Johnny's first visit to the room, Linda shows him the old piano that belongs to Ned (Lew Ayres), who used to be an accomplished pianist, and her own unfinished paintings, and the weight we are to give to the blockage and frustration of their creativity becomes clear from the fact that the room is associated primarily with their mother. The dawning of Johnny's perception, on the night of the party, that there is something more radically wrong in the family than he'd supposed comes out of a drunken outburst from Ned:

'Father wanted a big family, you know. So she [mother] had Julia straight off, to oblige him. But Julia was a girl, so she promptly had Linda. But Linda was a girl – it looked hopeless. So the next year she had me, and there was much joy in the land. It was a boy, and the fair name of Seton would flourish. It must have been a great consolation to father. Drink to mother, Johnny – she tried to be a Seton for a while, then gave up and died.'

What is wrong, from the Seton point-of-view, is that Ned and Linda have failed to negotiate their Oedipus complex satisfactorily – neither has been constrained to renounce their mother. Ned has been able to cope with his refusal to be the longed-for son only by becoming alcoholic, and retreating into a sterile, cynical embitterment. But as he himself puts it, 'unlike me, Linda always hopes', and the process whereby the Oedipal rebellion passes from the male to the female child is central to the film, and to our sense of its stature. Ned, it is clear, is incapable of breaking with the family: his attitude to drinking is akin to the 'I prefer not to' of Herman Melville's Bartleby, and as a challenge to the father it can't move beyond passive resistance. Indeed, he is quite lucid about the limitations of his strategy, and accepts its terms:

Linda: You get beaten, though, don't you?
Ned: Sure. But that's good, too. Then you don't mind anything – not anything at all. Then you sleep.
Linda: How long can you keep it up?
Ned: A long while. As long as you last.
Linda: Oh, Ned – that's awful!
Ned: Think so? Other things are worse.
Linda: But where do you end up?
Ned: Where does everybody end up? You die. And that's alright, too.

At the end of the film, when Linda finally leaves the house, she asks Ned to come with her. Mr Seton at once interposes – 'A trip now is out of the question. Please remember you have a position to fill.' What that position is has been implicitly defined, for Ned as for Julia, in the cigar scene, and Ned's significance in the dramatic structure is to be a middle-term between the two sisters.

Linda: You won't?
Ned: I can't.
Linda: Caught?
Ned: Maybe.
Linda: I'll be back for you, Ned.
Ned: I'll be here.

That a man rather than a woman should be placed in this position is remarkable, and the dialogue draws attention to the reversal of the conventional roles: 'I'll be back for you' is an emblematic 'male' line. This doesn't imply, however, that Linda, in rebelling as she does, is 'masculinised'. On the contrary, the film emphasises that she is able to respond to her oppression in that way rather than in Ned's precisely because she is a woman. Ned may not want to fill the position his father mentions, but he is very conscious of having it, and his alcoholism is a way of rejecting it and clinging to it at the same time.

Linda's 'You won't?' and his 'I can't' are both, in a sense, true: his inability to do anything, except to embrace a prolonged proxy suicide, is very much a matter of his particular relation, as the son and heir who remains heterosexual, to the phallus. Linda isn't in that position, and the playroom sequence culminates in the moment when she finally turns against her father in a way which realises the radical significance of Jo's commitment in *Little Women*. The dialogue must be quoted at length:

Linda: Listen to me, father. Tonight means a good deal to me – I don't know what, precisely – and I don't know how. Something is trying to take it away from me, and I can't let it go. I'll put in an appearance downstairs, if you like. Then I want to bring a few people up here – the few people in the world I can talk to and feel something for . . . That's alright with you, isn't it?
Seton: Your place is downstairs.
Linda: Once more, father: this is important to me. Don't ask me why. I don't know. It has something to do with when I was a child here, and this room, and good times in it, and –
Seton: What special virtue this room has I'm sure I don't see.
Linda: You don't, do you? No, you can't. Well, this room's my home. It's the only home I've got. There's something here that I understand, and that understands me. Maybe it's mother.
Seton: Please do as I have told you, Linda.
Linda: I suppose you know it's the end of us, then.
Seton: Don't talk nonsense. Do as I say . . .
Linda: You thought I'd come round, didn't you? You always think people will come round. Not me – not tonight. And I shan't be bothered here, either. Because if there's one thing you can't stand it's a scene. I can promise you one if you interfere – I can promise you a beauty!
Seton (ignoring her): Well, Johnny, so there's good news, is there?
Linda: Was mother a sweet soul, father? Was she exciting?

Seton: Linda, if you are not happy here, why don't you go away? I should be glad if next month you would take your maid and go on a trip somewhere. You distress me. You cause nothing but trouble and upsets. You —

Linda: All right, father. That's just what I'm going to do, after the wedding. No maid, though. Just me, Linda, the kid herself!

Seton: As you wish.

Linda: I've wanted to get out for years. I've never known it so well as tonight. I can't bear it here any longer – it's doing terrible things to me.

Seton: And you will leave this room now, please.

Linda: This room – this room. I don't think you'll be able to stand it long. I'll come back when you've left it.

If you had to chose a sequence to represent Hepburn's radical significance, this would do as well as another. There is obviously no question here of a desire to replace the father, but instead a repudiation of the function itself: when Linda tells Seton that he 'can't' see what the playroom represents, she makes the essential criticism which the context as a whole elaborates. What Linda 'can't let go' is the condition of female desire prior to the father's intervention, and the connotations of play, creativity and pre-Oedipal sexuality (Ned's as well as Linda's) which have by now accrued to the room are fixed, through the primary reference to the mother, as a metaphor for the repressed. The function of the Hepburn figure, in both *Holiday* and *Bringing Up Baby*, is to be the return of the repressed, and we need only compare these embodiments of it with the presentment of female Oedipal rebellion in the Gothic, which invariably signifies

Still: Susan Vance (Hepburn) and David Huxley (Cary Grant) in Bringing Up Baby.

castration (see, most obviously, *The Exorcist*, William Friedkin, 1973), to realise the way in which the Gothic metaphor necessarily constructs the repressed as a negative. It does so by defining it in terms of anarchic primal energies which are *per se* 'uncivilisable' – a definition which builds in an equation of 'civilisation' with patriarchy which must, in turn, assimilate transgressive female desire to the appropriation of the phallus. This concept of the repressed underlies those Freudian formulations (the id as 'a seething cauldron of excitements') that are most deeply informed by romantic psychology. The clearest analogue within the Gothic to Linda and the playroom is, perhaps, Rebecca's bedroom in *Rebecca* (Alfred Hitchcock, 1940) – again an oppositional home-within-the-home, associated with a relationship between women (at once maternal and lesbian) which defies and sets itself up against patriarchal regulation. But its connotations are entirely negative: Rebecca is explicitly identified with the devil and the power of 'aberrant' female sexuality with castration, so that while Hitchcock's film doesn't affirm De Winter (Laurence Olivier), it is left in the familiar position of being able to affirm nothing else.

In *Holiday*, the return of the repressed isn't 'archetypal', and does not connote regression: Linda embodies a conscious and intelligent allegiance to values and experiences which patriarchy necessarily inhibits, and it is the cost of the inhibition (the mother's death, Ned's alcoholic degeneration, Linda's 'it's doing terrible things to me') which the film rejects. Its way of following through the implications of rejecting them is, of course, evasive. The patriarchal organisation of sexuality has been correlated with the capitalist organisation of property, but all the film can propose, at this level, through Johnny and Linda, is that people who have just made an enormous haul on the stock market have enough money to opt out. The bifurcation, in the film's positive relationship, of the sexual and economic themes which are interrelated in the critique of the family is inevitable and scarcely surprising (Hollywood movies do not habitually affirm socialism), but this should not be allowed to divert attention from the substance of what *is* achieved. Similarly, while the ending does attach Linda to Johnny, sexually and, in prospect, economically, it is crucial that he does not appear as the agent of her 'spiritual education' (compare *My Man Godfrey*, Gregory La Cava, 1936): her opposition to what the Setons represent long predates his appearance, and her break with her father during the party is not motivated by desire for Johnny, or in any sense inspired by him. Indeed, he continues, albeit half-heartedly, to try to make a success of the relationship with Julia *after* Linda's attitude to her family has been made clear to him.

This brings up another fundamental difference between *Holiday* and *Little Women*. Jo is profoundly jealous of Brooke when he begins to court Meg, but though Linda is quite open about the effect that Julia's leaving will have on her – 'I don't know exactly what I'll do when you go. I've got to do something – get out, quit on it, change somehow, or I'll go mad. I could curl up and die right now'. – she is so far from being jealous, first of Johnny and latterly of Julia, that, on the one hand, she befriends Johnny at once and, on the other, refuses to make her love for him explicit until after Julia has rejected him. The difference is important because of what it makes of Linda's love for Julia and, inseparably, of her relation to the family. Jo's possessiveness is continuous with her identification with the father. Linda, whose commitment to Julia is both intense and disinterested, is identified with her mother – though not with her mother *as a Seton*: Linda values in her mother everything which her status as her husband's property repressed. It is essential to the film's meaning that Linda's relationships with both women (and with Ned) are characterised by a solidarity which is at odds with the proprietary nature of patriarchal heterosexual relations as the cigar sequence defines them. There, the 'little woman's' transition from father to husband, and the equation of 'deriving pleasure from' and 'having rights in', are dramatised through the cigar's dual value as commodity and phallus, possessed by men, and *through* men by women. In such a context, we give Linda's behaviour, after her entrance, its appropriate weight: the threat to extinguish the cigar, the spontaneous generosity of her delight in Julia's happiness, and her movement away from the father-daughter pair to look up at and address her mother's portrait above the fireplace acquire, in the juxtaposition, great critical substance.

The contrast is carried over into the opposition between the two parties. Linda's is *for* Julia, and takes place in the room associated with the mother (and through her, with pre-Oedipal desire): for Linda, it celebrates the community between the women, and between them and their friends, which, while founded on the patriarchal family, has become independent of and contradictory to it. Downstairs, the father's party is celebrating the cigar, and it is typical of Julia, at this stage of the film, that she should have agreed to both of them. Later, when Linda defends Johnny's decision not to remain in business after the marriage, the latent conflict between the two sisters emerges:

Linda: Julia, why do you want to shut me out in the cold like this?
Julia: I wasn't aware that I was.
Linda: But won't you just talk to me? Oh, please, Julia!
Julia: I don't know what there is to say.
Linda: Never so long as I remember has there been anything we couldn't —
Julia: If there's been any shutting out done, it's you who've done it, Linda.
Linda: Me!
Julia: Johnny and I have had a difference of opinion and you're siding with him, aren't you?
Linda: But he's right! He's right for you as well as for himself.
Julia: I think that's for me to decide.
Linda: Not Father?
Julia: Father has nothing to do with it.
Linda: Oh, no!
Julia: He happens to agree with me where you don't, that's all.
Linda: We've *always* agreed before – always!

While the beginning of this conversation exactly recalls Jo's with Meg ('You're getting so far away from me'), the intention is diametrically opposite, for Jo goes on to say 'D'you have to fall in love and spoil all our happy times together?' Linda is *defending* the marriage (even though she is by now in love with Johnny herself), and the significance of this can't be adequately described in terms either of Linda's self-sacrifice or of the suggestion that Julia can be 'saved' and educated by a man. The stress falls on the fact that Linda's feeling for her mother is associated by the film with the non-possessiveness of her feeling for Julia and, more generally, with the fact that, from Linda's point of view, the children are not rivals for the mother's affections (certainly not the father's) but, on the contrary, a solidary group constituted by its allegiance to the mother.

This is important in that, as Schneider argues, the Oedipus complex must be theorised as the construction not only of gender but also, and in the same moment, of an exclusive relation to the object of desire:

'So the exclusive acquisition of the heterosexual love object already bears the marks of a social form of organisation based on the exclusive, that is, "private", acquisition of the means of social production. Phallic Oedipal rivalry and aggression are the indigenous psychosexual sedimentation of a social form of behaviour which is governed not by the principle of co-operation . . . but by the principle of competition' *(Neurosis and Civilisation*, p.89).

The relevance of this to the cigar scene will be clear; and indeed, it is at this moment of agreement between father and daughter that Julia consents to Seton's grand public party, even though she has previously committed herself to Linda's. Thus the central point in the Linda/Julia dialogue is that Julia's 'opinion' is in fact Mr Seton's, and as the conversation continues it emerges that from Julia's point-of-view the sisters *are* rivals.

Julia: No – I think quite often I've given in, in order to avoid scenes and upsets and – oh, well –
Linda: Is that true, Julia?
Julia: You've always been the 'stronger character', haven't you? At least, people have always thought so. You've made all the decisions, you've always had the ideas –
Linda: And you've been resenting me right from the very – Oh, I can't believe it!

Julia finally plumps for Daddy, and thus for a particular way of desiring Johnny, and it is this – not rivalry for a man – which disrupts the sisters' relationship. Julia necessarily experiences it as rivalry – 'you're siding with him, aren't you?' And so she is, but the fact that she is also siding with her mother, and against construction as a 'little woman', has great significance for the *kind* of heterosexual relationship which is affirmed through Linda and Johnny. Were the logic of Linda's character to be fully realised, she would be bisexual – and *Holiday* can't do that. It can, however – and it's enormously to its credit that it does – construct a female character whose strength is not a matter of her 'masculinisation' and whose heterosexuality is defined by an identification with her mother, not as 'wife', but – with a radical explicitness – as a woman in opposition. From this perspective, Linda's unanswered question to her father – 'Was she a sweet soul, father? Was she exciting?' – appears, incontrovertibly, as the crux of the film.

Inasmuch as the play *Stage Door*, by Edna Ferber and George S. Kaufman is worth studying at all, it is as a paradigm of those bitter, querulous, snobbish 'thirties entertainments which are primarily dedicated to flattering their middle-class audiences with the proposition that theatre is superior to movies, and that theatre-goers do not so much watch plays as hold aloft the torch of culture against

Still: Ginger Rogers as Jean and Hepburn as Terry in Stage Door.

124

the encroaching darkness of barbarism. This exchange, apropos of 'motion-picture acting', is representative:

Terry: That isn't acting, that's piecework. You're not a human being, you're a thing in a vacuum. Noise shut out, human response shut out. But in the theatre, when you hear that lovely sound out there, then you know you're right. It's as though they'd turned on an electric current that hit you here. And that's how you learn to act.

Jean: You can learn to act in pictures. You have to do it till it's right.

Terry: Yes, and then they put it in a tin can, like Campbell's soup. And if you die the next day it doesn't matter a bit. You don't even have to be alive to be in pictures . . . An actress in the theatre, that's what I've wanted to be my whole life. It isn't just a career, it's a feeling. The theatre is something that's gone on for hundreds and hundreds of years. It's – I don't know – it's part of civilisation.

This kind of thing – which can still rake in money even at the upmarket end of Shaftesbury Avenue – is the ideology of theatre *par excellence*: confronted by the traditions of millennia we may purchase, as we re-enact the rites of middle-classness, a delicious self-approval at the cost of a little humility. Knowing that Lord Olivier is a more important actor than Robert Mitchum, and that *Othello* is more important than *Home from the Hill*, is one of those exquisite tactics for gaining access to one's own superiority without experiencing any of the concomitant disadvantages of conceit. The theatre/cinema motif is accompanied, in the Ferber and Kaufman play, by another, also representative (one may find it at its most loathsome in Noel Coward's *Present Laughter*) – the vilification of the 'high-brow'. For the theatre-goer, while wishing to know that theatre is part of civilisation, does not want to be troubled or disturbed by it, and is uneasily aware (having vaguely heard, in 1936, of Eugene O'Neill) that the bland, innocuous and reassuring fare that he or she in fact enjoys has been indicted for escapism of exactly the kind that dreadful Hollywood movies are supposed to provide. This gnawing guilt is gently laid to rest by the introduction, in the play, of an earnest young dramatist who aspires to write about 'life', and who is placed in the middle of the stage like a skittle and bowled over by the spectator's identification-figure:

Keith: The theatre shouldn't be just a place to earn a living in. It should be thunder and lightning, and power and truth.

Terry: And magic and romance!

Keith: No, no! Romance is for babies! I write about *today*! I want to tear the heart out of the rotten carcass we call life and hold it up, bleeding, for all the world to see.

Terry: How about putting some heart *into* life instead of tearing it out all the time?

At the end of the play, Keith sells out to 'Hollywood', and the spectator can feel not only that the highbrow is a hypocrite anyway, but also that movies and plays about 'life' are somehow each other's corollary: theatre, civilisation and the spectator's self-esteem can then be salvaged on the middle ground between them.

Everything in the play of *Stage Door* relates to these motifs, of which nothing is left in the film: most of the dialogue, and the conception of the characters and their inter-relation, are entirely new. For the present purpose, two other changes are crucial.

First, there is the film's marginalisation of male characters. Keith, the high-brow playwright and 'love interest' whom Terry rejects because of his decision to write for motion-pictures, is omitted. The play's film producer, David Kingsley, bears almost no relation to the film's Anthony Powell, who is a theatrical impresario and derives, as the casting of Adolphe Menjou indicates, from *Morning Glory*'s Louis Easton. Fundamentally, these differences subserve a radically altered conception of the *function* of the male characters. Keith is discredited as a possible partner for Terry because of his capture by movies, but as the play progresses, it emerges that Kingsley's heart, despite his bondage to the Globe Picture Company, is in the theatre, and that he is to be the patriarchal agent of Jean's ascent to stardom on the West Coast and of Terry's big break on Broadway. By the same token, he mediates, by committing himself to Terry, our rejection of Jean and of Hollywood:

'When they come into the theatre – when picture people take a really fine play and put a girl like Jean in it; when they use a play like this for camera fodder, that's more than I can stand. The theatre means too much to me.'

And, once Terry has redeemed him by reviving his passion for the boards, he can, as producer and husband, effect her subordination in the patriarchal happy ending:

Kingsley: No, I'm not one of those boys who puts on a play just so that his girl can act in it . . . By the way, you *are* my girl, aren't you?
Terry (brightly): Oh, yes, sir!

We are to have it, pleasantly, both ways: the 'success' of the two central female characters reaffirms the supremacy and desirability of male agency and spares the spectator the distress of contemplating 'failure', while at the same time confirming our relative evaluation of stage and screen. In the film, Powell and all the male characters are discredited, with astonishing system and explicitness, in terms of a project which affirms the value of the female community in the boarding-house *against* patriarchy.

The second crucial change is that the Jean and Terry of the play have no connection whatever with the characters of the same name in the film which have been rewritten for Ginger Rogers and Hepburn respectively. The Hepburn part was played on the stage by Margaret Sullavan, for whose persona of fragile but resilient idealism the Ferber/Kaufman Terry is clearly modelled. As a character, she is closer to the film's Kaye Hamilton (Andrea Leeds), and indeed, in the play, replaces her: for while the original *does* have a Kaye Hamilton, the film effects the crucial structural change of transposing her suicide (which occurs in the play's second act) to the end. Its position in the play, given the likeness between Kaye and Terry, is a function of the uplift of the ending: Terry's success counterbalances Kaye's defeat. In the play, Terry is *not* a newcomer to the boarding-house, and she and Jean are close friends from the outset, drifting slowly apart as Jean delightedly suffers herself to be engulfed by Hollywood. The film reverses this trajectory: Terry and Jean are bitterly antagonistic throughout, committing themselves at the end to a friendship the 'lesbian overtones' of which provoked the wrath of a contemporary critic in *The New Masses* (not so 'new', perhaps).

Stage Door represents a transitional point in both Hepburn's and Rogers's careers: it initiated, as I showed in Chapter Two, the strategy of casting Hepburn in comedy as a contemporary American heiress, and it was Rogers's first non-musical. While she had appeared in a number of Busby Berkeley musicals, Rogers was primarily associated, of course, with the partnership with Astaire, and she had been trying to persuade RKO for some time to cast her in a film without him. They did and they didn't: the best way to approach *Stage Door* is to see it as an Astaire-Rogers film with Hepburn in the Astaire part.

The similarities, once noted, are obvious. *Stage Door* has the show-business setting and the putting-on-a-show structure of many classical Hollywood musicals, and both the female group and the tough, street-wise camaraderie of its members evoke Rogers's roles in the Busby Berkeley-choreographed *42nd Street* (Lloyd Bacon, 1933) and *Gold Diggers of 1933* (Mervyn LeRoy, 1933). The development of the Jean-Terry relationship is analogous to the archetypal pattern of Rogers's films with Astaire: the couple meet, quarrel, are kept apart throughout by a series of misunderstandings, and finally get together at the end. Compare, for example, the scene in *Stage Door* in which Jean turns up unexpectedly at Powell's apartment and, finding him with Terry, concludes that she has been seducing him, with that in *Shall We Dance?* (Mark Sandrich, 1937), in which Linda (Rogers) finds Petrov (Astaire) with Irma (Ketti Gallian) and concludes that they are in love.

Most important of all, Astaire and Rogers (with Hepburn, RKO's major 'thirties stars) are used to dramatise class and sexual themes which have striking similarities with those I have tried to analyse in Hepburn's films: Hepburn's own remark about Astaire and Rogers that 'she gave him sex and he gave her class' certainly points us in the right direction. Like the early Hepburn, the 'thirties Astaire persona embodies contradictory class and gender signs. The legendary uniform for the dance numbers (top hat, white tie and tails or black tuxedo) connotes aristocracy, the *character* is invariably a 'good Joe', and the films make much of his hostility to, or unease within, an upper-class ambiance – consider, for example, the treatment of his relationship with the rich society girl in *Swingtime* (George Stevens, 1936), of the wonderful moment at the beginning of *Top Hat* (Mark Sandrich, 1935) where he disrupts, and expresses his contempt for, the decorum of the gentlemen's club with a quick burst of tap-dancing in the reading-room. As soon as he begins to dance, Astaire becomes Superman without special effects (his dancing always looks at once effortless and impossible) and polymorphously perverse. While the virtuoso solo-numbers, and some of the duets with Rogers, are dazzling celebrations of phallic potency (the 'Top Hat' number in *Top Hat*, where Astaire 'shoots' the male chorus with his cane; the 'Bojangles' number in *Swingtime*, with its extraordinary opening shot of Astaire sitting atop a pair of grotesque giant legs; 'Change Partners' in *Carefree*, Mark Sandrich, 1938, in which Astaire induces Rogers to dance with him by hypnotising her, and controls her movements with gestures of his hands), the romantic numbers are characterised by an incomparable refinement, delicacy and grace, and the style and register of Astaire's singing are not in the least conventionally 'virile'. The superhuman prowess of the musical numbers is in sharp contrast to the Astaire character's narrative helplessness (he is repeatedly the victim of coincidence and error, misunderstanding the agency of others, rather than the initiator of significant action), and, as Robin Wood has noted, the recurrent strategy of providing the Rogers character with alternative men who are connoted as 'effeminate' serves to reinforce Astaire's sexual 'normality' (Robin Wood, 'Never, never change, always gonna dance', *Film Comment*, September/October 1979, pp.28-31).

Top Hat, the finest of the series, and one of the greatest of all musicals, is exemplary in this respect: the perfect democratic American couple is affirmed in relation to three other couples which embody unacceptable class connotations and an imbalance of gender characteristics. Horace (Edward Everett Horton) and Bates (Eric Blore) are clearly to be read as gay, with Bates as fractious, nagging 'wife', and they are also master and servant. Horace is timorously married to Madge (Helen Broderick), and the excessive power of the wife in this relationship is contrasted, in the relationship between Dale (Rogers) and her fiancé, Beddini (Erik Rhodes), with a male effeteness (Beddini is a couturier) that seeks to overcompensate by means of a grotesquely exaggerated chauvinism inspired by an aristocratic code of chivalry. With the exception of Beddini, all these characters are treated with great affection, and the film's project is the creation, through Astaire and Rogers, of a norm in which gender roles have been at once revised and consolidated and defined as class-free (that is, American). Both the strategy and the tactics are crucial to the Tracy/Hepburn series as well, and I will return to them in Chapter Seven.

The mechanism by which the contradictions of the Astaire persona are mediated is the distinction/continuum between the dance numbers and the narrative, and we may find its exact analogue in *Morning Glory*: Eva is the all-American girl from the all-American small-town who, on stage, becomes Sarah Bernhardt. If Hepburn fails to gel ideologically, it is primarily because she is a woman, but also because none of the available narrative forms are able to regulate the contradictions as efficiently as the musical regulates Astaire's. There he is as Clark Kent, and there he is as Superman (that the Astaire/Rogers cycle is contemporary with the invention of the cartoon series is not coincidental): the form itself both foregrounds the opposition and demonstrates that it is a unity. The casting of Hepburn as 'doubles' (*The Little Minister, Sylvia Scarlett, Quality Street*) suggests an attempt to do a similar kind of thing, but because the strategy is not germane to the form it succeeds only in exacerbating conflicts which, in any case, are more intense in Hepburn because of her sex.

The Berkeley-choreographed films (in particular) had defined Rogers as tough, independent, working-class, worldly-wise (indeed, potentially unscrupulous) and sexual – even 'tarty': Anytime Annie in *42nd Street* is the subject of that legendary line, 'the only time she ever said no she didn't hear the question'. She is also, like Hepburn, a redhead (with all that that connotes socially), though the class ethos of the two personae is antithetical. The Astaire films (as well as the later work without Astaire) tend to cast her either as a working girl or as a working girl who has made good as a professional, and a number of them (*Swingtime, Shall We Dance?*) emphasise her class by assigning the Astaire character 'another woman' from the aristocracy. The films seek to preserve the ideologically positive connotations both of her class and her sexuality (the 'good broad'), which are crucial for the anchoring of the Astaire persona in democratic heterosexual normalcy, while using Astaire, conversely, to contain and soften the negatives.

Take, for instance, the opening scenes of *Top Hat*. Though the film isn't explicit about it, it's implied as clearly as it *could* be in 1935 that Dale, who is ostensibly modelling Beddini's creations, has become his mistress in order to further her career. She is thus associated from the beginning with sexual and class transgression: Dale is on the make, and cynically using a man in the process. Beddini is correspondingly 'feminised' – both his profession and his rhetorical assertion of his maleness bespeak an uncertain virility which Dale sees through and, memorably, deflates in her tart rejoinder to his favourite self-inflating catch-phrase 'For the woman the kiss, for the man the sword' – 'And what have you got for the children?' The sword, which Beddini is constantly threatening to use and never does, is later juxtaposed with Astaire's cane.

The scenes which introduce Jerry (Astaire) establish, on the one hand, a gender uncertainty which relates him to Beddini, and on the other a positive class mix which is set against Dale's class transgression. For the first *tour de force* solo, 'No Strings', he wears the Astaire class uniform (evening-dress), but his affront, in the opening scene, to the staid and desiccated atmosphere of the Pall Mall club has already dissociated him from the upper class, and identified him with the disruption of European formality by American energy. The 'international theme' is central to the film, and the finale, 'The Piccolino', celebrates, among other things, the regeneration of Europe by America: the song, we are told, was 'written by a Latin/A gondolier who sat in/His home out in Brooklyn/And gazed at the stars'. Moreover, Jerry's friend and colleague, Horace, who is a member of the club, corresponds to a type of 'good' British upper-classness – the amiable, bumbling P.G. Wodehouse moron (indeed, his relationship with Bates, while in some ways quite dissimilar can be related to the Jeeves/Wooster couple).

While 'No Strings' confirms, through the dancing, an image of phallic mastery, its lyric implies, ambiguously, either an easy, confident, heterosexual philanderer ('No dates that can't be broken/No words that can't be spoken') or a state of polymorphous sexual indeterminacy ('In me you see a youth who is completely on the loose; no yens, no yearnings; no strings, no connections/No ties to my affections/I'm fancy-free, and free for anything fancy'). The meeting with Dale which immediately follows (she has been trying to sleep in the room below, and comes up to protest about his dancing) takes up both lines of suggestion:

Jerry: . . . every once in a while I suddenly find myself – dancing.
Dale: Oh – I suppose it's some kind of affliction.
Jerry: Yes, yes, it's an affliction – St Vitus' Dance.
Dale: And it only occurs at this time of night?
Jerry: Yes – it only occurs at this time of night. As a matter of fact, I shouldn't be left alone.
Dale: Yes, I can see that. You probably should have a couple of – guards.
Jerry: I think you're very unkind to make fun of me.
Dale: Oh, I'm sorry!
Jerry: I wish you wouldn't leave.

Dale: Why not?

Jerry: I think I feel an attack coming on. *(He begins to dance)* There's only one thing that'll stop me.

Dale: Oh, you *must* tell me what it is!

Jerry: My nurses always put their arms around me.

Dale: Well, I'll call the house detective and tell *him* to put *his* arms around you.

The fact that Jerry is flirting with Dale reinforces the lyric's positive emphasis (Jerry is a normal heterosexual male), but the dialogue also indicates a potential parallel between Dale and Jerry and Dale and Beddini. The innuendo of the opening lines is clear enough: Jerry's affliction 'only occurs at this time of night', and Dale would prefer to sleep. Her attitude here is analogous to her failure to be impressed by Beddini's sword, and defines an autonomous sexuality which is not readily available to men and which, as in the other case, threatens to 'feminise' them ('I'll call the house detective and tell *him* to put *his* arms around you'). At the same time, aspects of Jerry which contradict the phallic prowess of his dancing seem to invite Dale's assessment of him: she retains the initiative throughout the dialogue, and her parting shot, which makes Jerry 'female', is provoked by his own comparison of himself to a child demanding its nurse.

These tensions are both newly articulated and beautifully resolved in the first *pas de deux,* which takes place in the deserted bandstand in the park. The sequence begins by reversing the dominant class connotations of the two stars. Jerry, in hot pursuit of Dale, has disguised himself as a working-class cabby, complete with Cockney accent; Dale, who has been out riding with some of Beddini's society friends, is immaculately turned out in riding-cap, tweed jacket and jodhpurs. The costume continues to imply of course, the 'unfeminine' inaccessibility of her sexuality, and her refusal of the female role which Jerry offers her is made explicit in the dialogue which precedes the number: in reply to his request to 'rescue' her (she has taken refuge in the bandstand from a rainstorm), she tells him that she 'prefers being in distress.' Her intransigence is disturbed when it begins to thunder – we discover both that she is afraid and that she doesn't know how thunder is caused. Jerry moves in at once, and explains it in terms of sexual antagonism:

'When a clumsy cloud from here meets a fluffy little cloud from there, he billows towards her; she scurries away, and he scuds right up to her. She cries a little and there you have your shower. He comforts her – they spark – that's the lightning. They kiss – thunder!'

If this lesson in *natural* history defines heterosexual relations in terms of male aggression, female frailty and irresolvable incompatibility, the ensuing song proposes a *cultural* form in which the conflict can be resolved. That form, of course, is monogamous patriarchal marriage, and the theme of the song, adumbrated in its title ('Isn't it a lovely day to be caught in the rain?'), is the way in which the couple both draws on and reconciles antagonistic natural forces. The process has three stages:

a) the cloud dialogue, in which an unacceptable form of male power is seen to create disharmony;

Still: Jean and Terry in Stage Door.

b) the song itself, in which aggression is replaced by, or channelled into, court-ship. The thunder frightened Dale, the song soothes her, though of course her fear is also the condition which allows Jerry to capture the initiative which he had lost in the hotel sequence. In so doing, he asserts his 'maleness', while his 'femininity' acquires a positive connotation as the softening of 'natural' force. Similarly, the fact that Dale succumbs renders her available to Jerry without discountenancing those elements in the character which distinguish her from the model of the 'feminine' implied by the 'fluffy little cloud';

c) Dale and Jerry then go, marvellously, into their dance – the brisk and exhilarating tap routine which is *de rigeur* at this point in Astaire/Rogers movies. Dance in musicals, of course, always has a sexual significance: here, the creation of the couple through dance both enacts the resolution of a particular set of class and sexual tensions, and also celebrates, in a specific inflection of the nature/culture antinomy, the preservation of a continuity between primal, natural energies and sexuality which has been regulated by patriarchy. This last motif is embodied in the form and organisation of the number: the dance takes place in a covered bandstand which is nevertheless open to the storm (it has no walls), and the transition from dialogue to song and, later, from the leisurely opening of the dance to its frenetic conclusion, are signalled by peels of thunder.

No description can hope to convey the wit, urbanity and delicacy with which *Top Hat* orchestrates its themes, but I have said enough, I hope, to indicate the common ground between Hepburn's 'thirties films and the Astaire/Rogers cycle.

There is a certain overlap of personnel between the two groups, and while I would attach no significance at all to the fact that George Stevens and Mark Sandrich directed both Hepburn and Astaire/Rogers movies, the role of Pandro Berman, who produced all but two of Hepburn's RKO films and all those of Astaire and Rogers, is clearly important. I am not competent to suggest the extent to which the contiguity between the two groups can be profitably discussed in terms of studio policy and executive decision, and research both into this area and the career of Berman (evidently one of the most intelligent and distinguished producers of the classical period) would probably yield valuable results. They wouldn't, however, substantially alter (though they might consolidate) the present argument, which has to do with the ideological material articulated through the three star personae.

The curious inverse relationship between Rogers and Hepburn is clear not only from the Astaire movies, but also from those which Rogers made after the team broke up. The structure of Leo McCarey's *Once Upon a Honeymoon* (1942), for example, is strikingly similar to that of *Top Hat*. Rogers plays Katie O'Hara, a Brooklyn burlesque queen, who is masquerading as a Philadelphia heiress, Katharine Butte-Smith, and who is attached, at the beginning of the film, to a European male (Walter Slezak) whom (like the characters played by Erik Rhodes in *Top Hat* and *The Gay Divorcee* and by George Metaxa in *Swingtime*) the film's imagery codes as 'impotent'. As in *Top Hat*, breaking caste (proletarian upward mobility and a gravitation towards 'Europe') is associated not only with the character's use of a 'feminised male' but also with her indifference to the hero's sexual invitation which undermines his potency, dramatised, in the 'fitter' sequence, through the vicissitudes of O'Toole (Cary Grant) with his metal tape-measure, which alternates between unrestrained erection and disappointed detumescence. Subsequently, Katie's sexuality and her betrayal of her origins are rectified through her association with O'Toole. The extent to which the construction of the Rogers character's sexuality as a successful blend of ordinariness, toughness and 'femininity' depends on the presence of a viable hero is clearly demonstrated by *Roxie Hart* (William A. Wellman, 1942), in which the connotations of unscrupulousness and sexual 'looseness' predicated by the Berkeley-choreographed films again become dominant. This is nowhere clearer than in the dance numbers – the black bottom and, in particular, the amazing tap routine on the staircase. While the solo is a *sine qua non* of Astaire movies, Rogers, in her films with him, never dances on her own. In *Roxie Hart*, on the contrary, Roxie's dancing celebrates energies which explicitly discount and exclude the male, and the hero (George Montgomery) does nothing in the tap sequence but watch in amazement as Roxie expresses and extols her own prowess. Indeed, the very title of the number ('Grab it by the horns and hit it while it's hot!') is clear enough about the nature of Roxie's desire, and the film can only subordinate it to domesticity by resorting, at the end, to a narrative ellipsis of quite amazing gratuitousness.

One of the most immediately striking things about *Stage Door* is the way in which it reverses the terms of one of the central privileged images of white American culture – the asocial male group. Whether we are dealing with the crew of the Pequod in *Moby Dick*, the fugitive couple of *Huckleberry Finn*, Whitman's songs or Henry David Thoreau's 'majority of one', the function of the image is normative: it defines a paradigm of classless American democracy which can only be realised through the rejection of American democracy as it is actually constituted. Typically, actually existing society is equated with 'domesticity', which is equated in its turn with a regime controlled by women – 'sivilisation', as Huck Finn puts it. The essential American community is, in this tradition, male and homoerotic. Women are excluded from it and a threat to it, and the 'Knights and Squires' chapter in *Moby Dick* is perhaps the most passionate and lucid statement of the continuity between male comradeship and the enactment of the democratic ideal ('the kingly commons'). By an extraordinary reversal, women appear as the oppressors of men, and while Melville at least, is partially attuned to the contradiction (*see*, for instance, his remarkable short story 'The Paradise of Bachelors and the Tartarus of Maids'), the misrecognition of patriarchal social forms as smothering matriarchies is at the root of the curiously blocked and restricted radicalism with which the great male American writers contest the inhibition of same-sex love.

In *Stage Door,* the group is female; it is a beleaguered enclave within established society and not external to it; and it is threatened not by 'domesticity' but by the social power of men. The two alternatives to the world of the boarding house which the film proposes – marriage and family on the one hand, professional success on the other – are explicitly discredited. 'Family' is represented by Terry's incestuously possessive father (Samuel S. Hinds), who sets out deliberately to wreck his daughter's career to prevent her leaving him by Kay's unspecified horror of 'going back'; by the photographs in Powell's apartment, ostensibly idyllic representations of his own wife and children but in fact, as Terry discovers, the originals of images fabricated for an advertisement; and by the letter from home to Eve (Eve Arden):

'Pa got laid off. My sister's husband has left her. And one of my brothers slugged a railroad detective. I guess that's all. Yes. Lots of love and can you spare fifty dollars.'

When Judy (Lucille Ball) at last unwillingly succumbs to matrimony, through sheer financial hardship, she is so loath to renounce the companionship of the other women that she has to be pushed out of the boarding house by force. Professional success involves prostitution and a willingness to submit to being 'moulded' by a male entrepreneur ('I'll be the sculptor, you'll be the clay'). Yet while the terms on which relations with men are possible are irremediably compromised and oppressive, the social/economic place of men is such that they remain a continually necessary reference point: they represent 'meat and potatoes', as Judy puts it. I wish to analyse the film in terms of the collision between its desire to affirm relationships between women as opposed to heterosexual relationships, and its reiteration of themes and motifs from earlier Rogers and Hepburn films which only acquire their logical pertinence from the need to accommodate the women to relationships with men.

One might begin with class, and the notion of the 'classlessness' of the democratic community. The disappearance of class is, of course, a crucial Marxist concept, but the thesis that the communist revolution creates the possibility, for the first time in history, of a classless society derives its theoretical substance from the objective structural position of the proletariat, which has no interest in the oppression of other classes. For Marxism, in other words, the supersession of class is the product of a history of class struggle. Bourgeois thought, by contrast, conceives of 'classlessness' as a human essence: 'all men are created equal'. At certain historical moments, this concept has great progressive force: radical Puritanism, for example, identified the Fall with the emergence of private property. It is increasingly absorbed, however, to the repertoire of bourgeois hegemony – the human essence is recovered and guaranteed *by the bourgeoisie*.

The crew of the Pequod is the classical American classless, male community:

'But this august dignity I treat of, is not the dignity of kings and robes, but that abounding dignity which has no robed investiture. Thou shalt see it shining in the arm that wields a pick or drives a spike; that democratic dignity which, on all hands, radiates without end from God; Himself! The great God absolute! His omnipresence, our divine equality!' (*Moby Dick*, Penguin 1972, p.212).

Two incompatible propositions are imaginatively conflated here. The crew's equality is attributable, firstly, to its members having all been created by 'the great democratic God'. According to this reading, 'equality' precedes the social and is alienated by it: class is an accretion which corrupts an original existential classlessness and which being produced by 'civilisation', can be contested by fleeing from it. Alternatively, the crew members' equality has to do with their being *men* in identical *class* positions, with their playing a particular part in the labour process: here, equality is produced within, and potentially opposed to, existing social relations. The fact that the existential definition of equality tends to prevail inevitably undermines its effective oppositional force: in that the claims of equality are asserted against 'the-social-as-such', rather than grounded in the struggles and experiences of groups and classes which relate to other groups and classes, they relinquish their hold on the antagonistic forces which they wish to challenge.

The importance, for the white male American imagination, of the image of an extra-social democratic community – America in spite of America, as it were – needs to be read in terms of a bourgeois critique of bourgeois rhetoric. The response to the perception that America is transparently *not* the classless land from which 'European' inequalities of wealth and status have been banished is the assertion, more or less confident, that the democratic germ can be nourished in a space forever beyond the society which exists. Lacking a consistent account of the objective discrepancy between bourgeois language and the real dynamic of bourgeois social relations, this discourse is condemned to an infinite re-gression somewhere at the end of which the bourgeois ideals can flourish in their pristine form.

The question is further complicated in that the American democratic community also serves to valorise male homosexuality, as the touchingly ingenuous imagery of the Melville passage makes clear. If 'civilisation' alienates the democratic essence, it also alienates men from themselves and each other: the group of equals holds out the promise of self-realisation through 'the dear love of comrades'. A bourgeois critique of the bourgeoisie goes hand in hand with a patriarchal critique of patriarchy: same-sex love is seen to be constrained by women, to whom the democratic essence is foreign, rather than by the social/sexual division of labour and its corresponding norms of gender. The account, in the opening chapters of *Moby Dick,* of the development of the relationship between Ishmael and Queequeg illustrates with exemplary clarity the conjunction of the community's homoerotic and 'democratising' functions: Ishmael is prepared for admission to the group by sleeping with a man and renouncing his class identity.

One of the crucial problems in *Stage Door* is that while the female group is partially defined in feminist terms, it is also used to embody the *ideological* concept of the democratic American community, and this double connotation generates the radical incoherence of the film's attitude to Terry/Hepburn. For the coexistence of these two meanings of the group entails two concepts of the nature of its solidarity, which is seen to derive, on the one hand, from the women's oppression as women, and on the other from their organic unity as democratic Americans. It hardly needs to be said that the latter concept, which not merely lacks but actively suppresses any sense of contradictory interests, or else redescribes them in language borrowed from the same mystifying rhetoric, is inherently anti-feminist, in that it refers democratic equality a) to God's creation, and b) to the enactment of the divine intention by the bourgeois nation-state. Since women were *not* created equal ('He for God only, she for God in him,' as John Milton puts it of Adam and Eve), and since the notion that equality is institutionally guaranteed by 'Americanness' is a fetish, the bourgeois democratic community is necessarily a patriarchal form.

Stage Door is torn between an impulse to affirm, on the one hand, a militant assertion of the equality of the oppressed in and against the social world external to the group, and to validate, on the other, a 'classless' equality within it. This contradiction is reflected in the uneasy co-existence of two models of class identity in the film, one defining it in terms of social/economic privilege and the other in terms of particular sets of tastes (Shakespeare) and a certain behavioural style. Terry has, in fact, renounced the privileges of her class in deciding to become an actress at all. She tells her father that she wants 'to achieve something by [herself] without the aid of the family millions', and the film makes it clear that her choice entails the refusal of the subordinate, private role assigned to women by her class. Thus Terry's real interests and allegiances, far from being antagonistic to those of the other women, are at one with them; her wish to define herself both *through* her labour and as a woman represents a commitment to their struggle. In her first confrontation with Powell when she storms into his office after Kaye's collapse, Terry appears as the articulate champion, at once intransigent and personally disinterested ('It doesn't matter about me'), of the rights of the actresses whom Powell treats so callously, and her denunciation of his exploitativeness, opportunism and complacency obviously has the film's support. From this point of view, there can be no question of a need to incorporate Terry within the community, since her very presence there embodies its demands and aspirations.

The hostility to Terry is provoked entirely by the class connotations of her manner, and it is significant that the film does not feel obliged to provide the slightest motivation for a spontaneous communal antipathy which Terry neither invites nor reciprocates. It is assumed that the animosity by which the women, and in particular Jean, are instantly possessed is sufficiently explained by the antithetical personae of the two main stars, and the first Hepburn/Rogers duologue,

Still: Terry and Powell (Adolphe Menjou) in Stage Door.

brilliantly written and played, asks us to read a bravura exposition of that antithesis as a substantial basis for the conflict which ensues. The opposed class ethos
imported by the actresses allows the film tacitly to presuppose the antagonism
of the characters they play. The effect of this strategy is paradoxical and contradictory. The incompatibility of style between Terry/Hepburn and populist images
of democratic classlessness allows the film to suppress the fact that her position
represents the group members' real interests, both as workers and as women,
and to transform a narrative which is potentially committed to the women's social
claims into an account of Terry's discovery of democratic feeling. It is thus
crucial that Terry should be separated from the other women from the start,
and that her espousal of their common interests should be subordinated to her
exclusion from their classless camaraderie. A centrifugal theme, built round
Terry's integration and the elimination of the group's internal conflicts, displaces
the latent centripetal theme of the struggle against oppression, in which Terry
would figure as a radicalising force.

At the same time, the strong positive response to Terry is manifested in the
sporadic, uncertain attempts to place her fellow actresses' hostility. Consider,
for example, the brief conversation between Terry and Kaye, in which the latter

responds to Terry's nervous attribution of the prevailing domestic tension to a fault in herself ('I'm beginning to feel that there's something definitely wrong with me') with the suggestion – apparently offered for endorsement – that the women's rebarbativeness must be referred to the uncertainty and instability of their social position ('They're young enough to have courage, but they're young enough to have fears, too'). Similarly, we seem to be asked to feel the perverseness of Jean's insistence on cultivating her resistance to Terry's offers of friendship ('We started off on the wrong foot – let's keep it that way'). The film's invitations here remain obstinately discrepant: it cannot be argued that Terry must undergo a democratic education in order to become part of the group and that the group's deliberate attempts to exclude her are, however understandable, irrational and misplaced.

This uncertainty is a fact of the objective difficulty of affirming the logic of the film's subjective allegiances. Given the clarity and astringency with which *Stage Door* perceives oppression, Terry's militancy (Powell actually calls her, with an irony the more anxious for the fact that he has been unwillingly impressed, 'my militant friend') is necessarily posited as a desirable norm. The positive evaluation is confirmed by linking Terry (like Cynthia in *Christopher Strong* and Linda in *Holiday)* to a heroic tradition of American pioneering: Terry usurps the role of the male adventurer who rejects the constraints of domesticity, while also clearly, and publicly, identifying herself as a woman and selecting, as the hostile landscape to be conquered, not the untracked wastes of the West but the institutions of male domination. The women in the boarding house are trapped in a vicious circle which continually reproduces their oppression. Refusing their sanctioned place within the family, they are compelled, in order to succeed in their chosen profession, to win the attention and assistance of the men who control the profession and through whom alone success can be achieved. Integrity resists such expediency: because the members of the group are women, they cannot, like the members of the Hawksian male group, honour the imperative of self-respect through the exercise of their skill. The two have been socially constructed in contradiction, and self-respect can only be maintained by embracing the extreme social disadvantage of unemployment. This disadvantage in turn creates another form of dependence on men, and encourages acquiescence in the very domestic role which the women sought to escape. Inasmuch as the film sustains this analysis, Terry is affirmed. Inasmuch as a classical Hollywood movie *cannot* sustain it with any consistency, the understanding of the community of women turns in upon itself, since the affirmation of the group's achieved cohesion as democratic microcosm is bought at the cost of domesticating the qualities which sustain Terry's challenge to patriarchy. The women's solidarity is disengaged from any concept of resistance.

The despair which hangs over the end of the film – the emphasis on what the women have lost in renouncing marriage and the family ('What'll we have? – some broken-down memories and an old scrapbook that no one'll look at') and a corresponding stoicism ('Don't be sentimental! Remember you're a ham at heart!') – bears eloquent testimony to the impasse *Stage Door* has reached. The only condition on which the group can be valorised as a female group also eternalises its existing relation to the patriarchal *status quo* which the film has discredited. Were the film less radical than it is, its problems would be considerably diminished. It is the fact that *Stage Door* regards patriarchal social relations as absolutely unacceptable and sets a supreme value on solidary relations between women, but cannot endorse socialist feminism, that compels it to freeze the opposition between the group and a world in which it is always oppressed, and on which it cannot act.

The same impasse appears even more clearly in the treatment of the 'feminisation' theme which *Stage Door* takes over from previous Hepburn movies: the film argues quite clearly, as I showed in Chapter Two, that Terry's transformation into a 'great actress' is immediately determined by her acquisition of 'femininity' from Kaye. The gender opposition is embodied in two contrasting acting styles. Terry wishes to 'act with her brain', and in the rehearsal sequence the intelligent regulation of feeling is identified with *absence* of feeling: Terry's acting is shown to be wooden and expressionless. Kaye's performances, on the other hand, are the product of inspiration and intuition ('genius'). If Terry is 'artificial' because her desire to think impedes the flow of spontaneous (that is, in ideological terms, genuine) emotion, Kaye is 'authentic' because the unmediated re-enactment of personal experience has evaded the cold touch of cognition. By a familiar cultural trope, this authenticity is seen to be continuous with 'femininity': inasmuch as women aspire to the exercise of reason, they relinquish their womanliness. The choice of *The Lake* for the play in which Terry appears, and the complex system of cross-reference to *Morning Glory*, make it plain that *Stage Door* intends an unusually explicit equation between character and star.

The incoherence of such a theme in a film which also makes critical use of the myth of Pygmalion and Galatea to discredit and discountenance the proposition that women should be the passive, pliable objects of controlling male intelligence, and which has no intention of preparing Terry – or any of the women – for a relationship with a man, is startling. For the positive corollary of what I have called the film's centrifugal theme – the subordination of struggle against oppression to the homogenisation of the group – is the creation of the relationship between Terry and Jean: the emergence of the democratic community of equals is paralleled by, and metaphorically embodied in, a cross-class friendship which is as frankly lesbian as it could possibly be, and which is valued as such. The radicalism of this conclusion hardly needs to be stressed: its conservative functions – the construction of a paradigm of bourgeois 'classlessness' on the one hand, the use of the 'learning of emotion' to recuperate the challenge of Terry's intelligent resistance to patriarchy on the other – are as nothing beside the dramatic integrity of a denouement which disdains the easy option of a 'nice' man, and in so doing effectively subverts the bourgeois/democratic model of equality with the suggestion that women can only have 'equal' relationships with other women.

Stage Door, then, has its internal contradictions: in that they are directly precipitated by Hepburn's presence, they are a salutary reminder that the implications of that presence exceed the limits within which even the most committed and intelligent of melodramas must operate. One feels, nevertheless, when one reviews the film's penultimate scene, or when one thinks of Bette Davis's rejection of her lover at the end of *Now, Voyager,* that here, for anyone willing to take the implication, is a progressive popular art.

6. Stars and Genre

One of the major limitations of Richard Dyer's monograph *Stars* arises from his discussion of the relation between stars and genre. Consider, for example, his account of the star 'vehicle', in the course of an assessment of the 'distinct and privileged place' which a star's films 'inevitably' have in the star's image:

'The vehicle might provide a) a character of the type associated with the star (e.g. Monroe's 'dumb blonde' roles, Garbo's melancholic romantic roles), b) a situation, setting or generic context associated with the star (e.g. Garbo in relationships with married men, Wayne in Westerns . . .), or c) opportunities for the star to do her/his thing (most obviously in the case of musical stars; . . . but also, for instance, opportunities to display Monroe's body and wiggle walk, scenes of action in Wayne's films). Vehicles are important as much for what conventions they set up as for how they develop them, for their ingredients as for their realisation. In certain respects a set of star vehicles is rather like a film genre such as the western, the musical, the gangster film. As with genres proper, one can discern across a star's vehicles continuities of iconography . . . visual style . . . and structure. Of course, not all films made by the star are vehicles, but looking at their films in terms of vehicles draws attention to those films that do not fit, that constitute inflections, exceptions to, subversions of the vehicle pattern and the star image' (*Stars*, pp.70-71).

The fundamental error here is the proposition that 'a set of star vehicles' is in any way 'like' a genre (the 'in certain respects' and 'rather like' testify, perhaps, to Dyer's own uncertainty about it). On the contrary, the existence of a genre, *and of a relation between the genres*, is a prior condition of the vehicle: vehicles constitute a distinct sub-set, more or less highly individuated, of conventional relations which always precede the star. It is thus extremely misleading to reduce 'generic context' to something as loose and vague as a 'situation or setting', for 'generic contexts' are inseparable from narrative determinations. Quite apart from the fact that Garbo is *not* primarily associated with 'relationships with married men', but with the '*Anna Karenina*' structure (elderly, post-sexual husband/ passionate younger wife/romantic lover), Dyer's suggestion that 'vehicles are important as much for what conventions they set up as for how they develop them' encourages us to forget that the possibilities of development are entailed in (or at least circumscribed by) conventions, and that a film's being a vehicle for a particular star is by no means the major fact in that development. The '*Anna Karenina*' narrative implies a dramatic trajectory which is not in the least contingent on the casting of Garbo. While it is clearly crucial to ask why it was that Garbo should have been consigned so often to a structure which channels transgressive female desire into adultery and then leaves it with a 'choice' between renunciation and death, it is equally clear that the vehicle pertains in this case to a generic form with particular limits and parameters.

The way in which Dyer uses the concept of the vehicle serves to conflate at least four different kinds of 'convention':

a) those associated with a genre;
b) those associated with the use of stars;
c) those associated with a particular category of star (e.g. stars who play action heroes);
d) those associated with an individual star.

If the word 'convention' is to retain any significant meaning, we must conclude, I think, that d) is *least* usefully conceived of *as* convention, but is one of the *most* important determinants of the way in which convention is inflected. The '*Anna Karenina*' story is an archetypal bourgeois narrative which, in one sense, Garbo cannot affect: the available outcomes (her films enact every conceivable variant), and even the complex pattern of sympathies which problematise our attitude to the heroine's 'crime', are givens. In another sense, of course, her effect is crucial, but it is precisely because her films are not 'like' a genre but embedded in one that we can specify what that effect is.

While Dyer's discussion of genre is perfunctory, it implicitly endorses – indeed, takes as given – the tendency, in Robin Wood's phrase, 'to treat the genres as discrete' ('Ideology, Genre, Auteur', *Film Comment* January/February 1977, p.47) from which so much genre theory has derived its characteristically solipsistic quality. If we take as our starting point, as Dyer recommends, the isolation of 'continuities of iconography, visual style and structure' within a single genre, we are condemned to reproduce in our analytical categories the divisions and distinctions implicit in the material itself. The genres present themselves as discrete, and a formalist analysis of them is inevitably tautological. Thus having first subordinated genre to vehicle, Dyer proceeds to define a set of vehicles as a genre, and produces yet another discrete entity.

The essential theoretical point here is classically formulated by Marx in the 1857 'Introduction', apropos of 'the method of political economy':

'It would seem to be the proper thing to start with the real and concrete elements, with the actual preconditions, e.g. to start in the sphere of economy with population, which forms the basis and the subject of the whole social process of production. Closer consideration shows, however, that this is wrong. Population is an abstraction, if for instance, one disregards the classes of which it is composed. These classes in turn remain empty terms if one does not know the factors on which they depend, e.g. wage-labour, capital and so on. These presuppose exchange, division of labour, prices, etc. . . . . If one were to take population as the point of departure, it would be a very vague notion of a complex whole and through closer definition one would arrive analytically at increasingly simple concepts; from imaginary concrete terms one would move to more and more tenuous abstractions until one reached the most simple definitions. From there it would be necessary to make the journey again in the opposite direction until one arrived once more at the concept of population, which is this time not a vague notion of a whole, but a totality comprising many determinations and relations' (Karl Marx and Friedrich Engels, *The German Ideology*, edited by C.J. Arthur, Lawrence and Wishart, 1978, p.140).

The 'real and concrete elements' of, say, melodrama 'remain empty terms if one does not know the factors on which they depend'; and it follows at once that one of these factors is the existence of the western and the small-town comedy – that is, the production and reapportion of a division of labour, as it were, between the genres within the institution of Hollywood. The condition of the irreducibility of the genres is precisely their historical reciprocity: in an apparently paradoxical but very real sense, they are different because of what they have in common, not in spite of it. The common ground is that profound conflict of interpretations within the culture – ineliminable because germane to the culture – which assigns conflicting meanings to a single term or set of terms. Each genre seeks to regulate this conflict by organising particular 'forms and keepings', and appropriate expectations, whereby specific manifestations and resolutions of contradiction appear as properties of the generic world. The definitions and evaluations of middle America in *Margie* (Henry King, 1946) and *Beyond the Forest* (King Vidor, 1949), for example, are diametrically opposed to each other, but each is appropriate to the context which the genre creates, and they do not seem, therefore, to be contradictory. While each genre has means and methods of its own both for the enactment and the harmonisation of conflicting values and allegiances, it also exists in a complementary relation to other genres – a relation which *in itself* subserves the negotiation of contradiction by controlling its possible dramatic presence. Lacanian film theory seems to have institutionalised the proposition that the naturalisation of spectacle in the classical narrative cinema must be referred to the suppression of the act of 'writing': the film, we are to believe, does not present itself as a text (Colin MacCabe's essay on 'Principles of Realism and Pleasure' in *Screen*, vol.17, no.3, Autumn 1976, is a classic statement of this position). Nothing could be further from the truth. Popular American movies presuppose an enormously sophisticated intimacy with the conventions of genre – an intense awareness of the logic of *this* dramatic world as distinct from *that* one – and Hollywood works by encouraging a kind of instinctual formalism which freezes a film as an instance of the categories it employs. The spectacle is naturalised not because its conventions are invisible, but because they are referred to themselves.

'If we approach genre from the point of view of its intrinsic thematic relationship to reality and the generation of reality, we must say that every genre has its methods and means of seeing and conceptualising reality, which are accessible to it alone . . . Every significant genre is a complex system of means and methods for the conscious control and finalisation of reality' (M.M. Bakhtin and P.N. Medvedev, *The Formal Method in Poetics*, John Hopkins University Press, 1978, p.133).

In that the Hollywood genres appear as autonomous units which are related to one another only inasmuch as they differ – in other words, in that the 'intrinsic thematic relationship to reality and the generation of reality' which the genres, at any historical moment, have in common is suppressed – the reading which a Hollywood film demands seems to have been exhausted at the point at which it is located in the 'means and methods' of the genre to which it pertains. The conventions which the film employs and in relation to which it is readable appear to form the horizon of its reference. It is not that the film does not present itself as a text, but that certain kinds of reading of the text appear to be irrelevant and inappropriate: the text does not generate and finalise reality, it is 'just a horror movie'. In this sense, genre is the film's commodity form, and its status as commodity is underwritten by the entertainment syndrome, which at once encourages the purchase of a film as an object of prospective pleasure and trivialises the pleasure.

Conversely, every Hollywood movie of whatever genre must at least allow for a conservative reading. No film can explicitly authorise the transgression, or assert the bankruptcy of the ideological absolutes without adopting, as protective camouflage, the ostensible affirmation of them which many Hollywood films offer *without* irony. Indeed, the very condition of the ironic happy ending is a happy ending which is *not* ironic. The effect of these two facts – the apparent autonomy and self-reference of the genres; the obligation of any film apparently to endorse, whatever its real intention, the norms which are massively reproduced within the culture as a whole – is to discourage any process of generalisation from the dramatic world to the reality inhabited by the spectator which fails to conduce to intimations of the rightness of the status quo.

One can say, in effect, that Hollywood both enables and contains a *Beyond the Forest*. Vidor's film is possible *because* it is 'just' a Bette Davis picture, and we all know the kind of thing that Bette Davis gets up to: the structural assimilation of the subversive product is given in advance. At the same time, this very guarantee creates a space for *Beyond the Forest,* and it has been a fundamental proposition of this book that even films whose *intention* is conservative can leave room, in the very pursuit of their project, for unauthorised use. If genre, and that subsection of genre the 'vehicle', assign Hollywood movies their commodity form, they also assign them a language of enormous density and complexity, the innovative and transgressive use of which can actually be facilitated by the film's status as commodity. It is because *Beyond the Forest* is just another Bette Davis melodrama that it can do the things that it does. This thesis has a number of important implications for the study of stars.

1) The contradictions enacted by stars *in their films* are always at least latent in a particular genre. *Now, Voyager* is a Bette Davis movie, but 'Bette Davis' is a subsection or inflection of melodrama in its relation to sophisticated comedy. The personae of John Wayne, Gary Cooper, James Stewart, Henry Fonda and Clint Eastwood are all quite distinct, but none of them can be discussed significantly without reference to the concept of the western hero which they have at various times embodied, or to the tensions within the myth of white American history, refracted through a specific contemporary moment, which the genre articulates.

2) It follows that the function of stars as embodiments/mediators of contradiction *in their films* must be rigorously distinguished from their other functions and meanings. Dyer argues, correctly, that Garbo's retirement is as crucial a component of the Garbo myth as any of her films, but this is to say no more than that the Garbo myth mystifies the significance of Garbo movies, which are highly particularised variants of a generic preoccupation with women's oppression and self-assertion. The Garbo myth is autonomous, homogeneous and self-sufficient: Garbo films are readable only in relation to, say, the films of Hepburn, Davis and Dietrich, which are embedded in turn in the historical situation of genre.

The phrase *'Queen Christina* is a Garbo movie' may posit either the film's commodity form or an analytic category, and it is genre which will determine the significance the phrase is to have. Clearly, the myth, its ramifications and its retroactive effect on the films are of fundamental importance. The last shot of *Queen Christina* is, as extractable fetish, a crux of the myth, but it also has a dramatic function, and describes the *terminus ad quem* of romantic passion for women – exclusion from history and petrifaction as an icon (Christina has just told her dying lover that she will never leave him). The shot embodies a tension between these two meanings, the second of which the myth subsumes in a plangent romantic melancholy which is supposed to represent 'essence of Garbo'. The tension, and the more radical tendency of the Garbo persona, can only be recovered if we see the film's ending as a term in a generic repertoire which is frequently invoked to contain the problems raised by Garbo. The essentialising tendency of myth is, in fact, a part of the process of containment, and obscures the significance which Garbo acquires as an actor in melodramas.

3) Many stars repeatedly cross genres. In some cases, a star is associated with a particular genre at a particular stage of his/her career – Garbo, for example, was cast exclusively in melodramas until her last two films. Some stars are virtually genre-specific: most musical stars, by virtue of particular skills, some western stars (Roy Rogers, Gene Autry), or stars like Boris Karloff and Bela Lugosi who are enveloped in the ethos of a specific character. It is most often the case, however, that major stars are associated simultaneously with several genres. Thus, for instance, during the 'forties and 'fifties Hepburn was cast both in comedies and melodramas, and James Stewart's 'fifties action movies and domestic melodramas with Anthony Mann are interspersed with his thriller-melodramas for Hitchcock.

This does not mean that the star's work constitutes a new generic entity, but demonstrates again the historical interpenetration of the genres. The historical conditions which produce the possibilities of the kind of action hero created in the Stewart/Mann westerns are also such as to create a space within the western for concerns and thematics which it has previously marginalised, and tilt it towards melodrama and the Gothic. The impulses behind, and the rationale of male action, traditionally taken for granted, have become crucially problematic (the process can be specified in detail in the great westerns of the late 'forties and their complement, *film noir*), and the function of genre as a regulator of contradiction is disturbed by the genre's own historical trajectory. The heroic adventurer, creator and guarantor of a law of which he is the conscious spokesman, becomes compulsive, divided and inarticulate – that is, 'melodramatic'.

If the Stewart case is exemplary of the tendency of the genres to inherit each other and reassert the terms which their conventions have sought to marginalise or exclude, Hepburn's oscillation between melodrama and comedy draws our attention at once to the differences and the parallels between the strategies which different genres adopt in order to settle similar problems. The fact that the careers of, say, Bette Davis, Barbara Stanwyck and Rosalind Russell reveal an analogous pattern should warn us that it is as dangerous to compartmentalise the stars as it is to hive off the genres. Let us juxtapose, by way of example, *The*

Still: Tracy and Hepburn as Pat Jamieson and Jamie Rowan in Without Love.

Philadelphia Story, *Ninotchka* and *Destry Rides Again* – three films belonging to different genres (sophisticated comedy, romantic comedy and the western respectively) and all made in the same year (1939). The three stars for whom the films are 'vehicles' – Hepburn, Garbo and Dietrich – had all been labelled 'box-office poison' by *Variety* in 1937, and each work aspired (successfully) to re-establish the star's commercial viability by modifying her image.

It should not be necessary at this stage to reiterate the nature of the overlap between the three star personae: while each is highly specific it is scarcely surprising, given the problematic nature of their sexual identities, that they should have become contentious at the same time. The specificity is reflected in the genre chosen for the comeback: the preservation of a continuity with previous roles is a condition for the appropriate resolution of their intractable elements. Thus the selection of romantic comedy for Garbo bespeaks an attempt to maintain her association with all-consuming romantic love while averting an outcome of tragedy and defeat: the conventions of the genre allow the romantic impulse to be secured within the bourgeois-capitalist status quo, and legitimate the theme of romanticism as rebellion which is so crucial a component of Garbo's melodramas. Similarly, the type of the saloon entertainer allows *Destry Rides Again* to reiterate the Dietrich image of vamp/*chanteuse* while detaching it from the ethos of the exotic foreign cabaret and invoking a generic language that guarantees its suppression; and the 'world' of sophisticated comedy is clearly indicated as the requisite medium for the foregrounding, and amelioration, of Hepburn's rebarbative 'upper-classness'.

The very possibility of using genre in this way is, of course, already suggestive. The condition, in each case, of deploying one genre in order to resolve or soften tensions exacerbated by another is the fact that the genres 'represent different strategies for dealing with the same ideological tensions' (Wood, 'Ideology, Genre, Auteur'). Analogously, the diverse generic strategies of the three films embody a common ideological tactic – the narrative moments are remarkably similar:

a) Each star/character is located, at the outset, in a position of social power. Frenchy/Dietrich is the 'real boss' of Bottleneck; Ninotchka/Garbo is a Soviet commissar; Tracy Lord/Hepburn is both a wealthy New England heiress and the *primum mobile* in her family.

b) This power is seen to be fundamentally undemocratic and un-American. Frenchy's authority is inimical to the 'law and order' of the organic frontier community, Ninotchka is a Bolshevik, and Tracy is a walking affront to every article of the populist faith.

c) The women's power is associated, moreover, with their resistance to sexual regulation by men. Frenchy deprives Callaghan (Mischa Auer), the comic emasculated male in *Destry Rides Again*, of his trousers, holds the men of Bottleneck in thrall by her sexual charisma, and insists on having 'what the boys in the back-room will have'. Ninotchka objects to 'the arrogant male in capitalistic society', and regards romantic love as a mystification of desire which

Still: George Kittredge (John Howard) and Tracy Lord (Hepburn) in
The Philadelphia Story.

Stills: Tracy Lord with George Kittredge (above), Dexter Haven (Cary Grant) and Mike Connor (James Stewart) in The Philadelphia Story.

serves to subordinate women. Tracy is a 'virgin goddess' who is unpossessable by men, and an astringent critic of the complementary male vices of sexual dependency and sexual opportunism.

d) A male educator reclaims the woman for capitalism and 'femininity'. Destry wipes off Frenchy's make-up, and commends her to 'live up to the lovely face' which it conceals: subsequently, Frenchy's commitment to Destry is signalled by her surrender to him of her equivalent of what the boys in the backroom have got, her lucky rabbit's foot (Destry remarks that he hopes it was 'a big strong rabbit'). Ninotchka discovers, through love, that the revolution must be postponed: 'Give us our moment!' Tracy learns that she has been unfair to all the men in the film and that her strength is the source of their weakness, and remarries the husband she had contemptuously rejected.

Some such project could no doubt be identified in many American films, with or without the complexities, ambiguities, disharmonies occasioned, in these cases, by the three stars themselves. The point to be made is that we have here a very striking and concrete case of the complementary relation between star personae and between the genres, and of the dialectical interaction between genre and vehicle. To cast Dietrich as a saloon entertainer is to assign to her a character with a particular place in the generic world (analogous to that of related types in other genres), a corresponding evaluation and a possible dramatic life which is severely curtailed by the conventions. While Dietrich's presence cannot avert the generic destiny of the character, the necessity of which is a determinant of the casting in the first place, by the same token the casting (it is, after all, Dietrich and not Virginia Mayo) has its implication for the obligatory reinforcement of the generic judgement on the character type. The upshot is a radical crisis of value and allegiance within the film, whereby the relative evaluation of 'law' and 'disorder', and indeed, the internal coherence of the categories themselves, is profoundly disturbed. One need only compare Frenchy/Dietrich with Chihuahua/Linda Darnell in *My Darling Clementine* (John Ford, 1946) to realise that while such a crisis is implicit in the genre, its *enactment* is not: the casting of a specific actor, clearly, is one possible catalyst of it (another might be the intervention of a specific director). The star *in his/her films* must always be read as a dramatic presence which is predicated by, and which intervenes on, enormously complex and elaborate themes and motifs, and thereby refers us to a particular state of the social reality of genre, and of the relation between the genres. It is, for example, symptomatic of Dietrich's effect on *Destry Rides Again* that in the final scene, after Frenchy's death, the film registers a sense of regret for her loss: as the triumphant patriarch walks down the street of the newly civilised town, a boy disciple at his side imitating his every movement, a wagon passes in the opposite direction filled with young girls singing Frenchy's first song, 'Little Joe'. Dietrich brings to the film the theme of song/dance as a positive return of the repressed characteristic of the musical, and in so doing generates an ambivalence within the film's definition of the old town from which it never recovers.

4) Any set of star vehicles reveals recurrent thematic and stylistic features whose particular operation and development are indeed determined by the presence of the star. There are, however, crucial distinctions and discriminations to be made. As Charles Affron points out *(Star Acting,* E.P. Dutton, New York, 1977, p.95), the production of a *coup de théâtre* around the first appearance of the star's face is a characteristic rhetorical strophe in many Garbo movies, and this draws our attention to the particular value and significance of the face for that star persona. At the same time, this device is a specific inflection of the convention of the star entrance – consider, for example, the introduction of Hepburn in *Morning Glory,* Dietrich in *Shanghai Express,* John Wayne in *Stagecoach,* Humphrey Bogart in *Casablanca.* The potency of this convention allows for such remarkable effects as that produced at the beginning of *Now, Voyager,* the film elaborately creating the expectation of an 'entrance' by Bette Davis which is then abruptly undermined. Conversely, some Garbo motifs – an emphasis, for instance, on the touching of and sensual communion with inanimate objects – are specific to Garbo. Father/daughter relationships are as central to Hepburn movies as they are rare in Garbo's *(Anna Christie* and *Queen Christina* are the key exceptions), and young wife/elderly husband relationships are as characteristic of Garbo as they are foreign to Hepburn. Neither of these thematics makes much sense if we extrapolate it from the language of melodrama, or ignore the fact that such differences are a function of distinct, but reciprocal interventions of the star vehicle *in* melodrama.

I wish now to make some of these points more concrete and exact by juxtaposing two films – *A Woman Rebels* and *The Old Maid* – which, while 'vehicles' for their stars (Hepburn and Davis respectively), are also very close generically. The comparison will demonstrate, I hope, the kind of relation that we can expect to obtain between stars and genre, and between stars who, for all their irreducible uniqueness, address the basic preoccupations of a common language.

A Woman Rebels was directed by Mark Sandrich for RKO in 1936, *The Old Maid* by Edmund Goulding for Warner Brothers in 1939. Both works derive from literary originals. The former was adapted from a novel called *Portrait of a Rebel* by Netta Syrett (of which I haven't been able to trace a copy): Anthony Veiller, one of the two scenarists (the other being Ernest Vajda), had already worked on one Hepburn film, *Break of Hearts* (1935), and subsequently co-scripted *Stage Door* (1937) and *State of the Union* (1948). The primary source for *The Old Maid* is a novella of the same name by Edith Wharton, one of four stories published, in four volumes, under the generic title 'Old New York' in 1924. It was the first to be written (Wharton composed it in 1921), and was initially conceived as one of two novellas to be collected as 'Among the Mingotts'. The 'unpleasantness' of its subject matter – illegitimacy – led to its being turned down by a number of periodicals when Wharton tried to publish it separately (the editor of the *Ladies Home Journal* remarked that 'it is a bit too vigorous for us'), but it was quickly bought up by *Redbook* as a result of the publicity attending Wharton's receipt of the Pulitzer Prize for *The Age of Innocence.* It was enormously more successful, critically and financially, than the companion volumes in 'Old New York', selling three times as many copies, and in 1935 a stage adaptation by Zoe Akins opened on Broadway with Judith Anderson and Helen Menken. The play was also a huge hit: it won the Pulitzer Prize for drama in 1935, ran for two seasons on Broadway, and subsequently toured for eighteen months.

The authorship of *The Old Maid* is an extremely complicated question. Casey Robinson's screenplay initiates a series of Robinson scripts for Davis which clearly form a series of thematic variations on each other – *All This and Heaven Too* (Anatole Litvak, 1940), *Now, Voyager* (Irving Rapper, 1942) and *The Corn Is Green* (Rapper, 1945). Despite the fact that two of these films were directed by Irving Rapper, it can be assumed, I think, that his presence is of marginal creative significance. Rapper is a competent but anonymous figure, and while he also directed *Deception* (1946), which reassembles the three stars of *Now, Voyager,* the relation between the two films isn't of the kind which can be discussed in terms of the inflection of a specific and consistent thematic. Both *Now, Voyager* and *Deception* are Davis melodramas, but the former is also recognisably a Robinson film with preoccupations that recur in his work without either Davis or Rapper (see, for example, that exemplary small-town melodrama *King's Row*, Sam Wood, 1942): *Deception* has nothing in common with *Now, Voyager* except its stars. At the same time, two of the films in the Robinson/Davis series – *The Old Maid* and *The Corn Is Green* – derive from literary originals.

The Old Maid is also very close thematically, however, to an earlier Davis film, *That Certain Woman* (1937), in which Robinson was not involved – but which was written and directed by Edmund Goulding; and immediately before *The Old Maid* Goulding and Robinson had worked together on *Dark Victory* (1939) which, while it stars Davis, stands apart from Robinson's other scripts for her. Similarly, Robinson had no hand in *The Great Lie*, directed by Goulding in 1941 from a script by Lenore Coffee, though the film is clearly a variation on *The Old Maid*, distinguished by a remarkable inversion of casting logic whereby Davis plays 'the Miriam Hopkins part'. To complicate the matter still further, Lenore Coffee went on to script, with John Van Druten, an adaptation of Van Druten's play *Old Acquaintance* for Davis and Hopkins in which neither Goulding nor Robinson were involved (it was directed by Vincent Sherman in 1943) but which again enacts an inflection of the structure and preoccupations of the earlier films.

I am no more interested in assigning an *auteur* to any of these films than I am in suggesting that the inferiority of *Old Acquaintance* to *The Old Maid* cannot be discussed in terms of who wrote and directed them. A number of conclusions can be drawn, however:

a) The star's presence is enormously important. While the consolidation of the thematic of *The Old Maid* as a peculiarly appropriate dramatic form for Davis cannot be simply ascribed to her – she cannot be said to be its 'author' – her presence is the main determinant of its persistence. It is therefore necessary to inquire why *The Old Maid* was crucial for Davis while similar thematic material seems eccentric for Hepburn.

b) *The Old Maid* was adapted from a novella by a distinguished literary melodramatist; *A Woman Rebels*, though it derives from an independent source, is intimately linked to this novella generically; *All This and Heaven Too* is extensively indebted to a major convention of nineteenth-century melodrama, the 'governess' theme – all this locates these films in a genre of some longevity.

c) The thematic of *The Old Maid* acquired a particular resonance and pertinence in the late 'thirties and early 'forties, the period of Davis's greatest box-office

Still: Flora (Elizabeth Allan) and Pamela (Hepburn) in A Woman Rebels.

popularity. Her stardom, in other words, is inseparable from a specific dramatic situation and its inflection. Hepburn was 'box-office poison' in the early part of this period, and her presence in *A Woman Rebels* entails a dramatic development which is inconceivable in a Davis movie.

We have to deal, then, with three terms and their imbrication – the star, the social present of a genre, and the history of its composition. Consider, to begin with, the structural/thematic continuities between the two films:

1) The relationship between two women – sisters in *A Woman Rebels,* cousins in *The Old Maid.* In each case, one of the women is rebellious and unconventional

– Pamela (Hepburn) and Charlotte (Davis) – and the other conservative – Flora (Elizabeth Allan) and Delia (Miriam Hopkins).

2) The conservative woman marries, the other has an affair and becomes pregnant by a man who does not reciprocate her love.

3) The relationship between the unconventional woman and her lover is broken off. In *The Old Maid*, Clem (George Brent) is killed in the Civil War; in *A Woman Rebels*, Gerald (Van Heflin), having seduced Pamela, marries someone else. Neither man knows about the pregnancy.

4) Pamela and Charlotte leave home to have their child in secret (in *The Old Maid*, Charlotte's absence is covered by a time-lapse). Both give birth to a daughter – Flora (Doris Dudley) in *A Woman Rebels*, Tina (Jane Bryan) in *The Old Maid*.

5) The conventional woman's husband – Alan (David Manners) in *A Woman Rebels*, Jim (James Stephenson) in *The Old Maid* – is killed in an accident.

6) Because of the social stigma attached to illegitimacy, Pamela and Charlotte can have a hand in the upbringing of their children only by pretending that they are not the child's mother.

7) A time-lapse occurs – dramatised in both films through a montage sequence – during which the daughter grows to womanhood.

8) The daughter falls in love, and Charlotte and Pamela's antagonism to the lover precipitates a confrontation between mother and daughter in which the latter, still unaware of her real parentage, accuses her mother of being an old maid who has never known love.

9) The film ends with a reconciliation between mother and daughter. In *A Woman Rebels* it is accompanied by Flora's discovery that Pamela is her mother, whereas in *The Old Maid* the truth is suppressed.

In both cases, we are concerned with a liaison between two classical melodramatic themes – 'the old maid' and 'illegitimacy'. Each of these themes has a number of modalities.

The Old Maid

1) The variant represented by Henry James's *Washington Square*, filmed as *The Heiress* (William Wyler, 1942), in which the heroine is seduced by a fortune hunter who deserts her when he discovers that he will not be able to gain access to her money.

2) The narrative exemplified by Hepburn's 'fifties 'spinster' films, in which a 'frustrated old maid' discovers herself through a brief interlude of romantic passion.

3) Narratives in which the heroine remains unmarried because for some reason she and her lover are *unable* to marry: usually, the relationship is impeded by the fact that the lover already has a wife and/or an illustrious social position which the relationship would compromise. *Back Street* and two of the Davis/Robinson films, *All This and Heaven Too* and *Now, Voyager*, all relate to this pattern.

4) Narratives in which the heroine 'never speaks her love' because of the constraints of social propriety and/or the inhibitions and lack of confidence produced by the convention that women should 'wait to be asked': for example, *Quality Street*, James's *The Spoils of Poynton*, Charlotte Brontë's *Villette*.

5) The structure with which we are immediately concerned, in which the heroine becomes an old maid because she has an illegitimate child. The prototype is to be found in one of the most popular of Victorian melodramas (as novel and play), Mrs Henry Wood's *East Lynne*. Here again, the heroine can stay with her child only by concealing her maternity (she becomes his governess), but in this case her transgression is punished by the child's death ('Dead! Dead! – and never called me "mother"!'). In this variant, and in the James texts, the frustration of the heroine's sexuality is intimately related to questions of property, and type 5) is distinguished from type 3) by virtue of the fact that while the heroine of the latter may also become a surrogate mother, the child is *not* her own.

Illegitimacy

1) Narratives in which the heroine's sexual transgression is publicly revealed and she is socially ostracised: for example, Nathaniel Hawthorne's *The Scarlet Letter*, *Way Down East* (both filmed, with Lillian Gish, respectively by Victor Sjöström in 1926 and D.W. Griffith in 1920), Thomas Hardy's *Tess of the D'Urbervilles*.

2) Conversely, narratives in which the transgression has been repressed, the plot turning on the threat of revelation. In George Eliot's *Felix Holt*, the illegitimate child has been brought up within the family as if he were legitimate, in Charles Dickens's *Bleak House*, the child is a foundling. This structure is clearly very close to type 5) of the 'old maid' theme, the difference being that in this case the heroine is married (though not, of course, to the child's father). In other variants (e.g. *Letter from an Unknown Woman*, Max Ophuls, 1948), the heroine's husband may be aware that her child is not his, and the 'revelation' theme may be marginalised (e.g. *Orphans of the Storm*). Significantly, the female protagonists of the Eliot and Dickens novels, Mrs Transome and Lady Dedlock, have a number of the generic characteristics of the 'old maid' – frustration, embitterment, loneliness, acerbity.

3) Narratives in which the woman is compelled by her lover to assume the secret and 'invisible' role of his mistress so that the children's' illegitimacy shall not damage his social standing – for example, Lydia Glasher in Eliot's *Daniel Deronda*.

It should be added, perhaps, that the theme of the social prevention of motherhood is also frequently dramatised through narratives in which the heroine's 'crime' is not an illegitimate child but adultery (*Anna Karenina*) and/or prostitution (Josef von Sternberg's *Blonde Venus*, 1932).

It will be seen, then, that the basic thematic material of *The Old Maid* and *A Woman Rebels* can be regarded as a specific inflection of a characteristic generic preoccupation with the contradiction between female desire and the ethical norms and economic structures of patriarchal capitalism. Both films work, moreover, by juxtaposing a woman who embraces the bourgeois norms with another who violates them, and by making the latter the movie's emotional centre. In what

Still: Phoebe, Dr Brown (Franchot Tone) and Susan in Quality Street.

ways do they differ, and to what extent can these differences be defined in terms of casting? The opening scenes of *A Woman Rebels* establish the central Hepburn motifs:

1) The rejection of the father's authority, both in his capacity as father and as a representative of the law – Thistlewaite (Donald Crisp) is a judge. The first scene, in which Pamela (Hepburn) is arraigned before her father for 'the violation of every rule of this house', is staged as a trial, and as she leaves, unrepentant, Pamela remarks, 'I should hate to be tried before you, either innocent or guilty. If you're unjust as a father, you must be doubly so as a judge.' In the following scene, as she and her sister, Flora, are preparing for bed, the nature of Pamela's rebellion against patriarchal authority is generalised when she says, of her father, 'He's only a man,' adding, 'I'm not afraid of him; I just don't like him.'

2) From the outset, the challenge to the father is inseparable from a conscious, articulated refusal of conventional female roles which is not contingent on, or inspired by, desire for a man. The main charge against her is the surreptitious removal of 'forbidden books' from the library and on being asked to explain herself she replies, 'I want to *know* things.' The scene culminates in her designation of Mrs Ellis's *Daughters of England*, offered by her governess, Miss Piper (Eily Malyon), as 'the Bible of English womanhood – every sentence is a holy command', as 'rubbish'. A few moments earlier Miss Piper has asserted that 'a woman must learn to feel her dependence', and Pamela's assertion of her independence is, characteristically, narcissistic (as opposed to romantic) and political,

in that its immediate referent is the position of women in general. It is not, in other words, simply a question of the particular, private confrontation being defined as representative by *the film:* the heroine herself sees that it is so.

3) The oppositional affiliation to women: the closest link here is with *Holiday.* Pamela's whispered injunction to Flora – 'Don't let him make you cry, that's what he likes' – parallels Linda's 'Don't let him bully you', addressed to Julia prior to another confrontation with the father (over Julia's engagement to Johnny). As in *Holiday,* the mother is dead, her death is associated with her oppression and defeat by patriarchy ('She was afraid of him, too'), and she represents for the Hepburn character physical and emotional possibilities which patriarchy inhibits ('He's never even kissed us – not once! . . . Mother kissed us, all the time'). Pamela, like Linda, is desolated by the prospect of losing her sister through the latter's marriage, and the film makes it clear that it is the grief and loneliness produced by Flora's departure which lead her to gravitate towards Gerald. The two sisters sleep together and, in an extraordinary scene, Gerald appears miraculously and inexplicably in the garden to which Pamela has retreated in tears after being unable to sleep now that Flora has gone. The fact that Pamela later passes off her daughter as her sister's child, and actually names her Flora, is thus crucially significant, and looks back to the lesbian theme of *Little Women.* Gerald becomes the medium through which Pamela can bear Flora's child and then, as active feminist, create a new family without a father.

It is, indeed, the radically different *nature* of the relationship between the two women which distinguishes *A Woman Rebels* most sharply from *The Old Maid.* Not only, in the former, are the women friends, but Flora dies immediately after receiving the news of her husband's death. In *The Old Maid,* Charlotte and Delia are rivals for Clem, and rather than the unconventional woman bringing up the child of the conservative one, it is Delia who, as the action progresses, gradually appropriates the transgressor's child. These two asymmetries within narratives which are structurally so close are immediately referable to the presence of a particular star.

Whenever Hepburn is cast as another woman's romantic rival, she invariably becomes friends with the woman and prefers to renounce the man rather than hurt her. The two most obviously extraordinary instances of this inversion of the universally acknowledged truth that two women in love with the same man cannot be friends are to be found in *Christopher Strong* and *Sylvia Scarlett.* The transformation of consciousness which enables Elaine Strong to tell Cynthia that 'marriage and children make almost any woman old-fashioned and intolerant', and to give her 'a mother's sincerest thanks' for the way in which she has helped Monica, in the full realisation that Cynthia and Strong have been having an affair, is one of the most remarkable features of Arzner's film, and the terrible ironies which accompany it don't in the least detract from the power generated by replacing an expected conventional confrontation with an expression of solidarity. On the contrary, the fact that, at this stage, the solidarity can only have the effect of restoring the balance of a patriarchal order which has been irreparably discredited (by imposing on Cynthia the most extreme form of self-sacrifice and reinstating the family which oppresses Lady Strong) is the essence of the irony, and of the film's critique of the effect of patriarchal heterosexual relations on relations between women. In *Sylvia Scarlett,* Sylvia saves Lily's life in order to restore her to Fane – in the conviction certainly, that this is what Fane really wants, but also moved by a sympathetic identification with Lily herself. The question is further complicated by Lily's sexual attraction to Sylvia, which enables the film to extend the analysis offered by *Christopher Strong* to include the male inhibition of erotic feeling between women: it is Fane's presence and the convention of 'exclusiveness' that governs the way in which Lily and Sylvia are able to relate to him, which impose on them the choice between rivalry and self-abnegation. In both films, the refusal of the convention which dictates *the former* permits the dramatisation of *both* as mechanisms which regulate, and defuse the radical potential of, an emotional commitment by a woman to a member of her own sex. In *Holiday,* Linda's love for Julia is such that she will permit herself to express her love for Johnny only after her sister has explicitly rejected him.

The most remarkable testimony to the difficulty of showing Hepburn as another woman's romantic rival is provided by the films with Spencer Tracy. While it is one of the cycle's most stable conventions that the Hepburn character has a relationship with another man, the reverse is never true, with the single exception of *State of the Union,* which is unique in this respect in the entire Hepburn canon – the opposition between Susan Vance and Alice Swallow (Virginia Walker) in *Bringing Up Baby* hardly works in these terms.

In *State of the Union,* the Hepburn character is relentlessly inscribed as 'mother', and the mother's role is seen to go with both total self-abnegating devotion to the husband and vicious rivalry with another woman. In this context,

Still: Hepburn and Tracy as Mary and Grant Matthews in State of the Union.

Hepburn's motherhood in *State of the Union* is inertly rhetorical. The fact of it is crucial to the project because that is the female role which is to be affirmed, but its value is baldly asserted rather than realised, and the children (and the idea of the family) are little more than obligatory stage machinery. While we may certainly infer from this a contradiction between the Hepburn/Tracy convention and parenthood, it suits the film's purpose to pretend that the contradiction does not exist.

It is worth noting in passing that Hepburn is still more prolifically maternal (seven children) in *Song of Love*, which I have not been able to see. A friend informs me, however, that its project (characteristic of the 'bio-pic') is, as far as Hepburn is concerned, close to that of *State of the Union*: in the interests of the greater glory of male creativity, Clara Schumann abandons her own career and rejects the lure of sexual passion, only resuming her work as a pianist after her husband's death, as a propagandist for and transmitter of his genius. The two works help to clarify one's sense of the generally conservative character of Hepburn's MGM period, in which the groundwork for her 'seventies and 'eighties films is prepared rather more thoroughly than might at first be apparent. The step from *State of the Union* to *On Golden Pond* is a short one, and it has been the distressing effect of the films of the 'forties to establish a great gulf between the contemporary Hepburn and the Hepburn of RKO.

Stills. Below: Clara Wieck Schumann (Hepburn), Robert Schumann (Paul Henried) and Johannes Brahms (Robert Walker) in Song of Love. *Opposite: Mary Stuart (Hepburn) in* Mary of Scotland.

State of the Union apart, when another woman is present, the relationship between the Hepburn figure and the hero can be secured only if the other woman renounces him, and the conclusion, in the light of the findings of the previous chapter, is clear enough. Hepburn has to be shown in solidary, comradely and potentially lesbian relationships with other women, and the problem in the comedies with Tracy is to get her to relate to the hero, not him to relate to her (except inasmuch the latter is an *effect of* the former): it is always she, rather than the Tracy character, who threatens to disrupt or impede their union. Romantic rivalry is at best irrelevant to the issues that Hepburn raises (she can't be shown to put a man before another woman's interests) and may, at worst, exacerbate them by making her attachment to the hero even more difficult. It is clearly significant that in *Stage Door* the other women's antagonism to Terry is entirely one-sided, never generates an equivalent antipathy in Terry herself (on the contrary), has nothing to do with rivalry for a man, and resists, as we have seen, coherent dramatisation.

The exceptions to this general rule are *Mary of Scotland* and a number of the late films (*Suddenly, Last Summer, The Trojan Women, A Delicate Balance*). John Ford's film is, in terms of Hepburn's other RKO movies, strikingly aberrant. The characteristic thematic of the 'thirties melodrama cycle about female monarchs coincides with the preoccupations of Hepburn's movies to the extent that both explore the ways in which patriarchal sexual relations impose renunciation on women: Mary (Hepburn) cannot be both an effective, powerful social agent and a lover. What distinguishes the two groups is the protagonist's attitude *to* her lover – a point which becomes clear if one compares *Mary of Scotland* with, on the one hand, *Queen Christina* and, on the other, *Christopher Strong*, the only other film in which the Hepburn character dies. Mary and Elizabeth are not sexual rivals, but Mary's final judgement on her antagonist (she tells Elizabeth that the latter is 'not even a woman' because she has preferred the exercise of power to sexual relations with men and that, consequently, 'it's you who've failed, not I')

Stills. Above: Violet Venable (Hepburn) and Catherine Holly (Elizabeth Taylor) in
Suddenly, Last Summer. *Opposite: Julia (Lee Remick) and Agnes (Hepburn) in*
A Delicate Balance.

is determined by the kind of romantic passion which expresses itself in Mary's
admission, earlier, to Bothwell (Fredric March), that 'perhaps I didn't really exist
at all until I met you.' Clearly, neither of these propositions has much to do with
Hepburn, and one isn't surprised to find her on record as saying that she
despised Mary and wanted to play Elizabeth. The attitude to another woman is
unique because *Mary of Scotland* is the only film in which Hepburn can be made
to assert 'Still, still, I win!' on the grounds that she has enthusiastically embraced
her own exclusion from history and action by 'falling in love'. Elsewhere, in
Christopher Strong or *Sylvia Scarlett*, the romantic impulse is accompanied by an
equal and opposite resistance, and while Mary, like Cynthia Darrington, effectively commits suicide (the rhetoric of the ending transforms her execution into
a kind of Catholicised *Liebestod*), the realisation of Cynthia's death embodies a
protest against, and critique of, the forces which have destroyed her, not a celebration of her 'dark victory'.

The appearance of antagonistic attitudes to other women in some of Hepburn's later films (most remarkably in *Suddenly, Last Summer*) is quite another
matter, and has to do with a tendency to cast her in this period as oppressive
matriarchs whose power is exercised within the family. *Suddenly, Last Summer* is
the first film in which Hepburn plays a 'monster' and, with three exceptions, the
first in which she plays a mother. Here, again, two of the exceptions – *A Woman
Rebels* and *The Sea of Grass* – prove the rule. In both cases, her motherhood embodies a transgression of patriarchal authority which is viewed sympathetically:
Lutie's son in *The Sea of Grass*, like Flora in *A Woman Rebels*, is illegitimate, and

her husband (Tracy) expels Lutie from their home when her second child turns out to be not the longed-for legitimate male heir but a daughter. Mrs Venable (Hepburn) in *Suddenly, Last Summer* is, on the contrary, the classic wicked mother in that her 'strength' takes the form not of breaking out of the family but of taking it over. Rather than expanding on the logic of the connections implied in this paragraph, it is useful at this point to juxtapose Hepburn with Davis:

1) Davis is *incessantly* cast in narratives about relationships of more or less insatiable jealousy, animosity, loathing and resentment between women, each of which takes the form of a mutual struggle for power: *The Old Maid*, *The Private Lives of Elizabeth and Essex* (Michael Curtiz, 1939), *All This and Heaven Too*, *The Little Foxes*, *The Great Lie*, *Now, Voyager*, *Old Acquaintance*, *A Stolen Life*, *All About Eve* (Joseph L. Mankiewicz, 1950), *What Ever Happened to Baby Jane?*, *Hush . . . Hush, Sweet Charlotte!* (Robert Aldrich, 1965) are obvious examples. The rivalry may be romantic, professional or familial (the struggle between mother and daughter, cousins, sisters), and usually two forms of rivalry pervade the same relationship, with the romantic rivalry as the master conflict. Davis can play either the victim or the oppressor (thus, for example, she is the monstrous mother in *The Little Foxes*, the suffering daughter in *Now, Voyager*), and sometimes both: Charlotte in *The Old Maid* is Delia's victim and the oppressor of Tina, and in *A Stolen Life* Davis plays both the 'good' and the 'bad' sister. Davis's first film was called *Bad Sister*, in which she played the 'good' sister.

2) Davis, unlike Hepburn, repeatedly plays 'wicked' women and 'bitches'. Jack L. Warner remarks of her first major role, in *Cabin in the Cotton*, that it was in this part that 'the magic quality that transformed this bland and not beautiful little girl into a great artist when she was playing bitchy roles' was first manifested: i.e. when the liaison between Davis's physical appearance and manner and a certain ideological category was first effected. She is regularly cast as a murderer – *Bordertown* (Archie Mayo, 1935), *The Letter* (William Wyler, 1940), *The Little Foxes*, *Beyond the Forest*, *The Nanny* (Seth Holt, 1965) – and other 'bitch' roles include *Of Human Bondage* (John Cromwell, 1936), *Dangerous* (Alfred E. Green, 1935), *Jezebel* (William Wyler, 1938), *Dark Victory*, *In This Our Life* (John Huston, 1942) and *The Anniversary* (Roy Ward Baker, 1967). This aspect of the persona, and its relation to Davis's charisma, is superbly formulated in the legendary ad line for *In This Our Life* – 'No one's as good as Bette when she's bad' – as fascinating an ideological conundrum as ever was. The alliteration of 'Bette' and 'bad', and the corresponding pun on 'good' (which we reduce at our peril, in Warner's manner, to 'good as an actress'), suggest that the ideological content of these terms, as applied to women, is centrally at issue in the Davis persona. The theme of *The Old Maid* is the meaning, and thus the possible application, of the word 'wicked'. Which of these women is 'good' and which 'bad'? Is either term in the least appropriate? What is the social specificity of their conventional meaning?

3) While Hepburn doesn't play 'monsters', Davis doesn't play feminists, and this distinction implies that their respective characters have very different kinds of consciousness and very different positions in relation to patriarchy. Neither, clearly, can be shown in happy domesticity, unless through the bluff of a happy ending which implies a future contentment without having to face the embarrassment of dramatising it. As we have seen, the characteristic Hepburn protagonist

Still: Lutie (Hepburn) and Brewton (Tracy) in The Sea of Grass.

challenges patriarchal authority *in a way which she knows to be normative* (that is, she identifies herself as a woman), and demands a position in a public world both as a man's equal and as a representative of her sex. The problem she raises, therefore, is essentially one of accommodation: how does one get a woman who has taken up this kind of position to relate to men? The Davis problem arises from the fact that she *does* relate to men: she is located within the 'private realm', the traditional sphere of female competence, but is for some reason incompatible with its norms. Davis repeatedly plays

a) women who *wish* to be married, but whose marriage is prevented by some external impediment. Thus Charlotte in *The Old Maid* cannot marry Clem because he loves Delia, and Delia impedes her marriage to Joe Ralston (Jerome Cowan); in *All This and Heaven Too* and *Now, Voyager* the Davis character's lover is already married, in *Dark Victory* she is terminally ill, in *The Private Lives of Elizabeth and Essex* she is Elizabeth I. These women are held by the persistence of a love which cannot be consummated in a position of suffering and narrative passivity; by the same token the social laws apparently 'tragically' impermeable, which restrain them, trap them in a world in which they cannot assume the logical female role to which they aspire. The key note is struck at the very beginning of *The Old Maid* when Charlotte says to Delia, apropos of the latter's rejection of Clem, 'I can't imagine not waiting forever' – a line which one might compare with that equally representative Hepburn moment near the end of *Holiday* when Linda, who still imagines that Julia's marriage to Johnny is to go ahead, compares the indulgence of unrequited love to Ned's alcoholism, saying 'it's like living on that stuff. I'll *have* to get over it.' Davis's 'spinsters' *cannot* marry, whereas even Hepburn's 'fifties 'old maid' cycle is unable to repress the feeling that Hepburn has become a 'spinster' because she *refuses* to 'get a man the way a man gets got'.

The fact that the Cukor/Hepburn version of *The Corn Is Green* eliminates any suggestion of a romantic relation between Miss Moffat and her pupil, emphasising her creative fulfilment through work which places her in a position of authority over men, while the Rapper/Davis version defines its protagonist in terms of the stoical sublimation of a romantic impulse for the realisation of which her work is a tragically inadequate compensation, is only superficially explained by reference to the respective age of the two stars when the films were made; the difference is, in fact, fundamental. When Davis plays a woman who occupies a position of great social power (*The Private Lives of Elizabeth and Essex*), or who commits herself to professional self-definition outside of marriage (*Old Acquaintance, All About Eve*), the film invariably stresses the ultimate barrenness of her achievement, its irrelevance to her 'real' needs: Margo Channing's 'you're not a woman [without a man]' is exemplary. The very title *The Private Lives of Elizabeth and Essex* is profoundly characteristic: the film is about the obstruction of private life by public status, and not (as so often in Hepburn's case) the undermining of professional integrity and independence by private life.

The most striking exception to this general pattern in Davis's work is *Now, Voyager,* which is also, significantly, the film in which she comes nearest to a feminist self-definition. It is indeed the case that her spiritual education is governed by men and romantic love (as it never is in Hepburn's case, where love is almost invariably a threat to her autonomy), and that it is just possible to read the film's astonishing ending in terms of the 'tragic' obstruction of passion by external forces. The dominant suggestion, however, seems clearly to be that Charlotte refuses Jerry (Paul Henreid) because his love is not of such supreme importance as to justify the renunciation of everything else – in this case, an achieved professional status and a non-patriarchal family which exactly parallels Pamela's in A *Woman Rebels*. The effective agency and independence that Charlotte has discovered through male intervention is more significant for her than the men themselves, and given the film's rigorous demonstration of the effect of the patriarchal family on women, the family without a man that is created at the end emerges as a powerful and substantial positive. Even here, however, we find a motif which is also common to *Dark Victory* and *The Old Maid* whereby the Davis character creates in fantasy the 'normal' role she is unable to live through. Charlotte's successful transgression is sustained by a private reconstruction of the order she has violated. In *The Old Maid*, romanticism, the loss of agency and interiority go inseparably together. When she visits her cousin's school, Delia tells her, 'You seem to be living inside yourself somehow.' She has nowhere else *to* live. Deprived of actual domesticity, and placed in a position which inhibits the possibility, or the consciousness, of an alternative to it (Charlotte agrees with Delia that 'it's a woman's duty to marry'), she can only struggle to maintain the integrity of the world within.

b) Davis can play, conversely, women who, having become wives and/or mothers, react to their oppression by being 'bad' (murder, adultery). This privatised and self-destructive self-assertion is the corollary of the passivity and suffering of the previous type: these two sets of characters are constrained either by the prevention or the attainment of marriage, by being unable to achieve domesticity or by having done so. Davis is supremely skilled in the dramatisation of the repression entailed by the domestic role or by an unfulfilled yearning for it, and all her characteristic mannerisms – the clipped precision of speech, the nervous clasping of the hands, the darting eye movements, the walk at once briskly self-confident and awkwardly poised and self-contained – bespeak the perilously unstable containment of accumulated intensities. It is this theme of the relation between interiority and the social curtailment of agency which links the two categories, with opposite but complementary reference to the role of 'wife'. It is of the essence of the persona's complexity that every time a Davis character says something of the order of 'I can't imagine not waiting forever', we hear a tacit intimation of Regina Giddens's line in *The Little Foxes*: 'I'll be waiting for you to die'.

The 'good'/'bad' dialectic noted above derives its substance from the fact that if the very notion of a woman's independent agency is ideologically problematic, the consequences of its inhibition are no less so. Waiting interminably to get a man and then, having got him, waiting for him to go, are equally undesirable alternatives, but they are also logically produced by the existence of an ideal female role which defines women entirely in relation to men. It is in this gap between an ideological norm (women should be passive, not active) and the perception of its immediately negative corollaries, whether a woman marries or not, that the question of the morality of action is generated. While it is also implicitly solved, in that the norm must eventually be reaffirmed, Davis's stardom expresses the tenuousness and difficulty of the solution – its shocking incoherence. Such a thematic is, of course, implicit in the genre; its realisation and its potency must surely be referred to the radical contemporary crisis in the understanding of women's traditional social roles and social functions engendered by the war. There can be no question of the films being *about* this; works of art can be *enabled* by historical conjunctures without adverting to them, and it is always necessary to beware of the reflection theory of artistic practice. Had Davis melodramas articulated their social 'moment' in that way, they could hardly have moved beyond *Since You Went Away:* it is the interaction between that moment and the preoccupations of the genre with which we are concerned.

The different nature of the issues raised by Davis and Hepburn is nowhere more clearly demonstrated than in the function of men in *A Woman Rebels* and *The Old Maid*. Consider, for example, the opening shot of the latter film – the rapid pan from the headlines of a newspaper announcing the latest news from the front (the narrative begins during the Civil War) to an item in the society column, tucked away at the foot of the page, announcing Delia's wedding. The shot defines immediately one of the film's crucial concerns – the reassessment of the content of history, the recovery for history of areas of experience which have been written out of it. This preoccupation is, of course, implicit in the genre, which characteristically displaces the identification of significant historical process with a tale of 'arms and the man', and takes as its material the facts condemned by such tales to appear as trivial, peripheral, contingent. *The Old Maid* is remarkable for the remorseless logic with which it grasps the meaning and implications of this generic datum. On the one hand, the male characters are treated, with a supremely cavalier indifference, as the merest narrative functions. Clem and Jim

Ralston (James Stephenson) are wheeled on to provide Charlotte and Delia with children, and then simply killed off; the world of male action represented by the war is reduced to a brief montage of stock footage. The film goes out of its way to inform us that Delia has a son, Jim (Rand Brooks), as well as two daughters, and then proceeds to ignore him: the one line he is given – a briskly consolatory 'Don't worry, mother, *I'm* here' at the wedding of Dee (Janet Shore) – makes it absolutely clear that his only function is to foreground the marginalisation of men.

The Old Maid recognises, on the other hand, the dialectical complement of the genre's reduction of the phallus to the indispensable George Brent – the corresponding emphasis on the contradictory consciousness engendered in women under social relations in which the organisation of emotional life is patriarchal. While Charlotte is obviously not Delia, the whole narrative movement is determined by the fact that Charlotte wants for Tina the kind of social/economic status that only Delia is in a position to give to her. Charlotte continually struggles against Delia's gradual appropriation of her child, but she is also compelled to collaborate with it because her original transgression, being romantic, is also radically contradictory, and it is this contradiction which gives the objective forces acting on Charlotte their subjective purchase. The film is meaningless if we think of Delia either as merely Charlotte's conservative antagonist or as the long-suffering victim of Charlotte's perverse intransigence described by Dr Lanskell (Donald Crisp). Delia is effectively monstrous – Charlotte's 'I could not have done to you what you have done to me' has the film's full weight behind it and embodies, in conjunction with Charlotte's denial of the charge of 'wickedness', the film's clearest judgement of the bourgeoisie: but it is equally clear that Delia could not have done what she does if she hadn't been able to win Charlotte's consent by appealing to assumptions they have in common. Charlotte's romanticism and Delia's 'consuming passion for the First National Bank' are two distinct but complementary forms of consciousness both generated by the subordination of women to men, and each woman manifests residual traces of the more striking characteristics of the other. Thus if Charlotte's concern that Tina should be in a position to 'find herself a husband and make herself a home' brings her close enough to Delia for the latter to have power over her, the intensity with which Delia sets out to capture Tina is fuelled by sexual jealousy and the desire to 'undo' Charlotte's relationship with Clem. It is this reciprocity, traced by the film to social relations which conduce to women's emotional and economic dependency, that provides the condition for the terrible violence which the women inflict on themselves and each other.

The contrasting strategies of *A Woman Rebels* are determined by a need which does not arise in *The Old Maid* – the privatisation of the protagonist, which, as we have seen, is precisely the source of conflict in the Davis film. The dramatisation of the mother/daughter relationship is crucial here. The sources of Charlotte's opposition to Tina's friendship with Lanning (William Lundigan) are complex and ambiguous, deeply rooted in the contradictions of her own position. It is in part a question of an intensely sympathetic but inarticulate consciousness of Tina's vulnerability as a woman whose uncertain social position and whose love make her dependent on a man: the staging of the scene in which Charlotte waits up for Lanning and Tina on the night of the party and then overhears their conversation in the hallway clearly recalls the earlier sequence in which Charlotte herself, already vividly aware that Clem does not love her, has returned to the same house with him late at night after making love, and is discovered by Dora (Louise Fazenda). At this level, Charlotte fears that Lanning will betray Tina, or exploit her sexually and condemn her to something like her mother's position. This is inextricably interwoven with an element of sexual repressiveness, whereby Charlotte visits her resentment of her own frustrations on Tina, for whose sake, after all, she has submitted to them: at some level, she is punishing Tina, both as a potential sexual transgressor (like herself) and as the immediate cause of her own self-abnegation. At the same time, she is implicitly challenging the commodity-status of women: she goes on to tell Delia that Lanning's parents will prevent the marriage (as, indeed, they wish to) because Tina lacks the requisite social/economic credentials which go with having a father's name. It is, of course, because she fails to take this challenge far enough that she can be cajoled by Delia into accepting Tina's legal adoption as a Ralston: her own suffering remains the condition of Tina's 'happiness' because, from the beginning, the identification of a woman's happiness with marriage has remained unquestionable for Charlotte. Indeed, her personal wretchedness has confirmed that identification. The tragic nature of Charlotte's position consists in the fact that, while her experience is attributable to the form of bourgeois heterosexual relations, it also supports and nourishes her allegiance to a bourgeois concept of a woman's 'normal life'.

Pamela's opposition to Flora's engagement in *A Woman Rebels* is entirely contingent on the arbitrary decision to make Flora fall in love with Gerald's son – that is, with her own brother. This ingenious narrative manoeuvre is determined in turn by the film's need to destroy Pamela's career as a feminist activist and to foreclose any possibility of her resuming it. Pamela visits Gerald in secret to request his assistance in breaking up Flora's relationship with his son, and when Gerald's wife learns of the meeting (a suspiciously nocturnal one) she sues for divorce. Pamela is unable to give the real explanation of her visit in public because of the repercussions it would have for Flora; the divorce goes through, and Pamela's credibility as a proponent of women's rights is ruined by the scandal.

The implications of this strategy are ambiguous, and they embody more clearly than anything else in the film the fragility of the equilibrium it wishes to achieve. We are clearly invited to regard Pamela's feminism as necessary and desirable; the problem is to suggest that its demands can be accommodated within a suitably reformed and ameliorated patriarchy. The solution is assisted by the film's historical setting: irony at the expense of Victorian patriarchs outraged by the idea of a woman being a shop assistant or a secretary or a journalist carries the comforting rider that the 'woman problem' has been superseded. The evidence that the film does not feel this to be adequate is given in its particular inflection of the illegitimacy narrative. While at the outset the illegitimate child can be used to motivate Pamela's activities, both by presenting a case of women's vulnerability to male turpitude and exploitation and by providing an objective impediment to domesticity and marriage, it also serves at the end to bar her from the public world before the deeper implications of her politics have been explored.

A good patriarch, Sir Thomas Lane (Herbert Marshall), has been vaguely on hand throughout in order to demonstrate that not all men are selfish, domineering and anti-feminist, and the film has also carefully instilled the suggestion that while Pamela's career has been freely chosen from passionate conviction, she would also have been willing to marry Lane were it not that the discovery of her 'crime' might harm him. Lane can then be produced at the denouement to tell Pamela that women really need men after all ('So weak, these modern women!') and to preside over a purely private reconciliation between mother and daughter beneath the looming canopy of the family, in which the recognition of the objective social functions of legitimacy, emphatically foregrounded by *The Old Maid*, can be suppressed. It might be argued that the very blatancy and gratuitousness of such tactics, and the dynamic of the Hepburn persona, disturb their effectiveness, but the nature of the intention is incontrovertible.

The Old Maid has no need for a Sir Thomas Lane: indeed it is the very fact that it has a less radical protagonist which spares it the necessity of compromising or recuperating its analysis of women's oppression. In an astonishingly perverse essay on the Robinson/Davis melodramas, Barbara Creed opines that *The Old Maid* sanctions the judgements of its lone male 'voice', Dr Lanskell ('The Position of Women in Hollywood Melodramas', *Australian Journal of Screen Theory*, no.4, p.29). It would be hard to be more completely wrong. About a third of the way into the film, Lanskell visits Charlotte's school for war orphans and, noticing that the children have taken to sliding down the banisters, asks her if there is nothing she can do to prevent them. After several of his suggested remedies have been rejected as impracticable, he advises Charlotte, with mounting irritation, first to stick nails in the banisters and then to 'shoot the lot of them!'

It is, perhaps, the most extraordinary moment in a work which, after repeated viewings, seems clearly to be one of the greatest American movies. Lanskell – played, appropriately, by the same actor who plays Pamela's father in *A Woman Rebels* – is an avatar of one of the classical generic types of the American melodrama, from Hawthorne's *The Scarlet Letter* to *King's Row*, from James's *Washington Square* to *Mandingo* (Richard Fleischer, 1975) – the patriarchal doctor as castrator, associated repeatedly with the repressive regulation of sexuality, particularly female sexuality – *The Locket* (John Brahm, 1946), *The Cobweb* (Vincente Minnelli, 1955) and *Marnie* (Alfred Hitchcock, 1964) are other obvious cases in point. The explicit presence in *The Old Maid* of the bourgeois patriarch's final solution to the problem of gender – castration, or preferably, for the sake of completeness, death – defines the context in relation to which Charlotte's struggle must be read, and it is scarcely surprising that later in the film Lanskell is to be found paying tribute to Delia's heroic endurance of Charlotte's 'frustration' – 'no woman like that was ever easy to live with'. Indeed! – though Lanskell isn't in possession of the film's irony, for the point is that only the timely deployment of nails in the Lovell banisters could possibly have made Charlotte 'easier to live with' for Delia and Dr Lanskell.

I have managed, I hope, to suggest the way in which the analysis of star vehicles becomes immediately an analysis of the inflection of determinate generic repertoires. In their films, Hepburn and Davis are complementary states of genre; their uniqueness and their reciprocity must be defined in terms of their respective relations to the family and heterosexual love as dramatised through melodrama, and it seems to me to be generally the case that vehicles can only be identified at all according to the principles adumbrated here.

7. Hepburn and Tracy

'I read *Huck Finn* going down the Yangtze' – Tess (Hepburn) in *Woman of the Year*.

The discussion of Katharine Hepburn's films with Spencer Tracy raises problems less of tact than of critical relevance. It is notoriously the case that the films themselves were for a long time reduced to an occasion to speculate about the personal relationship between the two actors – an impulse nourished rather than starved by the fact that the information needed to satisfy it was so difficult to come by.

'It was the end of a very private love story, that was also part of the story of Hollywood itself. As journalist Helen Dudar wrote in the *New York Post*, "for a quarter of a century, they were a quiet, durable, faithful, oddly-matched couple everyone in Hollywood knew about, and – uniquely – no one ever gossiped about" ' (Betty Puttick, 'Tracy and Hepburn', *Photoplay*, July 1980, p.43).

The very lack of gossip serves to intensify our fascinated scrutiny of the absent object, whose outline nevertheless can be sketched in, we are to gather, by reference to the films.

'*Guess Who's Coming to Dinner* is the ninth movie that [Tracy] and Miss Hepburn made together, over a period of twenty-five years, and when, at its climax, he turns to her and tells her what an old man remembers having loved, it is, for us

Photograph: Tracy and Hepburn with writers Ruth Gordon and Garson Kanin during the shooting of Pat and Mike.

who are permitted to overhear him, an experience that transcends the theatrical' (*The New Yorker,* quoted by Dickens, p.187).

Most journalistic writing about Hepburn and Tracy has consisted of a standard litany of apocryphal tales and a more or less explicit invitation to read the films as something akin to documentaries about their stars. The matter can't, however, simply be left there. The two most famous Hepburn/Tracy movies, *Adam's Rib* and *Pat and Mike* – both written by Garson Kanin and Ruth Gordon, and both directed by Cukor – are clearly informed by a tone of insinuating knowingness, and Kanin's little book *Tracy and Hepburn* (Viking Press, New York, 1971), revealingly designated by its author as 'an intimate memoir' and which one gathers was deplored by Hepburn, suggests only that the authors of *Pat and Mike* wish to make it clear to the spectator that they are in the habit of addressing the leading actors by their abbreviated forenames. Similarly, the last scene of *Guess Who's Coming to Dinner* is, obviously, in some sense 'about' its stars, and asks to be read not simply as the culmination of a fictional narrative but as a celebration of and valediction to their friendship.

One's quarrel, then, is with the connotations of the phrase 'transcends the theatrical'. The effect, in *Pat and Mike* and *Guess Who's Coming to Dinner*, of the tacit implication of the actors in their roles, is very different, but it is certainly impertinent (in both senses) to read either in terms of the miraculous dissolution of artifice: the realist fallacy is no less fallacious here than it usually is. The precise significance of the 'theatrical' here includes – indeed, is premised on – the hint of the 'extra-theatrical', and the interpenetration of the two – the symbiosis of actor and role characteristic of the star system – becomes increasingly the essence of the project of the Hepburn/Tracy films. The films are themselves very self-conscious about the tendency to extrapolate from the character which the star plays to the star-as-person, and this awareness is fundamental to their mode of operation.

One might reasonably begin with *Guess Who's Coming to Dinner* and its critical reception, despite the fact that the film is, in obvious and important ways, unrepresentative. Apart from *The Sea of Grass* and *Woman of the Year*, it is the only film in which the Hepburn and Tracy characters have a child (adopted in the latter), and it is further, and crucially, distinguished from *them* by the fact that the child does *not* precipitate the breakdown of the marriage. A related point is the complete absence of a feminist theme: the conflict in the Hepburn/Tracy relationship is generated not by the woman's demand for equality and autonomy, but by divergent reactions to the engagement of the daughter (Katharine Houghton) to a black man. This displacement of the content of dramatic conflict from the terms of heterosexual relations themselves, which are taken completely for granted, on to the theme of inter-racial marriage is accompanied, logically enough, by the marginalisation of the Hepburn character who, in that she questions neither her own position nor the desirability of the engagement, is automatically depicted as a spectator of the tensions experienced by other characters rather than as a dramatic agent in her own right. Her function, as in *On*

Stills: Guess Who's Coming to Dinner. *Top: Christina (Hepburn) and Matt Drayton (Tracy). Bottom: Christina and Joey Drayton (Katharine Houghton).*

Golden Pond, is to be a mere sympathetic witness of her husband's *crise de conscience*. Mark Rydell's film is, in fact, virtually a remake of Stanley Kramer's, the differences between them being primarily determined by the specific way in which each film invites us to extrapolate from the fictional characters to the actors playing them. Our knowledge of Henry Fonda's fraught relationship with his daughter, and of his imminent death, is as crucial to *On Golden Pond* as our knowledge of Hepburn's blood relationship to Katharine Houghton (Houghton is her niece), of her friendship with Tracy, and of *his* imminent death (here a matter exclusively of what we know of the actor, and not a realised dramatic theme) is to *Guess Who's Coming to Dinner*.

All that remains in the Kramer movie of the Hepburn/Tracy thematic is a 'fond' and schematised recapitulation of the familiar opposition between fervent, liberal-democratic idealism and crusty, but ultimately principled and flexible, republican pragmatism – a recapitulation, moreover, which effectively detaches the opposition from the issues which it was previously used to dramatise. One need only make the obvious comparison with *Adam's Rib* to see that the disturbance, such as it is, of the Draytons' marriage is, as it were, 'accidental' and contingent. In the earlier film, the viability of the relationship and, beyond that, of bourgeois marriage itself, is called into question by the partners' clash of convictions. In *Guess Who's Coming to Dinner*, their disagreement is an inert deposit of the actors' personae rather than a substantive theme with significant ideological resonance.

Contemporary reviews of the film repeatedly sounded a single note: the movie is dated, mawkish trash; Hepburn and Tracy are wonderful:

'William Rose . . . has written what I can honestly only call a load of embarrassing rubbish . . . Which brings me, thank goodness, to Tracy and Hepburn, and while either or both are on the screen the most savage criticism is replaced by gratitude. To me, at any rate, that craggy face and burly build, the exploding humour, extraordinary gentleness and toughness of old leather, have always represented the ideal man – and that is real film-fan talk. I found it very moving to see him in this, his last picture, talent, presence and personality all unimpaired. Miss Hepburn is, of course, unchanged and unchangeable. Anyone who feels as I do about this pair will go and see *Guess Who's Coming to Dinner* regardless of its fallacies and its hokum' (Penelope Mortimer, *The Observer*).

'*Guess Who's Coming to Dinner* is an inescapably sentimental occasion. It is the late Spencer Tracy's last movie, and he is coincidentally co-starred in it with his partner of eight previous movies, the glorious Katharine Hepburn. In the course of their long careers they have given us so much delight, so many fond memories, that the simple fact of their presence in the same film for one final curtain call is enough to bring a lump to your throat. They bicker fondly together in their patented manner, and for me, at least, their performances in this movie are beyond the bounds of criticism' (Richard Schickel, *Life*).

These are fully representative: review after review gives way, with that striking readiness and enthusiasm which implies what Volosinov calls 'choral support', to the most extravagantly uninhibited displays of plangent personal feeling about the actors. It is impossible, I think, to imagine any other screen couple

Still: Henry (Henry Fonda) and Ethel Thayer (Hepburn) in On Golden Pond.

being talked about in this way. The same critics might wish to express their admiration and affection for Astaire and Rogers or Bogart and Bacall, but neither partnership can be conceived as licensing such universal public confessions of emotion and involvement. Why should this be?

A clue is to be found, perhaps, in the final scene of *Guess Who's Coming to Dinner* – the 'democratic' speech which also figures in a number of other Spencer Tracy movies – *Boys' Town* (Norman Taurog, 1938), *Stanley and Livingstone* (Henry King, 1939), *Fury* (Fritz Lang, 1936), *State of the Union*. The function of the speech, in terms of the film's racial theme, is the liberal endorsement of a marriage between a black man and a white woman. Its actual theme is the supreme value of the couple, conceived of as isolated and embattled amidst implacably hostile social forces, the only protection against which is the unshakeable devotion and mutual commitment of the partners. This view of the couple is ostensibly justified by the specific context (an inter-racial marriage in a racist society), but it is at the same time explicitly generalised by reference to the marriage of Matt and Christina Drayton (Tracy and Hepburn), who are wealthy, white and middle-class; the passion and violence of the speech's language, and of Spencer Tracy's astonishing delivery, are strikingly at variance with the cautious reformism to which the film portentously commits itself. In a film characterised by the turgid factitiousness of its dramatic effects – by a false and self-serving sincerity – the speech is remarkable for its enactment of a genuine and substantially realised emotion.

The source of the emotion hardly needs to be pointed out, and the scene is indeed very moving, all the more so for our sense that it is potentially extremely distasteful and exploitative – Tracy's impersonal intensity manages to counter-act the dangers of corrupt and luxurious feeling obviously latent in a scene which intends to capitalise on an insinuated parallel between a fictional character and the personal life of an actor known, by all involved, to be dying. That parallel is, nevertheless, of the essence of the scene's ideological effect: the view of the couple advanced within the dramatic world is authenticated by the open reference to a couple which exists outside it. The couple, as the film defines it, is very like John Ruskin's concept of the family: it is a refuge and a solace in 'a world not right', an answer to the turbulence, uncertainty and potential hostility of social life. The unrestrained personal testimonials of the contemporary reviewers of *Guess Who's Coming to Dinner* correspond to and feel themselves to be justified by, the personal testimonial intimated by the film. Text and critics are drawn together in the celebration of a powerful ideology of the couple – an ideology given concrete life by the presence on the screen of Spencer Tracy and Katharine Hepburn in circumstances of which everyone who sees the film will be aware.

The point to be made is a complex one. It is obvious that the use of these actors to guarantee that ideology involves the suppression of all the problems about the institution of the heterosexual couple which are dramatised in previous Hepburn/Tracy movies. It is no less obvious that the operation to which Kramer's film commits itself is also enabled by its predecessors, which, while they may argue that the couple is, from the woman's point of view problematic, also assert that the conflicts can be contained. By the time of *Guess Who's Coming to Dinner*, Hepburn and Tracy mean 'tensions generated by the patriarchal couple can be resolved within it', and if the film can deny the knowledge of the cycle's feminist theme as completely as it does, and take its stars as the living guarantee of a couple which is highly patriarchal, it is because their simple presence implies that the issues which the film refrains from raising have been settled.

Compare the reviews of the last Hepburn/Tracy film with these of their first:

'As a lady columnist, she is just right; as a working reporter, he is practically perfect. For once, strident Katharine Hepburn is properly subdued' (*Time*).

'This is a sound script to start with, Spencer Tracy's steady, skilful, quietly humorous characterisation contrasted with Katharine Hepburn's tense, rather shrill portrait of an egotistic woman' (Eileen Creelman, *New York Sun*).

'Miss Hepburn and Mr Tracy are admirably paired. Mr Tracy's easy style with an undertone of firmness convinces one that his Sam is the man to cope with Miss Hepburn's combination of detachment and restlessness as Tess, the career woman' (*The Christian Science Monitor*).

These writers are well aware of what is going on in *Woman of the Year* (it would be hard not to be), and endorse it as completely as their latter-day counterparts endorse *Guess Who's Coming to Dinner*; in the interim, the ideological project which is transparent in George Stevens's film has been submerged. In 1942, it was apparent that the construction of the couple subserved the 'proper subduing' of the woman: by 1967, Hepburn and Tracy have come to embody what Roland Barthes describes, in *Mythologies,* as 'the natural glory of the couple'. Robin Wood has commented suggestively on Barthes's phrase:

Still: Matt and Christina Drayton in Guess Who's Coming to Dinner.

'Marriage, in fact, is too vague a word. The ideologically validated concept we are concerned with could be more precisely defined as legalized heterosexual monogamy. Its ideological power can be suggested by the fact that for most people in our society that is automatically what the term "marriage" conveys. Yet "marriage" could mean a lot of other things: the harem, for instance . . . The concept of legalised heterosexual monogamy . . . has been ideologically dominant in our society for hundreds of years, surviving many radical social changes. "The natural glory of the couple", however Barthes intended it, is a phrase to which most of us feel an immediate response even though we know that many actual couples live in unnatural misery and that "natural" is a highly problematic concept' (*Film Comment,* November/December 1976, p.23).

Stills. Opposite: Tess (Hepburn) and Sam (Tracy) in Woman of the Year.
Above: Mike (Tracy) and Pat (Hepburn) in Pat and Mike.

That implies well enough the nature of the potency of the final scene in *Guess Who's Coming to* Dinner, where the affirmation of the couple can't be distinguished from its naturalisation.

Two factors determine the movement from *Woman of the Year* to that kind of ceremonial – the conventionalisation, through repetition, of the first film's project, which has itself a naturalising tendency, and the publicity, the more telling for its lack of specific content and the reticence of its objects, surrounding the actors' friendship. If none of the later films is as virulent as *Woman of the Year*, it is because the ideological confrontation acted out through the stars is, progressively, at once routinised and particularised as what 'Kate and Spence' do: 'they bicker fondly together in their patented manner', as Richard Schickel has it. The pleasurability of the Hepburn/Tracy films is in direct proportion to the presence of a significant tension between an overall narrative movement towards conservative reassurance and a substantial enactment of real ideological problems and disharmonies. Thus *Pat and Mike,* in which the cycle's thematic has been safely inoculated as an inert, cosy, 'entertainment' formula by which we are to be disarmed, is merely embarrassingly arch, its grossly inflated reputation being comprehensible, it seems to me, only as evidence of the dazzling expertise with which it allows one to feel that the inequalities of patriarchal sexual relations, of which one has vaguely heard tell, can be convincingly rectified through the

Still: Amanda (Hepburn) and Adam Bonner (Tracy) in Adam's Rib.

private mutual accommodation of lovable, exceptional persons. Here, the Tracy/ Hepburn convention merely ritualises the removal of schematised impediments to a foregone conclusion. *Adam's Rib* and *Desk Set,* while they intend the consolidation of the couple to imply that objective social inequalities can finally be settled within personal relationships, also go some way towards acknowledging, if only through producing contradictions, that the nature of heterosexual relations has to be considered in terms of the organisation of power in bourgeois society as a whole.

One can roughly distinguish in categorising the heterosexual star-teams of the classical Hollywood cinema, between the 'romantic' and the 'democratic' couple. The former is itself susceptible to two distinct inflections, according to whether or not the couple's romanticism is regarded as normative. The films built round all these types have in common the assumption that it is not possible ideologically to celebrate the couple and the family as ideals at the same time. They seek to dramatise, that is, the area of tension between the exemplary *form* of adult sexual relations and their exemplary *function* – the creation of children.

Officially, of course, no such contradiction existed. As a category of bourgeois ideology, the couple (in such a context, the qualifying adjective 'heterosexual' is taken as read) is a function of the category of the family, and of the organisation through the family of the transmission of property and the socialisation of the young. The family is the couple's *raison d'être*. Yet it is evident that the association of the two is fascinatingly uneven and problematic. The intensity of our psychological investment in monogamy is directly determined by the exclusivity of the relation to sexual objects constructed by the Oedipus complex – that is, by the bourgeois family. It by no means follows, however, that this intensity, and the kind of demand for pleasure which follows from it, will automatically be satisfied by the recreation of the social conditions of its own origin. On the contrary, there is no easy transition from the residues of the Oedipus complex (a romantic investment in a 'special person' and an insistence on a privileged, proprietary relation to him/her) to the couple as a social institution, geared not to the satisfaction of erotic needs but to the reproduction of bourgeois social relations.

The two complementary avatars of the 'romantic' couple address themselves to this implicit disharmony between sexual romanticism and the institution of marriage. Normative romanticism can be sustained only by the suppression of marriage and family altogether – or rather, by their projection into a certain but undramatised future beyond the close of the narrative. When the family is present, romanticism appears as transgression, as a rebellion against bourgeois norms which is tragically doomed by the necessity of upholding them. The films of Astaire and Rogers, whose dancing enacts the popular cinema's most beautiful metaphor for non-reproductive sexual pleasure, are the classical expression of an affirmed patriarchal romanticism: the partnership of Garbo and Gilbert, in which that pleasure is synonymous with the breaking of laws, acts through the negative corollary of such an affirmation.

In neither case is the social equality of the partners a real dramatic issue. The equality of the 'tragic' couple consists in the exhaustiveness and reciprocity of the desire which compels them to violate the principles of 'the social' as such: they are 'equal' in their mutual abandonment of the possibility of social life. In the other case, the accommodation of romanticism to marriage enacts a utopian reconciliation of the transcendent and the mundane whereby the domestic institution is structurally unaltered, yet transfigured by the passion of the particular lovers. The question of real social equality is voided by asserting either that the existing social arrangements are absolutely inimical to, and repressive of, love, or that love alone can guarantee their authenticity and realise their essential spirit, the nature and content of 'love' being, in both cases, understood and unquestioned. (This is not to say, of course, that they need remain unquestioned: Minnelli's *Madame Bovary*, 1949, and Vidor's *Duel in the Sun* are distinguished cases of films which articulate the inter-relation of these two romanticisms as patriarchal forms and challenge both of them from the woman's point of view.)

The theme of the 'democratic' couple, on the contrary, is the creation of a heterosexual relationship based on the social/sexual/professional 'equality' of the partners: Tracy and Hepburn, William Powell and Myrna Loy, and Humphrey Bogart and Lauren Bacall are all variants of this type. I wish to argue that in the Tracy/Hepburn cycle, the term 'democratic' functions in an exemplary bourgeois sense: the films argue that the inequalities to which they point can be rectified within the status quo. It will be helpful to approach the cycle, however, by way of a comparison first with Hepburn's films with Cary Grant, and then with Bogart's with Bacall – two bodies of work in which the bourgeois understanding of 'democratic' sexuality is placed under much greater strain.

The four Grant/Hepburn movies can be divided for convenience into two pairs: *Sylvia Scarlett* (1936) and *The Philadelphia Story* (1940) – the first and last – on the one hand, and *Bringing Up Baby* and *Holiday* on the other. The latter two were both made, one after the other, in 1938; neither did well commercially, but they remain, perhaps, Hepburn's most progressive and most completely satisfying films. One is likely to be impressed first by the *differences* between the relationships of the central couples in *Bringing Up Baby* and *Holiday*: whereas in the Cukor film there is an immediate, and thereafter unbroken, rapport between the Grant and Hepburn characters, and the consummation of the relationship is impeded not by unresolved personal antagonisms but by both characters' generous misreading of Julia, the premise of Hawks's film is David and Susan's violent incompatibility. The differences are obviously crucial for the quite distinct trajectories of the two narratives, but it is more useful, in attempting to account for the significance of the differences, to start from the films' common commitment to the construction of a non-patriarchal heterosexual couple. It then appears that the essential distinction is a matter of the hero's sexual repression, and the corresponding presence or absence of a need to 'educate' him before the couple can be formed.

Johnny and Linda in *Holiday* are linked from the outset by their antipathy to the bourgeois world of capitalist free enterprise and patriarchal family, and by their common tendency to construct, around the figure of Julia, a fantasy that that world can be transformed or ameliorated by the intensity of their own commitment. The action demonstrates the untenability of that fantasy and moves towards the lovers' abandonment of it. The last third of the film is substantially flawed, understandably, by the extreme difficulty of being clear about the meaning or the consequences of this process – which is nevertheless passionately affirmed. No alternative is offered but the 'holiday' – an alternative about as clearly grasped as John Wayne's ranch in *Stagecoach*, to the end of which film ('Well, they're saved from the blessings of civilisation') the coda of *Holiday* is remarkably close; and the extreme perfunctoriness of the final scene only emphasises the fact that *Holiday* is so structured that Johnny and Linda never get a chance to talk to each other after the New Year's party where they discover that they are in love. The possibilities of the new relationship, and the characters' understanding of them, are not – and hardly could be – succinctly articulated. A related fact of particular importance in the present context is the film's consistent attempt to pass off as a 'bourgeois-democratic' couple two lovers who are also used to affirm values that are clearly unrealisable within bourgeois democracy. The rhetoric about Johnny's 'declaration of independence' and the similarity of Linda's character to that of her pioneering grandfather succeeds only in making itself felt as contradiction, for the sexual energies which are so powerfully substantiated through Hepburn and Grant are defined dramatically in terms of the rejection

Still: David and Susan in Bringing Up Baby.

of the Oedipus complex. Even as it strives to present as 'democratic' a couple whose realised dramatic status is non-patriarchal, *Holiday* enacts the fundamentally antagonistic tendency of the two concepts. Arguing that Johnny and Linda are the true patriarchal all-American couple, *Holiday* suggests that the patriarchal all-American couple cannot exist in America and that the sexual identity of its components is not patriarchal.

Bringing Up Baby is spared this type of contradiction because, as Robin Wood has pointed out, the values which Howard Hawks affirms are always "either irrelevant or antagonistic" to capitalist social relations (Robin Wood, *Howard Hawks*, British Film Institute, 1981 edition, p.176). It is an a priori of the Hawks world that the relationships which the films value are unrealisable within bourgeois society, and it is the films' last impulse to advance the contrary suggestion. In the adventure films, the absence of any commitment to that society, and thus of criteria of value or utility deriving from it, is made good by the creation of male groups, in which social cohesion derives from implicitly homoerotic personal attachments and a shared commitment to freely chosen, socially 'useless' labour. If the group activity explains and 'justifies' the male bonding, and provides the condition on which it can be celebrated, it is also true, conversely, that the group appears as an utopian social microcosm, founded not on alienation and estrangement but on self-realisation as the member of a community through pleasurable and mutually beneficial work. In the comedies, as Robin Wood has again noted, the antagonism to the bourgeois world which the adventure movies express by ignoring it erupts, the films celebrating the destruction of bourgeois order through the anarchic return of the energies it alienates. *Bringing Up Baby is* supremely anti-Gothic: it names the repressed and affirms it.

The Hawksian world view renders redundant (indeed undesirable) the ideologically normative view of the couple as producer of children and agent of social reproduction. Equally, the image of the 'democratic' couple, in its bourgeois acceptation, becomes problematic: if the bourgeois world is unacceptable per se, then the prospect of 'equality' within it is deprived of its status as an ideal. *Bringing Up Baby*, while it has obvious affinities with the other comedies, represents Hawks' most drastic solution to the problem of affirming a heterosexual relationship in the absence of any logical basis on which to do so: it comes as near as any film has ever done to celebrating the end of patriarchal sexuality. (Minnelli's *The Pirate*, 1948, is the closest parallel case, both films ending with the destruction of the phallus – the collapse of the skeleton of the dinosaur matched in that film by the breaking of the magic lantern – and an intimation, albeit ambiguous, of the polymorphous reorganisation of desire.)

Theoretically, the comedy of *Bringing Up Baby* is the comedy of male castration and humiliation, yet it is never actually felt as such: the process of 'humiliation' acquires a positive meaning, in that it constitutes the condition on which David (Grant) can learn, in the Hawksian terminology, to 'have fun'. His loss of dignity consists, on the one hand, in the loss of bourgeois status (which the film despises) and, on the other, in the rediscovery of the sexual energy estranged by the bourgeois ego: it is quite crucial that Susan erupts in response to David's unconscious resistance to his prospective marriage, and that she thus answers to a sexual identity which is not only already contradictory, but also already antagonistic to the 'destiny' of the heterosexual male. The parallel-in-contrast between Hawks's adventure films and his comedies establishes Susan as the disruptive bearer, in the bourgeois world, of the values of the group, now rendered explicitly in terms of the release of bisexuality and an antagonism to capitalist property. On her first appearance, Susan expresses her contempt for, and proceeds blithely to violate (by smashing several cars, stealing another and driving off with David poised hysterically on the running board), both bourgeois property relations and their 'reflection' in heterosexuality ('Your ball! Your car! Does everything round here belong to you?'). We are not surprised, then, to find Hawks, in a wonderful moment in the Peter Bogdanovich interview in *Movie* 5 (1962), describing Susan's effect on David in terms of his 'getting a little normal'. *Bringing Up Baby* does not know, of course (how could it?), what follows Susan's demolition of the dinosaur (the analogous uncertainty in *The Pirate* expresses itself in the confusions and contradictions of the final number), though the film is clear that the apocalypse is produced by David's final acceptance of Susan, and if it is unable to conceptualise the new 'normality' in detail, it recognises and affirms its preconditions.

The logic of *Bringing Up Baby* and *Holiday* entails the proposition that the democratic couple is incompatible with bourgeois social relations: in both films, the 'equality' of the partners is directly associated with the breakdown of Oedipal

Still: David and Susan in Bringing Up Baby.

sexual identities and the anarchic emergence of 'perverse' eroticism in which 'masculinity' and 'femininity' are no longer the property of a particular biological sex. The first and the last Hepburn/Grant films operate differently. In *Sylvia Scarlett* (which predates Grant's appearance as a major star and in which he does not play the romantic lead), Monkley's function is to embody a cynical, exploitative male opportunism which Sylvia is used to reject: the bisexual dynamic is acted out, with the very different emphasis and development which I analysed earlier, between Sylvia and Michael (Brian Aherne). Dexter Haven (Grant) in *The Philadelphia Story* is, as a character, not unlike Monkley, but the dramatic evaluation of him is reversed: his exploitativeness and irresponsibility turn out to be a venial weakness, incomprehensible to and exacerbated by female strength, and Tracy (Hepburn) must learn that he is really lovable after all. *The Philadelphia Story*, in fact, is as much the first Hepburn/Tracy film (its project is very close to that of *Woman of the Year*, which immediately followed it) as a reactionary appendage to Hepburn's films with Grant. In Dexter Haven, a conservative appropriation of the Grant persona, whereby male 'irresponsibility' and 'femininity' are deprived of the positive connotations which accrue to them in *Holiday* and redefined as a pathetic flaw which woman must devote herself to rectifying, serves the function of containing and vilifying the Hepburn figure's corresponding divergence from American female norms which passes, in *Woman of the Year*, to Spencer Tracy. In *Holiday* and *Bringing Up Baby*, the endorsement of the disturbance of bourgeois gender roles is enabled by the absence of any commitment to the bourgeois world in general. In *The Philadelphia Story*,

Still: Dexter, Tracy and Mike in The Philadelphia Story.

which touts for the bourgeoisie with a vengeance, the idea of castration triumph-
antly reasserts itself: the feminised man is a weakling produced by an emasculating
woman.

The Hepburn/Tracy cycle can be read as the corollary of the impossibility,
within the Hollywood cinema, of the more radical tendency of Hepburn and
Grant, who raise too disturbingly the prospect of a positive reconception of what
bourgeois sexuality experiences as castration. The 'femininity' of the Grant persona is inappropriate to the strategy of recuperating Hepburn for the patriarchal
couple, as *The Philadelphia Story,* which is able to come up with nothing better
than a character whose 'virility' Hepburn has undermined, is there to demonstrate. The Tracy persona, with its robustly assertive yet 'sensitive' masculinity,
and its combination of incorruptible integrity and forbearing irony, is perfectly
framed for the function the films assign it. To this extent, *Woman of the Year*
successfully rationalises the inherently unstable project of *The Philadelphia Story,*
which finds itself in the unsatisfactory position of arguing that Dexter Haven's
manhood is entirely contingent on Tracy's attitude to him. The evasive double-
think of the gun imagery at the end of *Adam's Rib* – Adam (Tracy) does and
does not have the phallus, men and women are the same but *'vive la différence'*
– is the nearest that the Hepburn/Tracy movies, with the problematic of castration
that they ultimately embody, can get to *Bringing Up Baby.*

Bringing Up Baby leads us to Bogart and Bacall, an account of whom, it
transpires at once, is really an account of Howard Hawks. The interest of *Key
Largo* (John Huston, 1948) and *Dark Passage* (Delmer Daves, 1947) consists solely

in the fact not merely that they are so utterly unlike *To Have and Have Not* and *The Big Sleep* in tone and significance, but also that they show no interest whatever in following through from them. The specific presence of Bacall in the partnership's last two films is, to all intents and purposes, redundant, and she could easily be replaced by half a dozen other actresses without seriously affecting meaning, mode or conception. This is suggestive in itself and, given the legendary status of the couple's collaboration with Hawks, provokes one to ask what it was about them that both made 'Bogart/Bacall' an axiom and inhibited the consolidation of the team.

One notes first, that the 'democratic' couples created in *To Have and Have Not* and *The Big Sleep* are dissociated from any concept of 'democracy' in the larger, national sense. There is nothing here of all that is implied by the title *State of the Union*, which makes explicit the link between the condition of the heterosexual couple and the condition of the commonweal which is as fundamental to the meaning of Hepburn and Tracy as it is alien to Hawks's Bogart and Bacall – or his Hepburn and Grant. When such a connotation emerges, in *Key Largo*, it is, like everything else in the film, purely rhetorical – broadcast, but conspicuously unrealised. The schema demands that a couple should be around to portend, in opposition to Edward G. Robinson and Claire Trevor, a revived national health, but it amounts to no more than gesture: the Bacall character is a mere ideological counter and has no function in the film except to inspire and commit herself, at the appropriate moment, to the moral renaissance of the hero.

The intimate connection between *Key Largo* and *To Have and Have Not* is crucial here: when I emphasised their complete dissimilarity in 'tone and significance', I had not forgotten the congruence of the narrative structures that can be abstracted from them. A summary of their plots, indeed, might suggest an identical project. In both, the Bogart character, at the outset politically uncommitted, is placed in a situation in which he must decide whether or not he will join the democratic struggle against fascism (in *Key Largo*, an incipient American fascism). Edward G. Robinson in Huston's film corresponds to Dan Seymour in Hawks's, and in both works Bogart's revulsion at the callousness with which these figures torment an alcoholic (Claire Trevor and Walter Brennan respectively) by withholding drink represents a decisive stage in the progress towards 'commitment'. The boat journey which ends *Key Largo* parallels the boat journey which Bogart is about to make at the end of *To Have and Have Not*, the trip expressing, in both cases, the hero's new-found allegiance to the democratic cause. As is usual in the 'commitment' film, the two movies relate the gradual consolidation of the forces of democracy to the formation of a heterosexual couple (though some 'commitment' films, of course, resolve the couple theme 'unhappily' – e.g. *Casablanca*).

What might seem, at first sight, to be the crippling weakness of *To Have and Have Not* – its absolute indifference to the impersonal, political dimension of Bogart's position, which is as completely submerged by Hawks as it is bombastically inflated by *Key Largo* – is, in fact, the condition of its remarkable strength. For the only structure available within the 'commitment' film for the conceptualisation of politics is a mystified opposition between 'the fascist menace' and 'the free American world', on the assumed polar antagonism of which the Broadway moral uplift of *Key Largo* (which is adapted, after all, from a play by

Maxwell Anderson) absolutely depends. Doubtless the limitation of Hawks's work is that the nature of his estrangement from 'the free world' and his perception of its 'unfreedom' are never articulated politically (and thus, more precisely, coherently and unambiguously), but such criticism, perfectly valid in itself, should also acknowledge the incomparable advantages which Hawks enjoys by virtue of his immunity to liberalism. The one indicated ideology for 'political' criticism in American culture would instantly recoup the Hawks thematic, and if his lack of the most rudimentary political sense leaves him no option but to dramatise his antagonism to bourgeois life through conventions which are notoriously problematic, it also checks the development of a conviction that that antagonism is anything but complete and irremediable.

The positive counterpart to the depoliticisation of political struggle in *To Have and Have Not* is the ironic critique of the inert bourgeois-democratic ideologies of the Hollywood 'anti-fascist' film, and of the aggrandisement of 'freedom', honour, duty and self-sacrifice that goes with them. If Bogart's commitment, and fascism, are 'personalised', they are also given a realised rather than a conventional content. In *Key Largo*, the meaning of 'fascism' and 'democracy' is known from the start, and the film ministers to a complacent confidence that the meaning is assured and our position morally unassailable. *To Have and Have Not* gives 'fascism' and 'democracy' a concrete reality which bears no relation whatever to the defence of an idealised American capitalism, and is able in so doing to dramatise that discovery of the personal bearing of objective social struggles which remains the necessary prerequisite of any valid political commitment without attaching 'commitment' to affirmed bourgeois norms.

Still: Adam, Kip (David Wayne) and Amanda in Adam's Rib.

Paradoxically, the apolitical nature of Hawks's categories in *To Have and Have Not* is the measure of their critical and progressive character.

The treatment of the couple proceeds from this. The couple in *Key Largo* is the merest ideological datum: the hero undertakes and successfully consummates an approved model of social action, dedicated to the protection of the bourgeois status quo (state and family), and the heterosexual couple is wheeled on as the logical guarantee of the finality and future efficacy of the act of purification. In *To Have and Have Not*, the disruption of the ideology which identifies 'civil society' with bourgeois society, and the dissociation of the hero's involvement in the democratic cause from a commitment to the bourgeois state, are accompanied by the creation of a couple which is correspondingly distanced from the idea of social reproduction. The traditional force of the happy ending, as it concerns heterosexuality, is to assert the permanence of the union as a necessary condition of its reproductive function and the satisfactory containment of sexuality, particularly female sexuality. Hawks emphasises the union's impermanence ('Maybe it's just for a day'): the partners will stay together as long as they are 'Having fun' – 'fun', as in *Bringing Up Baby*, being clearly defined, through the actors' incomparable repartee, as sexual pleasure.

Even more audaciously, *To Have and Have Not* violates the convention which hives off into two distinct 'types' the privatised sexuality of the hero's woman and the suspect public sexuality of the show-girl. Throughout, Hawks juxtaposes Bogart's increasing involvement with the resistance and Bacall's gradual adoption of the role of an entertainer in the saloon run by Frenchy (Marcel Dalio) – a role which draws her into an intimate, affectionate, creative relationship with another man. One might compare Hawks's treatment of the Harry/Slim/Crickett (Hoagy Carmichael) relationship here with that of the Adam/Amanda/Kip (David Wayne) triangle in *Adam's Rib*. Kip, like Gerald (Dan Tobin) in *Woman of the Year*, functions as a dire warning of the logical consequences of the Hepburn character's feminism for the male ego. Significantly, both Gerald and Kip get beaten up by Spencer Tracy at the end of their respective films, so as to assure us that the tentative accommodation of the Hepburn figure which Tracy is about to make doesn't entail a loss of virility. Kip is clearly coded as gay, and Adam's cryptic observation that Kip 'wouldn't have far to go' to become a woman makes the coding virtually explicit. Adam is also jealous of Kip's friendship with Amanda, the resentment focusing on the love-song which Kip writes for her and which subsequently provokes the couple's first serious row. (Kip's dual meanings as faggot and sexual rival are, of course, contradictory, but they are held together by the proposition that what Adam calls Amanda's wish to be 'a big he-woman' signifies castration from the man's point-of-view and a desire for a defective heterosexual from the woman's). The reconciliation at the end is signalled by Adam's appropriation of the song, whose lyric he amends to suggest the finality of the reunion and of the clarification of the blurred gender lines ('The battle was fun/But it's done/ It's through').

One of the central themes of *To Have and Have Not* is Slim's assertion of her right to sing in Frenchy's bar, and the movement towards the achievement of that right is paralleled by Harry's towards 'commitment'. Both movements define the realisation of a public, social identity independent of the partner, and both involve a relationship with another man. Harry is friendly with Crickett and

Slim with Eddie (Walter Brennan) – indeed, Slim is admitted to the union between Harry and Eddie through her uniquely appropriate response to the 'dead bee' routine – but in both cases, the second intimacy is substantially independent of the first and enables the expression of different, but equally important, needs and drives. The Harry/Eddie relationship, as always in Hawks, is implicitly homoerotic. Slim's relationship with Crickett is presented as a creative friendship: it is crucial that it should be thought of as fulfilling impulses that are not fulfilled by Harry and that, in being non-sexual, it should give positive acknowledgement to aspirations in the heroine that are not immediately erotic. This friendship, too, disturbs conventional gender norms: Crickett's spontaneous attraction to Slim explicitly doesn't take the form of sexual objectification, and the lyric of the first song they sing together, 'Am I Blue?', is not amended to accommodate a male voice (a fact which may be read, perhaps, as realising a pun on the line 'Was I gay?': *Bringing Up Baby,* made six years earlier, contains one of the first recorded instances of the use of 'gay' to mean 'homosexual'). The song which Slim eventually sings on her first appearance as the bar's entertainer, 'How Little We Know', both establishes her autonomous public identity and makes explicit the refusal to guarantee the permanence of Slim's relationship with Harry, the value of which isn't to be thought of either in terms of its lasting forever or of its capacity to realise everything the lovers want. The film ends, famously, with Slim's wiggle-walk across the bar to join Harry after her farewell to Crickett – a moment in which the expression of desire for the hero is rendered simultaneously as public performance and as the woman's celebration of her own sexuality.

To Have and Have Not is inevitably and obviously ambiguous, not least because the public identities achieved by Harry and Slim are so radically different in kind: the 'showgirl' and the 'hero's woman' are contradictory roles, but both are strictly defined in relation to men. The film remains extraordinary, in ways which the comparison with *Adam's Rib* brings out. Hawks is able to go further partly because he undertakes less: if the absence of any impulse to cut value to the cloth of bourgeois society is the film's greatest strength, the inability to dramatise the theme of sexual equality in a context of institutionalised social inequalities is the corresponding weakness. Hawks's total unconcern with the requirements of actually existing social relations both frees the film and simplifies the issues which it is required to confront, reducing some and eliminating others: *Adam's Rib is* condemned to liberal recuperation, but it also has more to comprehend. The Bogart and Bacall of *To Have and Have Not* are the inhabitants of a dramatic world which is at once peculiarly circumscribed and radically suggestive, and the sententious vacuousness of *Key Largo* suggests that they are possible only within it.

The Hepburn/Tracy films fall neatly into two categories – the comedies and the melodramas (a distinction slightly blurred by *Guess Who's Coming to Dinner*).

In the melodramas – *Keeper of the Flame* (1942), *The Sea of Grass* (1947) and *State of the Union* (1948) – the couple is disrupted by the conservatism, ruthless personal ambition and lack of democratic principle of the man, the woman appearing as the voice of a normative democratic idealism. In *Keeper of the*

Still: as Christine Forrest in Keeper of the Flame.

Flame, in which the characteristics of the man are taken to their logical conclusion (Robert Forrest is the leader of a fascist organisation), he is *not* played by Tracy, who is cast instead as Steven O'Malley, the reporter investigating Forrest's mysterious death. Here, the democratic couple which is eventually formed is in no way implicated in what Forrest represents (his widow, played by Hepburn, is shown to have been at first ignorant of his activities and subsequently opposed to them), and the blandness of the film is directly determined by the virtual absence of any dramatic/ideological tension between the Hepburn and Tracy characters who, while they embody two different class positions which will be bridged by marriage, are held apart merely by the requirements of the plot – Christine Forrest knows what happened to her husband and O'Malley (Tracy) doesn't. In *The Sea of Grass* and *State of the Union*, Tracy himself plays a version of the Forrest figure (an obsessive, tyrannical cattle tycoon and a corrupt Republican presidential nominee respectively), and the films trace the process of his self-realisation and recovery of integrity. *Guess Who's Coming to Dinner* relates partially to this pattern, though here the Tracy character's conservatism is given what we are to read as a rational basis, and has no connection with the self-serving abuse of political power.

The issue in the melodramas is not the woman's demand for autonomy and social rights, understood as a threat to the prerogatives of the male, but the

Stills. Opposite: Susan Forrest, Jason Rickards (Howard da Silva) and Steven O'Malley (Tracy) in Keeper of the Flame. *Below: Brewton and Lutie in* The Sea of Grass.

excess and abusiveness of the man's exploitation of his. Here, it is the man, not the woman, who violates the 'democratic' norm, and the woman's liberalism is correspondingly privileged. The crucial distinction from the comedies consists in the fact that in the melodramas the man's imperfect principles rather than the Hepburn figure's self-assertion impedes the woman's adoption of the normative female role. There is no question of her dissatisfaction with that role as such: the breakdown of the Forrest and the Matthews marriages in *Keeper of the Flame* and *State of the Union*, and Lutie Cameron's adultery and illegitimate child in *The Sea of Grass*, are all attributable to defects in the patriarch which alienate a woman who is not herself concerned to contest the terms of patriarchy. *Guess Who's Coming to Dinner* and *On Golden Pond*, which is, in effect, the tenth Hepburn/Tracy movie, take the use of Hepburn typical of this pattern to hitherto unprecedented extremes. In both films, her devotion to her husband is complete, and far from being permitted a rebellion against views and allegiances with which she disagrees she is required to 'understand' him, and to adjure third parties to 'understand' him too. Significantly, *Guess Who's Coming to Dinner* displaces the major political confrontation between Matt and Christina Drayton on to Christina's dismissal of her racist secretary (Virginia Christine), and the completeness with which the feminist theme of the comedies has been submerged can be gauged from the fact that the secretary is another woman – Christina's argument with the patriarch himself, in the ice-cream parlour sequence, is very notably watered down by cute comedy signifying Matt's 'ornery' lovability. Significantly, too, both *Guess Who's Coming to Dinner* and *On Golden Pond* use

Stills. Above: the Draytons in Guess Who's Coming to Dinner. *Opposite: the Thayers and their daughter Chelsea (Jane Fonda) in* On Golden Pond.

the Hepburn character to reconcile a potentially rebellious daughter to the father – a motif given the greater weight, in the latter film, by the casting of the Fondas, and the greater unpleasantness for its implicit anti-feminism; the reconciliation has Chelsea (Jane Fonda) becoming an honorary substitute, by performing a back flip-flop, for the male child for which her father has always resentfully longed.

In these films, then, where the theme is the man's departure from democratic norms which are deemed to have a real egalitarian content in principle, and where the narrative movement follows the man's return to the norm, the Hepburn figure is strongly affirmed in that her 'liberalism' embodies, by definition, the status quo which is to be endorsed. *Guess Who's Coming to Dinner* and (to an even greater extent) *On Golden Pond* dilute the theme even further by making concessions to the man which express themselves dramatically in the marginalisation of the Hepburn character and the suppression or recuperation of her criticisms of him. The uniform badness of the movies in this group (with the obvious exception of *State of the Union*) clearly proceeds from the banality of their project and the evasion of the significant ideological conflict involved in it. The endorsement of the Hepburn character is sanitised by making her husband's conservatism transparently unacceptable *in bourgeois terms* (or, in *On Golden Pond*, by making it heart-warming).

It is not, alas, by its disturbance of the conventions of the Hepburn/Tracy melodrama that Capra's film confirms the account I have given of them. *State*

Stills: State of the Union. *Above: Mary and Grant Matthews with Jim Conover (Adolphe Menjou). Right: Mary with Sam Parrish (Howard Smith) and Kay Thorndike (Angela Lansbury).*

of the Union is, of course, a far more profitable and interesting work than *The Sea of Grass* or *Guess Who's Coming to Dinner*, but the interest is primarily of the symptomatic kind: if the film is conspicuously not in possession of its material, the lengths to which it finds itself obliged to go at least allow it to expose, with stark clarity, the confusion and desperation of liberal-imperialist opinion at the brink of the Cold War.

The proposition that if only honest men could achieve power everything would be all right, but that, of course, power can never be achieved by honest men, is familiarly an ingredient of a certain kind of concern about the un-acceptable face of capitalist politics. The honesty of Grant Matthews (Spencer Tracy) before he becomes corrupted consists in his embodiment of a political position which, as the film conceives it, is above the political. He has no *parti pris*: having given a dressing down to Labour, he proceeds to give a dressing down to Capital. Both represent sectional interests rather than the interest of the whole, and the fact that they do so is not to be explained in terms of the real constitution of society but in terms of 'corruption'. If the representatives of Capital and Labour assert opposed interests, it is not because their interests actually *are* opposed, but because they are self-serving and rapacious. The pessimism of *State of the Union* derives from its commitment to an idea of social totality which it knows can have no possible existence; for if, at one level, the conflicts which impede the creation of such a totality are imagined to be of the order which can be re-solved by a 'change of heart' and not as the embodiment of objective structural

contradictions, the film is also committed to the commonsense assumption that the ideal solution is, in the nature of things, unrealisable. The idealism which can propose Grant Matthews as a solution is doomed to disappointment, and while the film sees that, it is unable to renounce, or think beyond, the ideal.

State of the Union is able to extricate itself from this stalemate only by asserting that the integrity with which Matthews affirms and, at the eleventh hour, returns to his principles, is valuable *independently* of the principles being realisable (that is, of any effectual use). The escape clause is prepared at an early stage in a remark by Mary Matthews (Katharine Hepburn) to her husband, when he is first tempted to compromise, that it doesn't really matter whether he becomes President or not so long as he sticks to his beliefs. This proposition has the crucial advantage of allowing the film to exact a high opinion of the beliefs without substantiating them – and in the face of the overwhelming evidence that they cannot be substantiated. The effect is of a peculiarly sentimental kind of double-think, whereby our faith in the efficacy of the one just man, and in the possibility, under his auspices, of the progressive reform of capitalism, is able to survive their defeat unchastened. For while we are to take comfort, at the end, in Matthews's recovery of his honesty and his declaration that, though powerless, he will continue to make his voice heard (how? – we may be moved to inquire, in the light of the film's account of the capitalist media), it is only too clear that the field now belongs to the corrupt. The machinations of Kay Thorndyke (Angela Lansbury) and Jim Conover (Adolphe Menjou) remain undetected in the climactic Dickensian 'unmasking', and they depart to find a candidate more pliable – less honest – than Matthews has proved himself to be.

Part of the fascination of *State of the Union* lies in the way in which, in 1948, it finds itself having to conceive of the ideal social totality: the basis of Matthews's

Still: Mary and Grant Matthews in State of the Union.

programme is a world government, 'with or without the Soviet Union'. There is even a reference, astonishingly, to the existence of nuclear weapons, and it seems to be implied that the alternative to world government is some form of world catastrophe. At one point, too, Matthews mentions anti-Communism as one item on a list of 'distractions' from the internal ills of the body politic. Ah, if that were all! McCarthyism, of which the makers of a film proposing a change of heart were necessarily intensely aware (and Hepburn, as I mentioned earlier, had just been briefly black-listed), was less a distraction than the ideological counter-point to the grand theme of post-war American foreign policy, its function being to redescribe imperialism as a crusade against Communist expansion. McCarthy-ism was integral to, and a condition of the reproduction of, the state which *State of the Union* aspires to reform. The 'with or without the Soviet Union' gives us the desperation, and the hopelessness, of the film's case. A world government *with* the Soviet Union is the government of a world which, though it remains structurally unchanged, has been miraculously transmuted by the change of heart – a world in which a decision to 'do otherwise' doesn't have to address itself to material conditions. A world government without the Soviet Union is a mystical inflation of classical Republican isolationism, and posits a world of fundamental contradictions which have neither effects nor disadvantages.

It would, of course, be inappropriate to convict a classical Hollywood film for its failure to embrace socialist internationalism (without which the idea of a 'world government' is merely inconsequent), but it does seem useful to make the connection between the film's attitude to the Matthews 'cure' and its attitude to the 'little people'. *State of the Union* has in common with a socialist position the perception that neither Capital nor the labour bureaucracy represent the interests of 'the people'. It differs from a socialist position not only in its conviction that Capital and the labour bureaucracy are complementary embodiments of self-interest (in fact, labour bureaucrats serve the interests of Capital by accommo-dating working-class demands to reformism), but in its understanding of what 'the people' means. Socialist internationalism is effected by a revolution in which the working-class and its allies – the class and the groups (women, blacks, gays) whose oppression is entailed by capitalism – liberate themselves. The world government of *State of the Union* is to be effected by a good man (very much a man) for 'little people' who, while they respond enthusiastically to his good offices on their behalf, are otherwise entirely subject, in his absence or defeat, to the bad offices of his antagonists. It is not the least of the film's problems (and they will be familiar from other Capra films) that the attitude to the people which it is prepared to endorse is rather like Conover's attitude to them – though of course, Conover can't appreciate their virtues quite to the extent that Matthews can. Whatever those virtues may be, the opposition between the inability to initiate significant political action which accompanies them and the resourceful agency of the powerful leaves *State of the Union* nothing to fall back on but the moral uprightness of the hero as an end in itself.

The film's predicament is cogently expressed in one brief, and apparently peripheral, scene. Walking home after the question of his running for the Presi-dency has first been raised, Matthews pauses briefly in front of the White House, where he is accosted by an elderly man, of European origin, who, assuming Matthews to be a tourist, undertakes to explain to him what the building is and what it stands for. Matthews replies curtly that 'it needs a new coat of paint', going on to add, in response to the old man's consternation, that he knows the house is the achievement of the struggles and the finest aspirations of the ages and that the spirits of the noblest man (Shakespeare, Thomas Aquinas, Plato and Dante, as well as the predictable American figures) reside within it – 'but it still needs a new coat of paint'. That is essentially where *State of the Union* stands. The film cannot make of the democratic affirmation anything more than rhetoric, and the failure of realisation in the sequence in question – the curiously uncertain mixture of high seriousness and comedy played out before a White House in fuzzy back-projection – is only inadvertently expressive; but for this very reason the rhetoric retains the power to cast its spell over any criticism that might be offered. All Matthews has to offer, in the end, is a paint job; and the blend, if that is the word, of a stridency and lack of conviction so characteristic of the film's worst scenes (in particular the prolonged, embarrassing ineptitude of the aircraft sequence) bespeaks its failure to be taken in by the only 'answer' it can imagine.

I mentioned above that Grant Matthews is offered as 'very much a man', and it is the film's most troubling aspect that its deeply reactionary sexual politics function as a solvent of the confusions and contradictions laid bare in its attempt to engage with the other issues – the ones that are seen as being political. The opposition between Mary Matthews and Kay Thorndyke exactly parallels that between Mary and Elizabeth in *Mary of Scotland*, and given the way in which *State of the Union* asks us to value the two women, the connotations of the Angela Lansbury character's surname need not be written off as fortuitous. Thorndyke is used, quite simply, to associate 'undemocratic' politics with the transgression of bourgeois gender norms, and thus to realise the significance of the play on words embodied in the title: Matthews and his wife, united by democratic prin-ciple, emerge as the bearers of a normative Americanism. The opening scene

Stills. Above: Davie Hucko (Aldo Ray), Mike and Pat in Pat and Mike. *Opposite: Tess and Sam in* Woman of the Year.

defines the intention with an amazingly schematic explicitness. Kay's father (Lewis Stone), dying of cancer, tells her that while he once regretted the fact that she had not been born a boy, he has learned to recognise that she has 'a man's mind in a woman's body'. He can now, therefore, surrender his power to her in every confidence that she is worthy of the gift, and the nature of the transaction is underlined for us by his handing Kay his stick. The renunciation of the phallus (and to a woman!) is Thorndyke's death warrant, and no sooner has Kay left the room than he blows his brains out.

Kay's pursuit and exercise of power, and the self-serving opportunism of her attitude to Matthews, are juxtaposed with Mary's exemplary devotion to husband and to hearth – a devotion so unswerving that she is even able, at the last minute, and in the teeth of her own convictions, to go through with the endorsement of Matthews's probity required for the television spectacular which is to sell him, as happy family man, to the American public. As in *Mary of Scotland*, the affirmation, through Hepburn, of the natural destiny of Woman is effected by making the character the bitter antagonist (here, uniquely in Hepburn's work, the sexual rival) of another woman who has sacrificed her womanhood to power, and both works move towards a confrontation between the two in which Hepburn voices the films' judgement on the other's aberration.

At some pre-conscious level, *State of the Union* is perturbed by its own anti-feminism, and the anxiety expresses itself in the kind of uncertain and unfocused comedy which seeks to soften the harsh outlines of a dubious sentiment to which the work is more or less committed by projecting either an extreme form of it or a *reductio ad absurdum* of the counter-argument on to characters who are signified as unpleasant or as 'comic relief', for the spectator's complacent rejection. Thus Mary is allowed to respond ironically to Conover's description of her as 'the loveliest plank in [her] husband's platform' ('That's a hell of a thing to say to a woman!'), and the businessman who invariably greets Mary with the observation that she looks 'good enough to eat' is presented as a crass buffoon. Most fascinating of all is the extraordinary (and, in narrative terms, gratuitous) little scene in which a comic Italian barber expounds for Matthews his wife's thesis that the world's troubles are attributable to the fact that it is men who hold the power, and that a woman ought to become President. If Conover's compliment makes sexism odious in the villain's mouth, feminism becomes funny in the hen-pecked dago husband's; and as though the daunting example of Kay Thorndyke were not enough to make it clear what female power would be, Mary is on hand to clinch our sense of the barber's wife's absurdity by remarking that a woman could never become President because 'she would have to admit she was over 35'. On the lips of Katharine Hepburn, the knowing joke is more peculiarly distasteful than it might otherwise have been.

The best of the Hepburn/Tracy comedies is *Desk Set* – it is to be preferred, I think, to *Adam's Rib;* if it lacks a Cukor, it is also exempt from the Kanins. Like *Pat and Mike,* and unlike *Woman of the Year* (which can only register its horror), *Desk Set* affirms the prodigiousness of its heroine; but whereas Pat's accomplishments are ideologically unproblematic (in that they are exercised, innocuously, in the field of professional sport, and connoted as 'exceptional' in a way which is reinforced by the knowing emphasis on Hepburn's own sporting prowess), the prodigiousness of Bunny Watson (Hepburn) in *Desk Set* derives its dramatic

Stills. Above: the research department in Desk Set – *Ruthie (Sue Randall), Bunny (Hepburn), Peg (Joan Blondell), Sylvia (Dina Merrill). Opposite: Adam and Amanda in* Adam's Rib.

value from the central theme of the conflict of capital and labour. She is the head of a television network reference library whose entire staff is about to be sacked so that the library's functions can be taken over by a computer designed by Richard Sumner (Tracy), and the action turns on the confrontation of the female workers with the male agent of capitalist 'rationalisation'. The clarity of the opposition is mitigated by the film's ulterior commitment to a notion of the 'dehumanising' nature of technology, whereby the women workers are continually redefined as 'people' and Sumner criticised for his defective human sympathies. Nevertheless, the real conflicts retain some force, and *Desk Set* remains unique among the comedies (as well as being the funniest) for its emphasis on the spiritual education of male conservatism.

In the comedies, of course, the couple is threatened not by the man's excessive conservatism but by the woman's excessive liberalism. The issue here is no longer the abuse by Tracy of democratic principles whose normative value is taken as given, but Hepburn's assertion that democratic principle is profoundly inequitable, and must be extended or reconceptualised altogether. Each partner's excess is shown as undesirable, in that the logic of each places the bourgeois state and bourgeois sexuality in jeopardy. The man's excess points to the oppression of the woman and to fascism (*Keeper of the Flame*) or an unacceptably

venal and inhumane capitalism (*The Sea of Grass*), the woman's to castration
and the breakdown of 'the rule of law' (*Adam's Rib*). The pun in the title of *State
of the Union* enacts in itself the meaning of Hepburn and Tracy: the ideal democratic couple, like the ideal democratic state, guarantees equality through the
evolution of a system of checks and balances which enjoins antagonists, through
debate and mutual accommodation, to arrive at a modus vivendi acceptable to
all. The creation of just such a couple at the end of the films underwrites the
viability of the larger order of which the couple is a part: the democratic reconciliation of a conflict between persons enacts in microcosm the resolution of the
objective, impersonal struggles to which that conflict refers. At the end of *Woman
of the Year*, Sam (Tracy) tells Tess (Hepburn), 'I don't want to be married to
Tess Harding anymore than I want to be married to Mrs Sam Craig. Why can't

you be Mrs Tess Harding Craig?' There, with an almost jarringly explicit in-genuousness, is the project of the Hepburn/Tracy comedy in a phrase.

If the comedies *are* comedies, it is because they wish to suggest that all that is valid in the Hepburn character's demands can be answered by the bourgeois status quo, while also making the logic of her actions appear absurd and un-reasonable: she goes too far, but she *does* have a point. Adam's 'I'm old-fashioned! I like *two* sexes!' expresses the film's ultimate allegiance to a problematic of castration (Mike is given a virtually identical line in the parallel scene in *Pat and Mike*): the comedies assume, in other words, that gender differences have a natural basis in biology. This is the essential law that Amanda has broken (though it is crucial to the film's project that her violation of it should be assimilated to an imputed hostility to any socially acceptable criminal law). Rendered as melodrama, Amanda's 'lawlessness' would automatically define itself as 'mon-strousness'. Melodrama provides no means of detaching a character's actions and behaviour from their tendency, so as to espouse selected aspects of the one and reject the other: indeed, the very principle of the construction of character in melodrama is incompatible with such an operation and obviates the need for it. An ideologically unacceptable character in melodrama can become acceptable only on the basis of 'the change of heart' – that is, an *absolute* shift from one position to another – and in some cases, including that of a female character defined as 'castrating', the absolute unacceptability of the transgression makes such a shift impossible.

Comedy here is the function of an intention to suggest that ground is being conceded to Hepburn *as she is*. Amanda is required, not to 'change her heart', but to recognise she was wrong to assume that her aspirations entailed the actions she performed. Her behaviour was less monstrous than irrational. Its apparent logic was, in fact, illogical, in the double sense that it had what we are to see as necessary (i.e. logical) consequences which she did not plan for or desire, and that its essential aim (i.e. the aim the film is prepared to endorse) could have been achieved by other more rational means. The comic mode is perfectly suited to the demonstration that behaviour which obeys a logic that is ideologically prob-lematic is based in faulty reasoning. In comedy, the behaviour is at once obviously logical and at the same time obviously unplanned-for and out of control. Comedy does not necessarily require the melodramatic 'change of heart' because, like tragedy, it can accommodate *recognition*: the collision between a deviant logic and the logic of the world has its upshot in a chastened perception of error which is authenticated by the evidence – the comedy – of their incompatibility.

In these terms, *Adam's Rib is* the polar opposite of *Bringing Up Baby*. Hawks's film affiliates to Susan's deviant logic and the anarchy precipitated by it, and ends with the hero's admission that he has never had a better time in his life. Here, the act of recognition involves not the rejection of deviance but its appre-hension as the new norm, and at once provokes the final collapse of the existing (bourgeois/patriarchal) order. *Adam's Rib* ends, conversely, with Adam's demon-stration to Amanda that 'no matter what you *think* you think, you really think the same as I do.' She isn't, the film seems at first to say, entirely wrong: the law *does* discriminate against women. In proving her point, she goes over the limit and breaks the basic natural law of gender differentiation. At one level, the film wishes to preserve a distinction between 'social' and 'natural' law, because

Still: Doris (Judy Holliday) and Amanda in Adam's Rib.

Amanda's victory in the courts is fundamental to the project: it endows her with a certain validity (without her the case would not have been won) while also establishing that women can obtain justice from bourgeois institutions. But what the film has given with one hand it immediately takes away with the other: Amanda comes, through Adam's re-enactment of the crime committed by Doris (Judy Holliday), to realise that the law is sacrosanct and that she really thinks what Adam thinks, thus allowing the film to recuperate its original concession that the law oppresses women. Doris's action and the action that Adam pretends to commit are established as the same 'kind of thing' – absolute transgressions of the 'rule of law'. The acknowledgement that the law embodies and protects the interests of specific groups and classes is suppressed, and the bourgeois legal code is tacitly assimilated to the natural law of gender identity as an inviolable absolute. By affirming Amanda's defence of Doris, and then exacting her admission that both she and Doris have 'broken the law', *Adam's Rib* contrives to have it both ways. Doris's husband *was* a louse, and Amanda's actions *did* lead to Doris's acquittal – but the women were wrong. Justice was done, but the law was broken. The film can thus appear partially to endorse a course of action with a determinate result while also securing a feeling of its illegitimacy and of the obvious unacceptability of its implications.

If the perilous instability of the project of the Hepburn/Tracy comedies can be deduced from the incoherence of *Adam's Rib,* it emerges even more blatantly in *Woman of the Year.* The extraordinary virulence and unpleasantness of George

Stills: Sam and Tess in Woman of the Year, *with Phil Whittaker (Roscoe Karns, above, bottom right) and Pinkie Peters (William Bendix, opposite).*

Stevens's film (which is very much the product of the same sensibility that informs *Alice Adams*) can be referred, in a sense, to its more rigorous consistency and its blithe indifference to the liberal proprieties. We are not left in the slightest doubt that 'the woman of the year isn't a woman at all', and it is clearly significant that the predominance of the impulse to punish and humiliate the Hepburn character tilts the film more sharply than any other of the comedies in the direction of melodrama. The affirmation of the 'democratic' couple absolutely necessitates the suppression of the family: the presence of children would in itself, by assigning to Hepburn the role of bourgeois mother, militate against the need to seem to honour her demand for autonomy. *Woman of the Year* ends, in the cycle's traditional manner, by proposing the concept of 'Mrs Tess Harding Craig', but it is distinguished from the other comedies by the blatant perfunctoriness of its gestures towards Tess's independence – a perfunctoriness determined by the connection it sets up between her commitment to her autonomy as a woman and her refusal of motherhood. The films' central scenes are entirely dedicated to demonstrating Tess's inadequacy as the mother of the orphan that she and Sam adopt, and their presence reasserts the normative relation between the couple and reproduction which the later comedies carefully suppress. Tess's resistance to patriarchal marriage and her rejection of the family are seen to be continuous with each other ('both of my men walked out on me'), and, as the corollary of their interrelatedness is the elevation of maternity to the status of the ideal female role, the film is unable to give Tess's position any positive meaning at all. Thus the process by which Tess is brought finally to acquiesce in marriage is endowed with all the characteristics of melodramatic 'punishment and change-of-heart': 'I'm tired of winning prizes – they're cold comfort. This time I want to be the prize myself.'

At one point in *Woman of the Year*, Sam, concerned to introduce Tess to his world, his interests and his friends, takes her to visit his favourite bar. They begin to talk, and in the course of a long evening Tess becomes very drunk. Launching into an account of her childhood, she describes herself as a 'girl without a country', and refers to a nomadic existence accompanying her father, an eminent diplomat, from one foreign posting to another. She was 'educated all over the world', and mentions having 'read *Huck Finn* going down the Yangtze.'

While readers of the most coruscating account of America ever written by an American may wish to ponder the ingenuousness of an attempt to enlist Mark Twain's novel in the particular cause of *Woman of the Year*, no irony beyond the obvious one is intended. We are not to think of the Huck Finn who, like Tess, finds domesticity oppressive, who would rather 'light out for the territory' than be 'sivilised' and who, confronted by the dictates of the law, bourgeois and divine, prefers to 'go to hell'. Nor are we to adduce a parallel between Tess on the Yangtze and Huck on the Mississippi. The function of *Huckleberry Finn* here is to be the exemplary *national* classic – a signifier of 'Americanicity', and of Tess's estrangement from it. She has, of course, read the book (that she has read everything is not the least of the points against her), but in an incongruous setting. She 'grew up by remote control', without a settled family life or a secure national identity, and now, while she is an expert linguist ('Women should be kept illiterate and clean, like canaries') and an authority on the history and culture of other nations ('Who can figure a dame who knew what was going on in Libya in 1803?'), she 'really [doesn't] know anything about American sport'.

The derogatory references to Libya and canaries are assigned not to Sam but to a minor character, albeit one of Sam's friends and colleagues, played by Roscoe Karns – an actor with an established persona of mean-minded, opportunistic cynicism. Far from serving to 'place' the sentiment, this strategy allows the film to affiliate to it while also distancing itself from the sentiment's proper logic, by which *Woman of the Year* is understandably embarrassed: the appeal for a smart laugh in response to the smart lines succinctly registers the ambivalence.

Because the Hepburn character's imputed violation of American 'democratic' principle in the comedies, unlike Tracy's in the melodramas, calls the content

of the principle into question, it is correspondingly more difficult to include her within an ideologically viable consensus. An acceptable balance must be found between what *Woman of the Year* understands by Huck Finn and what it understands by the Yangtze, though *Woman of the Year* itself is unable to come up with it; the odour of the foreign river is too powerful. We should not expect much more from the Hepburn/Tracy films than the evidence of the sleight-of-hand by which this balance is achieved, and it will have been apparent that I value the cycle as a whole less highly than Hepburn's two fully representative films with Cary Grant, *Holiday* and *Bringing Up Baby*.

The pleasures of the more publicised partnership are, by contrast, at once less challenging and more uneven. The generally received view that 'Kate and Spence were always at their best together' (Puttick) is highly questionable: it seems to me that, *State of the Union* and *Desk Set* apart, Hepburn and Tracy's co-starring performances consistently fail to attain the level of their best work on their own. The performances are, of course, technically remarkable, but too many of them are vitiated by the knowingness which becomes so intolerably cloying in *Pat and Mike*: the spontaneity too often seems too self-consciously and calculatedly winning, too much a matter of a flattering conspiracy of familiarity between the actors and the prospective audience. This want of freshness goes with the clubby atmosphere which seems to have prevailed on the set of the two films written by the Kanins and with the ideological ritual performed by the films themselves: the tacit reference to the actors on which the project depends so closely seems frequently to express itself in the tone and character of the acting. One notes with interest, in Cukor's interview with Gavin Lambert, that Tracy seems to have become aware of this:

'We were going to do another picture. Garson [Kanin] had a brilliant idea and wrote the opening of it. You were on a European train and you saw a lady in black sitting in one corner of a compartment, all alone. The camera moved very slowly up close to this lady – and it was Spence dressed as a widow. Then you discovered he was the head of a currency-smuggling gang based in Zurich. Spence was going to appear throughout the picture in different disguises. People in the State Department knew this chicanery was going on, and they got the best T-man from the Treasury – and it was Kate. She had this ruthless drive and purpose, and she was going to track him down and bring him to justice, like whoever-it-is pursues Valjean in *Les Misérables*. Then halfway through the picture she realises she's stuck on him . . . Maybe Spencer felt they were getting too old to do this kind of film. He felt "a joke's a joke", and maybe he was right. Life changes. There's nothing worse than doing a certain kind of thing very charmingly and then running it into the ground' (*On Cukor*, p.217).

This confirms one's sense of the spirit behind *Pat and Mike* ('a joke's a joke'), in which one may feel that the 'charm' is already unappetising, and one can only endorse Tracy's sense of the inadvisability of further collaborations with the Kanins. Cukor's outline of the projected third film classically expresses the dilution of the Hepburn/Tracy thematic into a cute star-turn.

It is hardly an accident that in the cycle's two best films, where the values embodied in the star personae are organised into a genuine dialectic, and where the self-conscious invocation of the actors themselves is least in evidence, the acting is correspondingly depersonalised and more genuinely inventive. The roof-top question-and-answer session in *Desk Set* is comic acting of a quite staggeringly high order.

On re-viewing *Desk Set*. I continue to regard it far more highly than any other in the Hepburn/Tracy cycle, though the resolution of its themes is far more conservative than I have implied above. We are to believe, at the end, that the computer which Sumner (Spencer Tracy) had installed was never intended to do workers out of their jobs at all. Capitalist rationalisation and full employment turn out to be by no means incompatible, and it transpires, in a winning and duplicitous irony, that the redundancy notices which all the workers have received were issued in error because of a computer malfunction. The computer needs people, and people are freed by the computer – and all without the necessity of a change in the mode of production! In the final scene, the reconciliation of management and labour is assimilated to, and guaranteed by, the formation of the democratic couple, and we are assured of the creative reciprocity of technology and 'the human touch' by the role played by the computer in Sumner's proposal of marriage.

But such things are, after all, not very surprising, and the film's themes are sufficiently in it, and dramatised with enough complexity, inventiveness and wit, to support the judgement that the conventional preference for the Kanin/Cukor films is unacceptable. One notes, in particular, the emphasis throughout on the comradeship and solidarity of the female group – a theme which virtually disappears from Hepburn's work after *Holiday* (the formation of the partnership with Tracy is clearly relevant here) and which links *Desk Set* to her most challenging and profitable period. Consider, for instance, the function of the three Victorian ballads ('Hiawatha', 'The Night Before Christmas' and 'The Curfew

Still: Richard Sumner (Tracy), the research department and the computer in Desk Set.

Still: Mike Cutler (Gig Young), Bunny and Richard in Desk Set.

Shall Not Ring Tonight') from which Bunny Watson (Hepburn) recites extracts in the course of the film. They provide much more than a *tour de force* for the actress, though they do that, and it is, indeed, the wonderful skill with which Hepburn executes them (in what is, in general, one of her finest performances) that realises their thematic significance. Each is associated with an affirmation of the energies of the female group, at the three crucial moments of its first appearance, the threat of its dissolution through Sumner's intrusion, and its final triumphant resurgence. In each case, the value of Bunny's prodigiousness is not simply substantiated, but shown in its essential relationship to the group, and the pleasures which Hepburn provides here create our commitment to what the group represents. While the film's resolution of the conflict of labour and management is undoubtedly reactionary, it is absolutely crucial to our sense of the superiority of *Desk Set* to the other Hepburn/Tracy comedies that any ending which attempted to establish the heterosexual relationship or harmonious industrial relations at the expense of the female group would be repudiated by the spectator. The group's presence endows the critique of male presumptions enacted in the quiz sequence and the treatment of Bunny's exploitation by Mike Cutler (Gig Young) with a content and a force entirely absent from *Adam's Rib*, in which, for all the academic deference to women's rights, friendships between women have no place at all. *Undercurrent* apart (one values the great performance of *Long Day's Journey into Night* somewhat differently), *Desk Set* is Hepburn's most rewarding film after the 'thirties.

8. The Old Maid

'This, however, was in the future; what Basil Ransom actually perceived was that Miss Chancellor was a signal old maid. That was her quality, her destiny; nothing could be more distinctly written. There are women who are unmarried by accident, and others who are unmarried by option; but Olive Chancellor was unmarried by every implication of her being. She was a spinster as Shelley was a lyric poet, or as the month of August is sultry. She was so essentially a celibate that Ransom found himself thinking of her as old, though when he came to look at her (as he said to himself) it was apparent that her years were fewer than his own. He did not dislike her, she had been so friendly; but, little by little, she gave him an uneasy feeling – the sense that you could never be safe with a person who took things so hard' – Henry James, *The Bostonians*.

In a society in which women as a group are defined predominantly in relation to men, there are numerous mechanisms whereby the woman who, as an individual, is *not* can be resecured, despite herself, for the appropriate generic category. 'Spinster' and 'old maid' are terms which designate an unmarried woman in such a way as to refer her to a man to whom she does not relate. The central fact about the spinster is the absence of men, an absence which both defines her objective status and implies a lurid image of its subjective consequences: the emotional life of the spinster consists exclusively in a perpetual seething torment of ungratified heterosexual desire. A woman's essence being realised in her union with a man ('maids' should be young), the spinster's other achievements, actions and aspirations are as nothing beside her unwilling betrayal of her nature. They are, indeed, in accordance with the vulgar understanding of sublimation, lamentably inadequate substitutes for the 'real' fulfilment she cannot achieve.

An unnatural type may be found pathetic, funny or threatening. As a figure of pathos, the spinster evokes a more or less ironic or forbearing compassion: she is a poor, wretched woman who hasn't had a proper life, and who therefore has a rightful claim on the understanding and indulgence of those who have (this attitude is extensively dramatised, and placed, in *The Old Maid*). At the opposite extreme, the spinster may be felt to have been depraved or unbalanced by the frustration of her needs, and is perceived correspondingly as psychotic (Sister Ruth in *Black Narcissus*, Michael Powell, 1947) or demented (Miss Havisham in Dickens's *Great Expectations*). The spinster as a comic figure occupies a middle ground between these two poles. In the case, for instance, of Margaret Rutherford's incarnation of Miss Marple, the tone of the comedy is positive: Miss Marple's spinsterhood, and her proprietary attitude towards and intellectual superiority to her 'Dr Watson' (Stringer Davis), are components in her endearing, asexual, British eccentricity. On the other hand, the knowing ridicule heaped on Lucy Shmeeler (Alice Pearce) in *On the Town* (Stanley Donen and Gene Kelly, 1949) is pre-eminently the comedy of misogynistic anxiety, all the more distasteful for the relentless high spirits with which the film makes its sentimental

Still: Cynthia Darrington (Hepburn) with Harry Rawlinson (Ralph Forbes) and Monica Strong (Helen Chandler) in Christopher Strong.

commitment to the 'normalcy' of its central couple.

It is particularly important, for the present purpose, to take note of the fact that the description of an unmarried woman as a spinster may be employed *strategically* as a means of denigrating and devaluing an active decision to reject heterosexual marriage in favour of some form of autonomous self-realisation. The basis for such a strategy in the nature of women's experience under patriarchy is clear enough: it is discussed, in relation to the work of a number of nineteenth-century female writers, by Sandra Gilbert and Susan Gubar in their brilliant book, *The Madwoman in the Attic.*

'Also like Jane Eyre, Lucy (in *Villette*) represents all women who must struggle towards an integrated, mature, and independent identity by coming to terms with their need for love, and their dread of being single, and so, like Jane, Lucy will confront the necessity of breaking through the debilitating roles available to the single women the Victorians termed "redundant"' (*The Madwoman in the Attic*, Yale University Press, 1979, pp.406-407).

The crucial significance of solidarity – of collective organisation and collective consciousness – for oppressed social groups consists in the fact that any radical deviation from a norm is deprived, by definition, not simply of social support but of the self-confidence generated by it. The 'struggle towards an integrated, mature, and independent identity' in a deviant role – and here the experience of women and of gays have much in common – must contend with more than the material obstacles of legal and professional discrimination. Bourgeois heterosexual relations are so organised that, for heterosexual women, love and independent, creative self-realisation are structured as mutually exclusive alternatives. This is the subject of *Christopher Strong,* which concerns itself with the nature of the social terms which impose renunciation on the female protagonist: there is no position in which Cynthia (Hepburn) can realise needs and desires which, though felt with equal intensity, have been rendered culturally incompatible. She has to choose, and the choice, whatever it is, involves loss and damage. Arzner's film also raises an intimately related issue – the anxiety generated by breaking as an isolated individual with a social norm the viability of which has been consciously rejected but which is everywhere reproduced as natural and inevitable. Compare, for example, the scene in which Cynthia wonders whether she has been foolish to chose 'a lonely life' with that in which, viciously and unfeelingly berated by Monica (Helen Chandler) with having 'missed everything' of value in life by never having had a relationship with a man, Cynthia replies that 'I'll have missed the kind of torture *you're* going through now.' The two positions are, of course, contradictory, but the contradiction is obviously inscribed in a situation in which loneliness is the corollary of Cynthia's choice (heterosexual involvement entails loss of independence), and which makes that choice, however prestigious, appear unnatural. Cynthia can thus appear as a feminist model to other women ('You gave us courage for everything') even as her isolation undermines her personal confidence in the decisions and actions which have created the model.

Consider Sylvia Plath's poem 'Spinster', from her first published volume, *The Colossus* (Faber & Faber, 1977, p.68). The protagonist, walking in the country 'with her latest suitor', recoils in puritanical, fastidious distaste from the irregularity and disorder introduced by her lover, whose 'gestures unbalance the air' and make

> Her gait stray uneven
> Through a rank wilderness of fern and flower.
>
> How she longed for winter then!—
> Scrupulously austere in its order
> Of white and black
> Ice and rock, each sentiment within border,
> And heart's frosty discipline
> Exact as a snowflake.
>
> . . . She withdrew neatly . . .
>
> And round her house she set
> Such a barricade of barb and check
> Against mutinous weather
> As no mere insurgent man could hope to break
> With curse, fist, threat
> Or love, either.

At first glance, the poem seems merely a locus classicus of self-oppression that inertly reiterates a banal cultural truism: the spinster, frigid and sterile, withdraws appalled from the anarchic abundance of natural fertility and the vital creative energies of the male. Indeed, it could fairly be said – which is part of the point – that that is the dominant meaning of the piece, for what is at issue in Plath's poem is the way in which the protagonist's commitment to an integrity of identity is imagined through the ideological concept of the spinster. The key terms are the word 'discipline' and the phrase which immediately qualifies it – 'exact as a snowflake'. Considered in abstraction from the context created by the writing, the nature imagery – the conventional opposition between winter and spring – gives the 'discipline' a negative connotation – ice, rock, frost, snow imply sterility, the seasonal death of natural creativity. Conversely, the inert conventional meaning is challenged by 'rank wilderness' – the hectic plentitude of the April morning is itself barren, even an image of decay ('rank'). The critical disturbance of the Romantic metaphor of the seasons provides the basis for the positive definition of 'discipline' to which the poem proceeds: the discrepancy between 'rank wilderness' and the traditional meaning of spring makes it impossible to read the April morning, and the lover associated with it, as black marks against the woman. Plath employs the nature metaphor so as to make 'winter' mean a self-defined femininity achieved through the most exacting self-regulation – the 'discipline' is self-creation as a woman – and 'spring' the destructive, uncreative male violence of the satyr. The automatic understanding of winter as a threat to spring (now less convention than cliché) is invoked and then at once inverted.

The significance is clinched by the use of language itself. The first image of spring which the poem gives us is that of 'the birds' irregular babel', by which the protagonist is 'intolerably struck': spring is at once the confusion of tongues and an experience of violent assault. In the final lines, Plath reasserts the connection between the physical threat of 'insurgent man' and an aggressive incoherence of language ('curse, fist, threat'): the poem's structure makes of the voice of the birds, the harbingers of spring, a form of masculine speech which is not only antagonistic to the woman ('By this tumult afflicted') but alien and meaningless for her ('bedlam spring'). On the other hand, the qualities of winter – the scrupulous austerity, the discipline, the exactitude – are also the linguistic qualities of the poem, the work created by the woman writer: 'heart's frosty discipline' is dramatised in the poised, ironic urbanity and lucidity of the verse movement. The very form of the poem enacts the criticism of the barrenness of winter implicit in the imagery.

The ambivalence, and poignancy, of 'Spinster' consists in the fact that, while it contests the ideologies embedded in the word it takes as title, it is also captured by them. The nature of the ambivalence is betrayed in the final line – 'Or love, either' – the only moment in the poem where the male lover acquires, unambiguously, a potential positive meaning. While the protagonist's very identity is threatened by everything he represents, he is also the prospective source of 'love', and this conflict of thought and feeling is inscribed in the writing: Plath both inhibits and questions the positive significance of the male nature-god and, unmistakably, makes the woman's resistance the object of irony.

> But here – a burgeoning
> Unruly enough to pitch her five queenly wits
> Into vulgar motley —
> A treason not to be borne.

The value of the 'burgeoning' is rejected, but the poem is quite unable to sustain a commitment to the sensibility which makes the rejection (though it comes very close): the attempt to formulate a positive meaning for an oppressive social image is doomed to failure by the very feelings which the image calls into being.

'Spinster' allows me precisely to focus the arguments I wish to put forward about Hepburn's 'old maid' films, which work assiduously on the anxieties which disturb the coherence of this poem by a distinguished woman writer. Norms have a material as well as an ideological form: they exist not only as ideologies but as institutions. Thus the transgression of norms is not simply unsanctioned; aberrant desire also lacks a given medium through which to realise itself. The logical development of Plath's poem is stalemated because, while the male-dominated couple is inimical to the woman's 'discipline', it is also experienced as the condition for the satisfaction of sexual desire, and the protagonist is left to choose between surrender and self-abnegation. The starkness of the alternative cannot be written off to Plath's ideological innocence: norms impede the imagination of alternatives for the very good reason that the society which deposits the norms places objective obstacles in the path of a successful realisation of the alternatives. 'The couple' functions as an imaginative blockage in 'Spinster', because the institution which might permit the imaginative reconciliation of the need for autonomy and the need for love hasn't even a possible existence for the writer, who, in its absence, finds herself in a position where both needs are imperative and both alienating. The poem's irony is of that curious kind which seeks to place a situation at the distance necessary for scrutiny while lacking the secure position which such an activity implies, and which ends by confirming the situation's intractability. Hepburn's 'spinster' films are very exactly attuned to the cultural situation which nourishes the incoherence of Plath's poem, and of its relation to the Hepburn persona.

It will have become apparent that the various phases of a star's career are im-plicit in the others. Each phase can be regarded as a specific attempt to solve the problems produced by the ideological material organised in the persona, and given that the range of possible permutations is determinate, we might expect that any particular one will be accompanied by the shadow, more or less pronounced, of its counterparts. The extreme difficulty of getting Hepburn's characters married is apparent from the very beginning of her career. Initially the difficulty is at least partly contained as a function of Hepburn's erotic status as the 'son-daughter', whose sexuality, at once frailly virginal and robustly as-sertive, is channelled towards the father. But quite apart from the fact that this function is contingent on Hepburn's 'youthfulness', it is also, as we have seen, perilously unstable.

The potential spinsterhood of Hepburn's characters is determined by two factors – the contradiction between marriage and autonomy on the one hand, and between marriage and a commitment to women on the other. Characteristic-ally, in Hepburn's most radical 'thirties films, the two difficulties are continuous with each other, and can be resolved only by subordinating the dramatic logic generated by a specific work to the logic entailed in its conventions. Only *Holiday* and *Bringing Up Baby* attempt to define a heterosexual relationship which is actually in line with the tendency of the persona rather than a check on it. Of

Stills. Above: Linda with Susan (Jean Dixon) and Nick Potter (Edward Everett Horton) in Holiday. *Opposite: Alan (Robert Taylor), Lucy, Ann and her father (Edmund Gwenn) in* Undercurrent.

the two, Cukor's film is the more devious and problematic. *Bringing Up Baby* alone, taking full advantage of the anarchistic licence and excess of farce, can celebrate the overthrow of gender differentiation, yet the very extremes of Hawks's film, which takes the Hepburn persona to its limit, demonstrate all the more clearly the nature of the problems confronted by Hepburn's other films.

The Hepburn spinster cycle consists of four of her seven 'fifties films – *The African Queen, Summertime* (alias *Summer Madness*), *The Rainmaker* and *The Iron Petticoat*. Both of Hepburn's 'fifties movies with Spencer Tracy – *Pat and Mike* and *Desk Set* – are permeated by motifs which derive from this cycle – a fact which lends additional force to the proposition advanced in the previous chapter that the ideological equilibrium effected by the Hepburn/Tracy partnership is a very vulnerable one. The cycle's characteristic thematic is anticipated, in all essential details, in *Undercurrent*, but since Minnelli's remarkable melodrama is a critique of the ideologies affirmed by its successors, the significance acquired by the thematic is profoundly different. *Undercurrent*, as a 'Freudian-feminist' melodrama – the term employed by Thomas Elsaesser to designate the major cycle of 'forties movies, inaugurated by *Rebecca*, about the insidious domestic persecution of a married woman – has in common with later Hepburn 'spinster' films a vulnerable, sexually inexperienced female protagonist and the equivocal, charismatic trickster who seduces her. But the melodramatic sub-genre to which *Undercurrent* primarily pertains has for its themes the oppressive power relations of bourgeois marriage, and the psychological organisation corresponding to them: the premise of the films is that marriage, as a social form, creates the condition for, and legitimises, the woman's oppression by making it socially invisible, and that the psychological violence of which she becomes the sanctioned victim is necessarily produced by the Oedipal construction of sexuality. Minnelli's exploration of the determination of adult heterosexual relations by the residues of the Oedipus complex, and of the way in which these same residues, sublimated as romantic dream, offer the illusion of liberation from the hideous real liaisons built on the same basis, has not the least affinity, dramatically or ideologically, with *Summertime* or *The Rainmaker*, which appropriate selected elements of the narrative of *Undercurrent* for an exactly contrary end.

The structural features of the cycle can be quickly defined though not all of them are fully developed by all the films:

1) Hepburn plays a repressed, middle-aged, unmarried woman. In three of the films, the Hepburn character is living, as a domestic assistant, with male relatives – father in *Undercurrent*, brother in *The African Queen*, father and brothers in *The Rainmaker*. In *Summertime* and *The Iron Petticoat* she plays an established professional, without domestic attachments, who is exposed through travel to the disruptive influences of an alien culture.

2) In *Undercurrent* and *The Rainmaker*, the Hepburn character is under intense pressure from her family to marry – pressure which she resists. Again, in both

films, and in *Pat and Mike,* she is provided with a persistent suitor who is defined generically as an 'average guy', and whose attentions she does not encourage.

3) Conversely, where there is no pressure and no suitor (*Summertime*), or where it is the Hepburn character's attentions which are not reciprocated (*Desk Set*), she is shown to be desperate for the lack of them.

4) There is an obligatory scene in which the Hepburn character remarks on her own unattractiveness and undesirability, provoking either another character's ambiguous disclaimer (*Summertime*), the suggestion that she is only unattractive because she 'won't do anything about herself' (*Undercurrent*), or the assertion that men don't necessarily demand glamour (*The Rainmaker*). All these replies effect minimal variations on a common project, the point being that a) the character *thinks* herself to be unattractive, b) we are to understand that she really is so, and c) the important thing from a woman's point of view, whether she is attractive or not, is the way in which she is perceived by men.

5) The Hepburn character falls in love with a charismatic confidence-trickster, whom she must learn to trust unconditionally in the teeth of the available evidence. In the process, she discovers that her initial scepticism is a reflection not on his duplicity but on the lack of self-confidence which leads her perversely to shun the thing she most desires. In *The Rainmaker,* the trickster is explicitly a fertility god, bringing rain to barren, parched mid-western soil; *Summertime*

Stills. Below: Ann and Alan in Undercurrent. *Opposite: Starbuck and Lizzie in* The Rainmaker.

inflects the same idea in gastronomic terms ('You are like a hungry child . . . *eat the ravioli!*'). This motif, clearly, is a sentimental, reactionary inversion of *Washington Square*, it being crucial both that the woman should commit herself to the man before he is proved to be trustworthy and that it should eventually transpire that he deserves her trust. The narrative, in other words, affirms the life-giving properties of the male while exacting from the woman an exercise of faith which, because it lacks guarantees, places the maximum emphasis on the extremity of her need.

The Tracy characters in *Pat and Mike* and *Desk Set* have points in common with the trickster, though the predominance in these films of the specific conventions of the Hepburn/Tracy movie produce a strikingly different development.

6) If, in *Summertime* and *The Rainmaker*, the woman's reward for her faith is the discovery that she is desired, her punishment is that her supreme experience cannot be sustained. It is, again, a case of having one's cake and eating it: the fact that the woman is left with only the memory of the most significant moment of her life inflates the value of the man, and binds the woman permanently to him in spirit, while condemning her to remain unsatisfied. She must discover what she has missed in order to know what she has lost. The transience of the affair relegates the life which precedes and follows it to the realm of the in-authentic: her past is an absence of the man, and her future a memory of him.

The Iron Petticoat, the most crass and reactionary of the 'fifties remakes of *Ninotchka* – significantly, it postdates both *Summertime* and *The Rainmaker* –

Still: Vinka (Hepburn) and Chuck Lockwood (Bob Hope) in The Iron Petticoat.

refuses the romantic reconciliation which *Jet Pilot* (Josef von Sternberg, 1957) and *Silk Stockings* (Rouben Mamoulian, 1957) have in common with the Lubitsch original so as to accommodate the ending to the Hepburn pattern, and in so doing illustrates something of the wider cultural basis of the 'spinster' cycle as a whole. But for the fact that Jane Hudson (Hepburn) is not a Communist, *Summertime* is already *The Iron Petticoat:* the project it enacts simply by virtue of casting Hepburn – 'the feminist of her early films has become a spinster eager for love', in that felicitous phrase of Romano Tozzi's which I quoted earlier – expresses exactly in relation to women what the *Ninotchka* theme expresses in relation to Soviet 'Communism'. Just as feminists are really love-starved old maids, so Russian commissars are really desperate for the joys of capitalism, and, once ingrained resistance has been broken down, each type succumbs with a passion all the more violent for the years of deprivation.

The description of ideologically threatening figures as repressed is, of course, understandably, a common ideological stratagem. Its function is to defuse, discredit and familiarise the threat by dissociating the aberrant type from an oppositional *ideology* and attributing the aberration to defective desire. It follows at once that the most efficient means of authenticating this stratagem dramatically is to submit whatever type is in question to a return of the repressed, such that the systems of value and belief which are to be recuperated appear as psychological defence mechanisms, designed to contain, but in fact powerless to withstand, the drives within – drives which appear correspondingly as the 'nature' which repression has denied. The interest of *The Iron Petticoat*, as a peculiarly 'fifties document, lies in its assimilation of the project of Hepburn's spinster films to McCarthyism. The very title of Ralph Thomas's film tells its own story. Behind the Iron Curtain lies an unpenetrated plenitude: the Soviet Union is the unfuckable, and the independent woman the Red menace, in the language of desire. Russians and feminists must be punished, first of all for not wanting what they ought to want, and then, since they really want it after all, punished further by being unable to have it. Above all, they must recognise their defectiveness themselves, thereby guaranteeing the tacit suggestion that anti-bourgeois ideologies are merely the false appearance of thwarted need. The nature of the intention is confirmed by the decision to cast, opposite Hepburn, Bob Hope – the most reassuring and chauvinistic (in both senses) of American comedians, whose persona is premised on the assumption, clearly correct, that the cynicism, complacency and amorality of American self-reliance can be most successfully affirmed by blurring the outlines of its more obviously deplorable traits with a little gentle satire.

7) The 'spinster' films repeatedly create sequences in which the Hepburn character is verbally or physically humiliated. This practice has its origins in two contradictory impulses. While it is essential to the project that the heroine's 'awakening through love' should be affirmed, it is notoriously the case (as works as diverse as the novels of William Faulkner and the operettas of Gilbert and Sullivan amply demonstrate) that the expression of desire by a middle-aged woman is in itself appalling. The spinster can be reviled quite as much for her yearning for, as for her renunciation of, sexuality, for her attempts, as it were, to de-repress herself as much as for her repression. The inexhaustible arsenal of degradations assembled by *Summertime* is triggered to go off whenever the heroine experiences romantic longing for the 'wonderful, mystical, magical miracle' which will, we are to believe, make a 'real woman' of her. Enchantment with the beauty of Venice is immediately answered by the discovery of a sewage out-let; lonely fantasies of acquiring a male companion evoke an urchin selling pornographic postcards; an attempt to take a photograph of the shop run by Renato (Rossano Brazzi) is inevitably the occasion for a fall into a canal.

It is the prevailing tone of undisguised animus which so strikingly marks off the Hepburn 'spinster' cycle from the Davis films of the 'forties and late 'thirties which I discussed in Chapter Six: *Now, Voyager* provides the most illuminating comparison. Casey Robinson's screenplay might seem, at first sight, to present two incompatible lines of argument – the first, to the effect that Charlotte is awakened and transformed by the intervention of men, and finds her identity and significance in roles that are contingent on them; and, contrastingly, a second to the effect that male agency is merely the catalyst for the creation of a female agent who is at last able to construct a world from which men have been ex-cluded. It is, in fact, the film's distinction to have proposed a third position. *Now, Voyager* is about the way in which Charlotte negotiates the constraints and sanctions of patriarchy (which she can't, as an individual, eradicate) so as to produce a compromise in which, rather than sacrificing all her needs to one of them (love), she is able to fulfil something of them all. The compromise isn't indeterminate, but it remains the case that Charlotte does, at the end, make her own history – though not under conditions of her own choosing *(Now, Voyager* may be read, in fact, as an exemplary enactment of the Engels maxim). It is crucial that the option of 'all for love' should be explicitly there, and that it should be refused because it doesn't suffice – crucial in that Charlotte's compromise (which is clearly endorsed by the film) entails the recognition of the potency and legitimacy of the things which Charlotte is *not* prepared to give up. We may feel that it is rather sad that she cannot marry Jerry too (or we may not), but the film certainly doesn't wish us to think that she should have done, given what she has to lose.

The contrast with Jane Hudson's renunciation of Renato at the end of *Summertime* is as extreme as it could be. Jane leaves him not because loving him is an option which, in its exclusiveness, its automatic foreclosure of other demands, is felt to be unacceptable, but merely because 'you and I would only end in nothing'. She has nothing to go back to: her life without him has been, by this time, thoroughly devalued, and she 'will always love [him]'. The act of renunciation is pure loss, and its integrity is further undermined by the implication that she is, in any case, simply pre-empting fortune: even if she stayed, the relationship would fail. The film isn't explicit about why it would, but since it certainly wouldn't be Renato's fault (we are required to accept his alibis for his evident duplicity, believe that he wishes Jane to stay and forget that he is, in fact, already married), we can only conclude that it would be hers. *Summertime* asserts not only that the heroine's life is worthless without men, but also that, through some subtle flaw of her own (the flaw involved, presumably, in having become a middle-aged spinster), a life with men is impossible anyway.

The renunciation of Starbuck (Burt Lancaster) by Lizzie (Hepburn) at the end of *The Rainmaker* makes a different but related point. Here, the heroine is not condemned to tortured celibacy but provided with another man, a 'patient Dobbin', in the form of File (Wendell Corey), whom Lizzie chooses in preference to Starbuck when the latter persists in idealising her as 'Mélisande' – the lyrical pet name with which he has endowed her in bringing her to the recognition of her own beauty. The File/Starbuck opposition is determined by one of the classical ideological polarities of the Hollywood cinema – the antinomy of settled, domesticated male and potent wanderer. As it affects a female protagonist, this opposition presents a choice between, on the one hand, subjugation and sexual deprivation as wife-and-mother and, on the other, transgression and pleasure. In many of the most distinguished explorations of this form of sexual triangle – *Blonde Venus, Shadow of a Doubt* (Alfred Hitchcock, 1943), *Madame De . . .* (Max Ophuls, 1953) – both alternatives are dramatised as being, for the woman, equally unsatisfactory in that the two men are seen to embody mutually exclusive, but objectively complementary, forms of patriarchal oppression.

The Rainmaker manages to come up with a marvellously inclusive reactionary reading of this structure. Even narratives which don't begin to doubt that the heroine finds all she desires in a charismatic male lover usually allow her the logic of her transgression (whatever reparation is finally exacted for it), or at least present her ultimate containment within the home as 'tragic'. *The*

Still: Jane (Hepburn) and Renato (Rossano Brazzi) in Summertime.

Rainmaker, having argued that Lizzie discovers herself, her sexuality and her need, through Starbuck, then requires her to opt for File – because 'Mélisande is a name for one night, but Lizzie can do me my whole life long'. Lizzie, in fact, needs both men: we are to rest assured that the local sheriff can, in the long term, satisfy the desire that only his ideological antagonist could call into being. It is rather as if *Now, Voyager* had decided to propose that Charlotte could be happy with Elliot (John Loder). *The Rainmaker* has as little to say about why Mélisande is a name for one night as *Summertime* has about the necessary transience of any relationship Jane might have with Renato: all that is necessary is that the heroine should know these things to be so. While the use to which this knowledge is put is different in the two films, they both naturalise an anti-feminist ideological stratagem by reference to the heroine's perception of 'the truth'. Both women, having been awakened to their true nature by men, 'freely' renounce them – one because she plainly sees that permanent felicity is only to be found in marriage, and the other because she plainly sees that, for the old maid, it is always already 'too late'. The two endings are, in fact, complementary. Both films punish the independent woman by redefining her as a frustrated spinster and getting her to acknowledge what she has always really wanted, but whereas *Summertime* contents itself with a negative confirmation of the role of spinster (independence is desolating and marriage unobtainable), *The Rainmaker* moves on to a positive confirmation of the role of wife, its loftier ambitions placing it, as we have seen, in the curious position of asserting that the feelings appropriate to *romance* generate the attitudes conducive to domesticity.

The contrast between Davis's 'spinster' films and Hepburn's alerts us to a major cultural shift, the most striking symptom of which is the progressive impoverishment, and then virtual disappearance, of the woman's film in the 'fifties. (*All That Heaven Allows* and *Magnificent Obsession* are there to demonstrate the recalcitrance of the language with which Sirk had to cope.) Both the astonishing efflorescence of the genre in the early 'forties and the clarification of its thematic can be related to the radical change in the composition of the domestic American audience occasioned by World War II: the particular social moment crystallised the significance of the woman's film rather as the 'seventies crystallised that of the horror movie. The Davis films are not concerned to construct a House of Correction for the spinster: rather, she becomes – like her antecedent, the governess of nineteenth-century women's fiction (*All This and Heaven Too* makes the genealogy very explicit) – the focus of an obsessive concern with the problematic and contradictory nature of the normative female role (motherhood) and the organisation of desire which it entails. The films are not to be conceived, of course, as somehow inertly 'reflecting' their conjuncture: the contemporary crisis in the social position of women is refracted through the conventions of a genre which enables a peculiarly systematic and acute engagement with what the contradictions exposed by that crisis fundamentally imply. The conventions constitute, in other words, a creative medium which allows the present to mean more: it could hardly be maintained that the issues raised, and the destination reached, by *Now, Voyager* were simply snatched out of the air. (I had better add, perhaps, though it shouldn't need saying, that I don't imagine the conventions of the woman's film – or any conventions – to be neutral or indeterminate, or that they penetrate to 'essential truth'. If they enable a complex exploratory dramatisation of a contemporary social dynamic, they do so within specifiable limits and conditions.)

The context of the Hepburn 'spinster' films, on the contrary, is the massive reinforcement of the domestic role characteristic of the American 'fifties. Of course, neither the films' strategies nor their acerbic tone are unprecedented. In *The Philadelphia Story*, Hepburn is already being castigated as a 'perennial spinster', and the men (father and ex-husband) whom she must learn to trust, forgive and love, very strikingly prefigure the trickster hero of the spinster cycle. Indeed, the famous silent opening scene of Cukor's film – Tracy, having expelled Dexter from their house and symbolically castrated him by breaking one of his golf clubs, is rewarded by a hearty punch in the face – acts out both the motivation and the tactics of the later films. But in 1940, Hepburn is still 'the golden girl' as well as the 'essential celibate'. It is the ageing of the star which, coinciding as it does with a period of ideological retrenchment, allows the project of *The Philadelphia Story* to be purged of its ambivalence. Hepburn was 43 in 1950, and Marilyn Monroe was already defining the new norm of beauty (and its corollaries); vituperation could now be indulged, disembarrassed of helpless fascination.

It is appropriate here, to add a note on *The African Queen* – the 'spinster' film that corresponds least closely to the narrative schema I have extrapolated from the group. The difference is immediately apparent in the casting. It is of great significance, in *Summertime*, that Hepburn should fall in love with a character played by Rossano Brazzi. Whereas the casting of George Brent in Bette Davis movies subserves the films' critical engagement with their conventions (Brent's nullity is the essential point), Renato as personified by Brazzi really *is*, we are to believe, the potent charmer that Jane takes him to be. In terms of the 'international theme' which H.E. Bates's script (and original story) lift from Henry James, Renato (an antique dealer) is Gilbert Osmond, imported from *The Portrait of a Lady* and endowed with a heart – and loins – of gold. The redescription of the American Princess as an old maid effects a corresponding transformation of her seducer, and the exploitative trickster-patriarchs of Hepburn's first three films (Christopher Strong is, as I have noted, particularly close to Osmond) become the rejuvenating trickster-sons of *Summertime* and *The Rainmaker*. The confidence trick which destroyed the heroine's autonomy is perceived as beneficent and redemptive, the 'faded rosebud' (Ralph Touchett's judgement on what Osmond offers Isabel Archer) becomes an oasis in the desert.

The presence in *The African Queen* of Humphrey Bogart – a star of Hepburn's generation and, like her, an 'axiom of the cinema' – signifies in itself a different project: leaving aside the significance of the Bogart persona, the star weighting is necessarily incompatible with the kind of thing that *Summertime* sets out to do. In fact, any interest that *The African Queen* can be said to have consists, on the one hand, in its refraction of the spinster project through a narrative structure that draws equally on Bogart's films with Bacall and Hepburn's with Tracy, and on the other, in its confirmation of the kind of relation that obtains between John Huston and Howard Hawks (and of one's assessment of that relation).

The African Queen makes much of the strength and resilience of Rose Sayer (Hepburn), and of her crucial importance as a narrative agent. It is she who conceives and, through moral authority, enlists (much against his will) the hero's support for the central action – the hunt for and destruction of the German

Still: Charlie (Humphrey Bogart) and Rose (Hepburn) in The African Queen.

gunboat – and throughout she remains indispensable to its successful execution, performing tasks as difficult, dangerous and exacting as her male companion's and displaying a spiritual fortitude and indomitable strength of purpose far in excess of his: on several occasions, when Charlie (Bogart) wishes to abandon the undertaking, only Rose's commitment to it keeps him going. In terms of her narrative function, then, and the moral qualities contingent on it, Rose is a very different figure from Jane Hudson and Lizzie Curry, neither of whom has any active narrative role whatever.

It seems to me that we pay the appropriate tribute to the film's sexual liberalism by recognising in it a level of calculation unknown to *Summertime* – a film which the staunchest admirer of the art of David Lean could hardly accuse of any unnecessary ideological sophistication. *The African Queen* has learnt from the Hepburn/Tracy movies all that it is capable of learning from them – which is to say that it has acquired a formula for the representation of the hetero-sexual couple. The film proceeds to extrapolate this formula from the real ideological tensions which, however confusedly and inadequately, the Hepburn/Tracy films seek to organise, and to reduce it, with arch knowingness, to a show-case for its stars. The self-referential, self-congratulatory quality of *Pat and Mike*, its insufferable tone of 'cutie-pie', can be traced to an identical operation: evidently *The African Queen* proved itself a dire catalyst for tendencies just held in check in *Adam's Rib*. In both cases, the Hepburn/Tracy convention has ceased to bear any but the most gestural relation to the theme of the social inequality of the sexes which the convention purports to dramatise, and the convention is simply indulged for its own sake with an effect of insidious, sentimental recuperation – the insidious sentiment manifesting itself as 'charm'. Here is Miss Hepburn, a shade prim and unvanquishably idealistic, yielding so touchingly to the promptings of womanhood. And here is Humphrey Bogart as a lovable old soak, 'minding his own business' yet again (*Casablanca, To Have and Have Not*), and being won over once more for the democratic struggle. The characteristic 'commitment' theme of Bogart's 'forties films, rendered by Huston with unctuous, bombastic rhetorical inflation in *Key Largo*, is thrown off here with the portentous lightness of touch that befits a Huston *divertissement*.

The enormous popular affection which has always surrounded *The African Queen* testifies, of course, to the potency of the 'charm' – to the slickness and expertise with which Huston goes through the moves. To admirers of, say, *To Have and Have Not* and *Stage Door*, the charm cannot but appear meretricious, in that its sole function is to disarm us before the film's actual operations by appealing to a knowingness about the personae of the actors. Rose begins life as that all-purpose emblem of female sexual repression, a religionist – in this case a missionary rather than the familiar nun. Charlie begins life as an earthy, ego-tistic solitary. In the course of the action, the woman acquires the knowledge of desire from the man, and the man discovers from the woman disinterestedness and the possibility of acting on principles which transcend immediate egotistic ends. Woman bears the concept of culture and schools man in democratic altru-ism: in return, man introduces woman to her physicality, the inhibition of which is the negative corollary of her civilising power, and schools her in the nature of her sexuality. The scene in which Charlie takes tea with Rose and her brother (Robert Morley) before the massacre which initiates the narrative movement

Still: as Rose Sayer in The African Queen.

gives us the essential data. Charlie, whose stomach rumbles at table, is vital but ungenteel; Rose, who preserves the amenities in the wilderness, is refined but nonplussed by the body. (The scene's simple comedy turns on the social taboo which demands that the needs which the consumption of food is designed to satisfy should not intrude themselves on the ritual of the meal itself.) And it is not, in fact, agency (which as a missionary she already possesses) but the body – the body as being for, and fulfilled through, the male – that Rose discovers: one of the film's most famous lines, Rose's 'I never dreamed a mere physical experience could be so exhilarating' after the successful negotiation of the rapids, defines succinctly the metaphorical nature of the voyage as far as Rose is concerned, and its relation to the presence of Charlie. Subsequently, much mileage is got from Rose's gradual thawing and her sexual innocence ('Oh, Charlie!'), the effect being of a massive appeal to a general knowledge about the ingenuousness of spinsters, who become so terribly lovable as they undergo their spiritual education. A complacent patronage is built into the 'affection', and the relentlessly inscribed 'charm' inures to, invites complicity with, the ideological banalities which the film sets out to reinforce.

The banalities work – as in a sense they clearly do – because of the factitious substance they derive from the convention of the 'democratic' couple implied by the casting. The substance is factitious in that while *The African Queen* shows no interest in creating a democratic couple (on the contrary), it is sufficiently canny to detect in the *convention* the chance of a histrionic *tour de force*. To conceive of the convention in that way is in itself to neutralise it, and consolingly to suppress the contradictions which it generates, while at the same time drawing from it certain formal elements which flesh out, and subtly mystify, the work's actual tendency.

A Note on Crying

'Another thing that happened was I was very proud I got Katharine Hepburn to cry, because I thought she was a cool person. Not at all – if she wants to cry she turns it on. But I was very pleased with the rushes, and I said to Pandro Berman, "Gee, Pandro, did you see the stuff? I think she gave a terrific performance." He said, "Well, Mr Mayer doesn't think so." So I went to see Mr Mayer. I said, "What are you talking about, Mr Mayer? She's terrific in that scene – she cries all through it." He said, "The channel of the tears is wrong." I said, "But, Mr Mayer, Mr Mayer, that's the way the girl's face is made!" He said, "There's another thing – some people cry with their voice, some with their throat, some with their nose, some with their eyes. But she cries with everything! And this is excessive" ' (Elia Kazan, interviewed by Stuart Byron and Martin L. Rubin, *Movie* 19, pp.2-3).

An actor's mannerisms are the actor's persona in microcosm; they embody the dynamic of the persona in a condensed form. But they are not thereby in any simple sense 'personal'; they pertain to specific traditions of performance. Laurence Olivier's rolling eyeballs are distinctively 'Olivier', but they also signify, beyond that, a conception, shared by actor and audience, of appropriateness and excellence in the enactment of classical theatre – a conception with a long history (consider Dr Johnson's remarks on Garrick) and apparently limitless powers of self-renewal.

While numerous traditions of performance fed into, and helped to determine the nature of, classical film acting, the most important is that which derives from nineteenth-century theatrical melodrama. The nature of melodramatic acting cannot be separated from the melodramatic conception of character. The characters of melodrama are not densely realised individuals but social types, produced by the isolation of certain class and sexual features in a cryptic and compacted form. The characters in, say, *Way Down East*, have no detailed psychological life: their dramatic status consists in their exemplary embodiment of a specific point of balance of one or more of the film's overlapping thematic oppositions – town *v.* country, aristocracy *v.* petit bourgeoisie, Old Testament retribution *v.* Christian charity, oppressive masculinity *v.* suffering femininity. Classical melodramatic characters embody social forces, values and ideologies which are in principle impersonal, and they do so in a polemical manner: melodrama appeals very directly for our affiliation to, or rejection of, its actants on the basis of the objective social conflicts to which they refer and of which they represent a particular resolution. This conception of character is closer to allegory than to realism, and in America, peculiarly, the radical (but deeply problematic and contradictory) secularisation of allegory as Gothic melodrama establishes itself as the fundamental domestic literary tradition, entering Hollywood through D.W. Griffith. The principle of melodramatic character survives the final superannuation of the vestiges of Puritan moralism (which are in Griffith, despite

Still: Adam and Amanda in Adam's Rib.

appearances, already superficial), though these persist as reactionary possibilities in the terms of the horror movie, for reasons which I have suggested elsewhere ('The Symbolism of Evil', *The American Nightmare*, Toronto Film Festival, 1979, pp.34-42). In other genres, the possibility of defining 'individuality' in social terms, in an implicitly didactic mode, permits that inflection of melodrama towards epic theatre undertaken in the work of Douglas Sirk.

Melodramatic acting is a function of this understanding of persons. Characters in melodrama are defined not only through their narrative functions and their, as it were, epigrammatic enactment of a social position (in such a way as to demand a value judgement), but by elaborately formalised codes of performance. In classical melodrama we recognise the villain by his relation to other characters and by his thematic content ('aristocratic/cynical/ womanising' or 'proletarian/ brutal/drunken'), but also because he acts 'villainously'. Melodramatic characters signal their narrative function to the spectator through the concrete objective correlatives (in dress, deportment, vocal delivery and intonation) assigned them by the genre. The definition of characters as exemplary social types is matched by an acting style based on schematisation (a specific villain is presented as an instance of his generic category) and the externalisation, as gesture, of subjective states. This style is, necessarily, anti-naturalistic and inclined to 'excess', and it too, like the principle of 'character' survived the disintegration of the relatively simple ethical polarities which, in Griffith's films, already exist in a contradictory relation to far more complex thematic structures. The Hollywood star system is an enormously sophisticated development of this tradition of character and performance, and is inconceivable without reference to it.

Stars play certain kinds of parts, and the elaboration of the star system brings with it the possibility of minutely particularised inflections of generic thematics. The fact that a certain generic type can be played by a wide range of different, popular star actors, and that profit is to be had from the cultivation of more, similar yet different, conduces in itself to complex thematic development (though not, of course, intentionally!). Even as the star system is premised on theatrical melodrama, it precipitates a rapid transformation and refinement of it. The individuation of a generic type through the actor playing the type will tend to the specification of contradiction *within* it rather than merely *between* it and other types, as well as to the amplification of the range of types.

Like the acting of classical theatrical melodrama, Hollywood star acting is inclined to excess. Obviously, the principle of 'typage' persists – James Cagney, Edward G. Robinson and Humphrey Bogart all manifest 'gangstericity' – but accompanied by a principle of particularisation, the constant reinscription of the persona: besides 'gangstericity', Cagney displays 'Cagneyness'. Cagney's descent of the staircase at the end of *Yankee Doodle Dandy* (Michael Curtiz, 1942) remains one of the most exhilarating moments in the cinema, not because the actor's ebullience and energy *transcend* the film's project at that point (essentially, the construction of imperialism as entertainment) but because they *contradict* it: the energy is that of the anarchic lumpen-proletarian, produced by and aveng-ing himself on the late capitalist city. As George M. Cohan descends the stairs of the White House, we see the shadow of another figure running up them with a machine-gun. Our exhilaration is a response to an excess produced by the enact-ment of contradiction, and if the excessiveness of star acting may serve, like that of classical theatrical melodrama, to enforce (for affirmation or rejection) a coherent, non-contradictory generic type (John Wayne's excess is usually, though not always, of this order), it may also employ the mode for an opposite purpose, and objectify contradiction in the form of gesture and behaviour. In comparing Katharine Hepburn with Bette Davis, I suggested that Davis's mannerisms function in this way, and the embarrassment which, as anyone who has taught the films will know, so often greets some of the greatest star performances – Jennifer Jones in *Duel in the Sun*, Dorothy Malone in *Written on the Wind* (Douglas Sirk, 1956), Davis in *Beyond the Forest* – testifies to the still-scandalous audacity, matched by great technical powers, with which the acting gives tangible form to the most disturbingly contradictory subjective states.

Louis B. Mayer was right: Hepburn's most notorious mannerism is excessive, and Kazan's anecdote helps us to focus its significance. Weeping is a classical signifier of feminine weakness and emotionalism. A man's tears are so striking, and so distressing, a confession of vulnerability because incompatible with the notion of manliness. 'I thought she was a very cool person': there is a striking tension between the associations which the Hepburn persona immediately invokes (female strength, assertiveness, confidence, intelligence) and the automatic cultural connotations of one of the most characteristic features of the actor's performance style. This tension correlates with the excessiveness to which Louis B. Mayer objects, though he doesn't go on to point out that the intensity and elaboration of the signs of crying in Hepburn's performances are typically produced not by a surrender to tears but by resistance to them: she 'cries with everything' because of the struggle involved in trying not to cry at all. The mannerism dramatises that struggle. The decisions which Hepburn characters have made, and the stresses and obstacles to which they are consequently exposed, create a real vulnerability, the surrender to which would at once be appropriated by the very imagery of female weakness and susceptibility which they transgress. The mannerism refers to a woman in a social situation which continually generates distress but which, because it does so, makes it all the more necessary not to give in, not least because the expression of distress, in being given an a priori social meaning (women are weak), has been partially alienated. Hepburn's crying, that is, signifies both the emotional cost of a woman's struggle under patriarchy for a sensibility which hasn't been brutalised, and a stoical determination to continue to resist: thus related, both the vulnerability and the strength acquire a strong positive meaning.

Consider two moments in Cukor's *The Corn Is Green*. Miss Moffat (Hepburn) is visiting the local squire (Bill Fraser), hitherto a dedicated opponent of hers, in order to persuade him to become the patron of her protégé, Morgan Evans (Ian Saynor). The squire has money and prestige, and while she loathes everything he represents, Miss Moffat is determined to put him to her own uses. Her strategy in the scene in question, which is wonderfully funny, is the flattery of the complacent male ego. She compliments him on the decor of his study, hideously adorned, in the Hemingway manner, with trophies of the hunt ('What a perfectly delightful room! It's so – *manly*'), and relentlessly plays up that constitutional feminine weakness which is so much in need of male support and assistance. In the course of her disquisition, which is obviously having the desired effect, she mentions that 'there are so many times when one longs for the qualities of a man' – qualities which she proceeds to adumbrate: 'the courage of a lion, the cunning of a fox . . .', adding in a sotto voce aside, after a brilliantly judged pause, 'the skin of a rhinoceros'.

The second moment occurs in the scene which follows, when Miss Moffat informs Morgan of the success of her mission, which will enable her to enter him for an Oxford scholarship. Morgan's resentment of her immediately erupts:

he accuses her of not being really interested in him, and takes out on her the fact that their relationship is calling his manhood into question amongst his peers, who now know him as 'the school-mistress's little dog'. Deeply hurt, Miss Moffat replies that she has spent money, energy and time on him – her time ('Two years is valuable currency') – and that she has, in fact, devoted herself single-mindedly to his interests ('I've laid awake making plans – plans for you'). Hepburn plays the scene with a regulated intensity which conveys both the extent of the character's pain and her determination to retain her self-control, her self-respect and her impersonality: she presents everything she has done for Morgan as a statement of fact, and refuses either to cloud her own case or to appeal to him through a release of emotion. Nevertheless, she is moved to tears, and when she at last permits herself to personalise her remarks to Morgan, it is to bring that against him: 'I haven't cried since I was younger than you are, and I'll never forgive you for that.'

The juxtaposition of the two scenes (among the finest in the film) has obvious point and felicity. Miss Moffat *hasn't* the skin of a rhinoceros. The enlightened opportunism to which her social powerlessness as a woman condemns her does not damage her integrity, but is obviously galling and demeaning in a way which is only partially mitigated by a sense of irony. Her reward is to be told by Morgan that he 'don't want to be thankful to no strange woman for nothing.' *His* integrity can't withstand the idea of being helped by a woman – and a woman, too, whose interest in him doesn't express itself in lavish devotion and isn't incompatible with a commitment to ends of her own. The upshot is the definition of a strength and an integrity which are not only more valuable than those embodied by the two men, but which are also produced by a struggle with the conditions of patriarchy. Morgan's behaviour is so much more insulting than the squire's because it momentarily breaks through the stringent self-discipline required to function under such conditions, and turn them, as far as possible, to advantage. Far from indicating weakness, the fact that Miss Moffat cries is part of the strength, which counts the more for the difficulty of coming by and maintaining it. The squire's strength, by contrast, is a mere fact of his social position and the easy rhetoric of the Hemingway ethos. Crying in Hepburn movies always generates this order of meaning.

With her Mary Tyrone in *Long Day's Journey into Night*, Jane Hudson in *Summertime* is one of Hepburn's greatest and most excessive performances. One wonders what Louis B. Mayer would have thought of it, since here Hepburn cries not merely 'all through' one poor scene but throughout the entire movie. The performance is pitched consistently on the edge of hysteria, but displays at the same time an astonishing precision of intelligent judgement. The apparently unrestrained intensities are rigorously controlled and organised. I have already given an account of what I take the project of *Summertime* to be; what I wish to emphasise here is the way in which Hepburn's 'excess' (which has neither the exquisite tastefulness of David Lean's *mise-en-scène* nor the vulgarity of its intention) generates a meaning which runs counter to it. One is struck by the violence of the performance – a violence which appears as a conflict between desire and resistance. In one sense, this is perfectly in line with the film's argument: the problem arises because Hepburn's intensity gives the woman's

Still: Jane and Renato in Summertime.

psychological anguish – the cost of that conflict for her – a dramatic centrality which the film cannot properly sustain. The cost, indeed, rapidly becomes more real dramatically than its occasion: the blandness of the male lead is cruelly exposed, and we are preoccupied more than we should be with the intolerable nature of the woman's situation and the rationality of her hysterical response to it. The film wishes us to feel that Jane shuns what she most desires. Hepburn makes us feel that Jane's desire makes her appallingly vulnerable, and gives the fierceness of her resistance, first to the indulgence of romantic fantasy, and then to the desperate impulse to believe that Renato embodies it, a weight and logic which override the film's attempts to devalue it. The performance implies everything that the film cannot afford to admit: it makes present the oppressiveness of a cultural situation that entails a norm (a woman should have a man) by which the woman, socially and emotionally, has everything to lose. The fact of oppression is there only in Hepburn's hysteria, but that is the most substantial, the most intensely and consistently realised fact in the dramatic world. Like Ingrid Bergman's performance in *Autumn Sonata* (Ingmar Bergman, 1978), Hepburn's Jane Hudson is an exemplary case of acting as counter-text: in both cases, the performance creates complexities which the film needs to suppress, and in so doing makes the film's project untenable.

Epilogue: The Star as Monument

'A woman my age is not a particularly interesting object in our society, and that's a fact' – Katharine Hepburn, interviewed by Rex Reed, New York *Daily News*, 28th January 1979.

In our culture, the myths of age as the occasion of heroic renewal or tragic self-inquisition and self-knowledge – of the confirmation of power or the discovery of its limits – are centred on men. We remember Tolstoy's agony, not his wife's. The great male stars of the Hollywood cinema end up as 'grand old men' – embodiments of the splendour and resilience of patriarchal authority, or emblems of a nobler former time doomed to be superseded by an age in which men are not giants. The tone of the 'ageing westerner' movies of the 'sixties is elegiac: the hero's power is the nobler, its moral force the purer and more convincing, for the pathos of physical debility and the spectacle of a degenerate race unworthy of its fathers. The tone of the contemporary female equivalent, *What Ever Happened To Baby Jane?*, is derisive and grotesque: the women's past glory is the more pathetic for their current decay. The cinema has tended to confirm the longevity of male, and the transience of female, potency. If it was possible for Clark Gable, Cary Grant and Ronald Colman to appear as romantic figures at an age when the complementary representation of a woman as being sexually desirable would be felt to be implausible, the latter-day incarnations of Bette Davis, Joan Crawford and Tallulah Bankhead suggest an impulse to revile and humiliate – to exact retribution for their previous eminence by dwelling on decrepitude, defining assertiveness as 'camp' and enacting knowing parodies of the star's thematic in a series of increasingly cheap and tacky B-pictures.

The latter stages of Katharine Hepburn's career have been, in one sense, less demeaning: indeed, they continue to be elaborately adorned with all the signs of eminence and distinction. Avoiding both the cameo part and the lower depths of the exploitation market, Hepburn has appeared exclusively, since 1960, in prestige productions – many of them (increasingly, of course, for television, but also for the cinema) filmed versions of the great dramatic works of our and other times, their prestigiousness enhanced by the collaborating personnel. She has won three more Academy Awards, bringing her total to an unprecendented (for an actor) four, and has continued a triumphant career in the theatre. Most significantly, perhaps, she has become an all-American institution – an institution of a kind that compels one to define the sense of disappointment and unease which, from the perspective of this book, the glories of the 'sixties and later provoke.

'Millions of people still care very much what she does because she represents decision, order, character, taste, standards, integrity and determination – qualities as rare as Christmas bluejays' (Reed).

There was a time when, though fewer people probably cared what she did, Katharine Hepburn represented something rather different; or rather, when the qualities described had a meaning which was not such as to warm the heart, and flatter the disposition, of Rex Reed and his readership. One feels both that much of what was valuable about Hepburn has been lost, and that there is a connection, intimate but complex, between the monument that she now is and the offensive aberration that to so many she once was. One is struck at once, in considering Hepburn's late films, by the diversity of the strategies embodied in them. All of these strategies are ultimately conservative, but their contradictoriness across the obvious points they have in common is important and suggestive. I have already noted that Hepburn is, for the first time, consistently located within the patriarchal family as wife-and-mother at this stage of her career, and while the films are linked by the attempt to construct some kind of ideological equilibrium between Hepburn's 'independent' image and the familial role, they reflect, taken as a whole, the difficulty of such a project. I say 'taken as a whole' because the contradictions are never significantly dramatised or clearly focused in any one work. Let us consider the various dramatic options.

1) The Gothic Mother

There is no more infallible method of discrediting female strength and authority – no surer means of defining them in terms of castration – than by creating a situation in which they are exercised inside the family. The adulterous heroine – the wife whose transgression of familial law takes the form of an absolute break with her role – can, of course, be presented conservatively, but need not be. But the woman who observes the form while defying the spirit of patriarchal marriage, who exploits a social position which is technically unimpeachable so as to disturb the 'natural' distribution of power which the family should embody, is instantly a monster. Not only is she dominant where she should be subordinate: at the same time, her seizure of power becomes socially invisible – is grotesquely substantiated – because of the legitimacy she derives from what she seems to be.

The sexual disorder implied by this kind of transgression – the conflict between the appearance of patriarchal order and the subterranean dislocation of the normal Oedipal arrangements – generates the Gothic mode, as *Rebecca* classically attests. The absent titular protagonist of Hitchcock's film uses the mystified popular understanding that she is herself respectably castrated in order flamboyantly to indulge desires which have entirely escaped male regulation, and which are for her husband (though not, because of Hitchcock, for us) diabolic ('It doesn't make for sanity, does it, living with the devil?').

Mrs Venable in *Suddenly, Last Summer* is an archetypal bad matriarch in this sense. Rebecca, of course, has no children (her stomach cancer, which she mistakes for pregnancy, testifies to her sterility), and her castrating powers are expressed through the violation of the couple – the denial of her husband's sexual rights, the appropriation of his name as a suffix to her own (dramatised in the omnipresence of her initials), the heterosexual promiscuity, the lesbian relationship with her maid. According to a familiar cultural wisdom, Mrs Venable's emasculating properties manifest themselves in the homosexuality of her son, Sebastian, whose appetites, indeed, she further nourishes by procuring for him. The decadent, incestuous involvement of the Venables, which has displaced

Stills. Above: as Eleanor of Aquitaine in The Lion in Winter. *Opposite: as Violet Venable in* Suddenly, Last Summer, *with Montgomery Clift as Dr Cukrowicz.*

and finally extinguished the father, is juxtaposed with the robust heterosexual health of Catherine (Elizabeth Taylor), whom Mrs Venable wishes to have committed because she knows the grisly story of Sebastian's proclivities and their appropriately apocalyptic come-uppance.

Hepburn has prided herself on the fact that 'I wouldn't play hatchet murderesses or alcoholic mothers or loonies when I was young, and I won't play them now . . . And I won't play a senile, dithering old lady locked in a sewer' (Reed). It is certainly true that she has, on the whole, eschewed the genre that claimed a number of her contemporaries. Doubtless, too, if one is going to play a demented, castrating mother, it is classier to do it in a controversial adaptation of a much-touted play, however meretricious, than in *The Anniversary*, the Bette Davis equivalent (also complete with effeminate son). Nevertheless, the ambience of *Suddenly, Last Summer* continues to persist, at least as an undercurrent, in a number of later films – *A Delicate Balance, The Lion in Winter* and one of her Broadway successes, *A Matter of Gravity* (the last two again associating the strength of the mother with the gayness of her male child).

2) The 'Good' Mother

If *Suddenly, Last Summer* discredits female strength by defining it in terms of the perversion of familial norms, the project of *Guess Who's Coming to Dinner?* and *On Golden Pond* is to dramatise the perfect compatibility of wifely subordination and 'independence'. 'Dramatise', perhaps, is hardly the word: the reconciliation of the contradiction between feminine submissiveness and feminist self-assertion is effected simply by Hepburn's playing the part. 'There isn't the least discrepancy,' *On Golden Pond* seems to say, 'between being what Katharine Hepburn now mythically represents and the kind of total devotion to your man

which inspires you to tell him that he's your knight in shining armour. On the contrary, the completeness of the devotion is itself a sign of the strength and completeness of autonomous identity.' The wives in these films are mere spectators of their husbands' existential crises, equipped so perfectly to provide tactful moral support, in the form of worship, because they have themselves no crises to undergo. This kind of acknowledgement of female strength is, of course, thoroughly back-handed, in that it is bought at the cost of the assertion that the strength should be devoted to men (men are little boys) and that its function is the inflation of the patriarch, whose survival of his crisis provides the final dramatic coup (men come through heroically). If *On Golden Pond,* as one of a cycle of films about the reinstatement of the father (*Kramer* v. *Kramer,* Robert Benton, 1979; *The Great Santini,* Lewis John Carlino, 1979; *Tribute,* Bob Clark, 1985; *Middle-Aged Crazy,* John Trent, 1980; *Ordinary People,* Robert Redford, 1980; *Author! Author!,* Arthur Hiller, 1982), has a distastefulness all its own, it is because the partial mystification of the strategy of doing dirt on the mother, characteristic of these movies, is generated by the presence of Hepburn and Jane Fonda, the resonance of whose personae serves to diffuse the sentimental conservatism of the project.

3) The Tragic Mother
It is notable that the roles of Hepburn's later years in which she has been able to usurp the realm of tragic experience (her Mary Tyrone in *Long Day's Journey into Night* and her Hecuba in *The Trojan Women*) are both classical parts in respectful re-enactments of 'masterpieces'. That is to say, these are enterprises in which, whatever the merits, demerits or significance of the work that is sanctified (and from the point of view of kudos, Edward Albee is hardly distinguishable from Euripides), the invitation to adopt an attitude quite distinct from that which we would normally strike in front of a movie tends determinedly to predominate; they are enterprises, too, which don't aim for box-office records and have no prospect of wide distribution.

Stills. Below: as Hecuba in The Trojan Women, *with Irene Papas as Helen. Right: as Mary Tyrone in* Long Day's Journey into Night.

Both *Long Day's Journey into Night* and *The Trojan Women* are woman-centred, and in both the Hepburn character is the focus of the tragedy. That the theme of women's social powerlessness (in the O'Neill, of women's entrapment within the family) should organise the tragic experience is indeed important, and Hepburn's performances are consummate: one cannot imagine a finer account of Mary Tyrone. The point to be made, however, is that the films can follow their sources in positing this theme only because they *are* transpositions of 'great plays': Hepburn's other matriarch roles are quite different in character, as *The Lion in Winter*, a work bent double by pretentious gestures towards tragic significance, most clearly demonstrates. The fact that 'there are no parts for older women' (let alone parts of the grandeur of Mary Tyrone and Hecuba) was clearly crucial for Hepburn's decision to play them, but while, for anyone familiar with the thematic of her work, the casting acquires an important meaning, the whole character of the film subdues the familiar, complex dialectic of persona person and part which the other late films so insistently foreground. In *Long Day's Journey into Night*, we contemplate Hepburn's greatness as an actress: the projects of *Rooster Cogburn* and *On Golden Pond* entail a demand to think of her as a person existing outside the fictional world.

The significance of the distinction between *Long Day's Journey into Night* and the complementary reactionary images of *Suddenly, Last Summer* and *On Golden Pond* is clear: the ageing woman can take on a cultural value comparable to that of the ageing man only in works in which, by virtue of their highbrow status and their separation from the commercial mainstream, the star's presence is deprived of much of its star meaning and function. The example of Lee Grant's magnificent *Tell Me a Riddle* (1980), constructed by its distributors, half-heartedly, as an 'art' movie, and foredoomed to failure and marginality (disgracefully, the film has never been released theatrically in Britain) confirms the point, and there is little reason to doubt that the woman's being revolutionary as well as old didn't further the film's case.

4) The 'Independent' Woman

Two motifs constantly repeatedly emerge in Hepburn's late films: the theme of intransigent survival, of the stoical endurance of the intolerable, and that of a striking – eccentric, even fey, but impressive – exceptionalism. These motifs appear not only in the films, but in Hepburn's own remarks to the press.

'The thing about life is that you must survive. Life is going to be difficult and dreadful things will happen. What you do is to move along, get on with it, and be tough. Not in the sense of being mean to others, but tough with yourself and making a deadly effort not to be defeated' (Hepburn talking to David Lewin, *Daily Mail*, 20th May 1968).

'It's so endless to be old. It's too goddamned bad that you're rotting away. Really, it's a big bore for anyone with half a brain. But you have to face it, and how you do it is a challenge' (*Time*, 16th November 1981, p.55).

'I'm sick and tired of a whole generation of kids who say "I'm tired" or "I'm nervous" or this and that. If you're tired, give yourself some gas and get to the top of that hill. Why you can't do something is of practically no interest at all to me, unless you say – I'm trying to walk up a hill and I've got a size-eight foot and I'm wearing a size-five shoe and I can't take another step. To this I would say – take off your shoe and hop on my back and I'll carry you the rest of the way. But it's a poor habit in life to blame anyone but yourself for anything' (Reed).

'Me, I'm like the Flatiron Building. All I can say is I could never be anyone else. I don't *want* to be anyone else, and I've never regretted what I've done in my life even though I've had my nose broken a few times doing it' (Reed).

For many years Hepburn has been able to select her own projects, and it seems reasonable to suppose that the parts she chooses to play in some way embody for her values and attitudes which are of cardinal importance in her own living.

The admirable qualities bespoken by these very representative remarks – the combination of robustness, generosity, personal pride and unselfpitying resilience – do not require comment; what concerns me is the use to which they have

Still: as Eula Goodnight in Rooster Cogburn, *with John Wayne in the title part.*

been put in the construction of 'Katharine Hepburn', the all-American monument, and the way in which the objectively contradictory character of the remarks themselves makes them available for such a use. Their tone is so very different from that of 'I Did It My Way' because they are spoken by a woman, and have behind them a life and a body of work which command, on political grounds, the deepest gratitude, respect and admiration: the contrast with Mr Sinatra's performance of that stomach-churning sentimentally self-aggrandising eulogy of male amoralism is extreme. Yet it is what the remarks have in common with the patriarchal song – a philosophy of self-reliant individualism – which allows the flatly contradictory element, the woman's voice, to be recuperated, and creates the possibility of a bourgeois myth of the permissibly independent woman.

The myth is permissible because of the woman's uniqueness – her *absolute* difference, and *Rooster Cogburn,* perhaps the most distressing and distasteful of Hepburn's late films, exposes the myth's logic with unusual clarity. 'She is what she is because that's what she wants to be – and that's how I take her': the price of John Wayne's acceptance of the terms of the women's movement is revealed at the close, when Eula (Hepburn) is required to return the compliment: 'You're a credit to the male sex, and I'm proud to have you as my friend'. Eula is not, of course, a credit to the *female* sex: the magnanimous salute from the Hollywood cinema's supreme patriarch, as from one wonderful old-timer to another, conspicuously neglects the attribution of exemplary status. It may be possible to make of Katharine Hepburn a 'grand old lady', but only superficially on the terms in which John Wayne is a 'grand old man'. What is stressed in the woman's case is her eccentric differentness – a differentness from the run of her sex which, while it provides the condition for her elevation to the rank of patriarchal institution (in the appropriately patronising manner), also generates the nagging resentment and antagonism inspired by a sense of abnormality. 'You've got more backbone than femaleness': this is good, in that it makes Eula/Hepburn an honorary man, but also, therefore, jarring, and the uncertainty of the film's laboured humour follows naturally enough from the difficulty of creating a positive meaning which has immediately negative corollaries. The category of 'differentness' is the film's trump card, but it is also a difficult card to play with any precision, and it is at times quite unclear whether we are being asked to find Eula splendid or ridiculous.

A similar uncertainty pervades several other late movies (*The Madwoman of Chaillot, Love Among the Ruins*), whose general classiness is clearly the major factor in convincing us that Hepburn's fate has been so very different from Davis's. 'Magnificent exceptionalism' turns out not to be cleanly separable from 'dementia' – the connotations of the latter remain latent within it, and give the handsome recognition of the sterling qualities of 'the old girl' a distinctly unpleasant undertone. The recognition takes place entirely on patriarchy's terms: not only does it necessitate a tribute from the woman so honoured to the most reactionary images of 'maleness' (a motif which links *Rooster Cogburn* to *On Golden Pond*, thus emphasising the essential insignificance of the apparently major difference between a 'good wife' role and the celebration of gutsy independence), but it also instantly recoups itself by simultaneously affirming the woman's superiority to, and parodying her divergence from, the female norm. Hepburn's being more and better than a mere woman entails her being less and worse, and if *On Golden Pond* is to be preferred to *Rooster Cogburn*, it is because Hepburn's assignment to a female role that no one will have the least trouble in approving obviates the need to programme to auto-destruct every tribute to the glories of female emancipation.

Only *The Corn Is Green*, from this period, merits partial exemption from such strictures, on grounds implied by its genuine differences from its contemporaries. Hepburn is *not* cast, here, opposite a patriarch of legendary eminence (a Wayne, a Fonda, an Olivier) in a formal gesture of parity which is undercut at every point by the realised project. The 'differentness', too, is more substantially perceived as a strength, and as a *woman's* strength, met continually by male resentment, resistance and anxiety and asserting itself through determined struggle against material social obstacles: the reading of the strength *by men* as 'eccentricity' or 'aberration' is foregrounded in the film. There is also an attempt to organise the contradictions of the late Hepburn persona (contradictions turning as we have seen on the relation between independence and the role of wife) into some kind of suggestive dialectic – a project enabled by the material itself, with its theme of displaced motherhood that proposed *The Corn Is Green* as an exemplary Davis subject in the 'forties. The film follows Emlyn Williams's play in its snobbish, misogynistic treatment of the venal nymphet whose alluring but fatal body threatens to sabotage the hero's ascent into the petit bourgeoisie, and this narrative *donnée*, combined with the fact that the Hepburn character's strength is, ultimately, for the benefit of a man, certainly locate *The Corn Is Green* as a late Hepburn movie: Miss Moffat is indeed distinct from the rest of her sex (and from its sexuality) and a man is the beneficiary of the improvement. Nevertheless, the film merits a marginal distinguishing note – it *is* possible to watch it without *consistent* anger and embarrassment.

I have argued elsewhere ('Sideshows: Hollywood in Vietnam', *Movie* 27/28, Winter 1980/Spring 1981, pp.4-5), that the ability of the great Hollywood movies to dramatise ideological contradiction so acutely must be referred to the comparative safety, in the culture as a whole, of the norms and institutions whose value and coherence the films contest. Their safety is embodied, I suggested, in the viability, and the separateness, of the genres; and the use of genre to articulate the very conflicts and contradictions implicit in conventions which function dominantly to contain, regulate and naturalise them is contingent on a situation in which such conflicts are acutely present socially but have not yet acquired a concrete political status – have not yet crystallised, that is, in organised, collective struggle.

The point can be extended to include the star system, which, in the cinema, is articulated with genre, on the basis of the individuation of social conflict characteristic of bourgeois narrative. The great female stars are, obviously, pre-women's movement, and the fact is most usually cited, perhaps, as evidence of the drastic limitations of the works built round them. In one sense, of course, this is true, but it is the converse proposition which is surely the more striking. It is precisely because there was no women's movement, and nothing corresponding to one, that the films of Hepburn and Davis, say, were able to dramatise, within conventional forms which provided mechanisms for the standardised resolution and localisation of conflict, the most fundamental issues about the position of women under capitalism – issues which could not possibly be raised, in a mass entertainment medium with a commodity form, if they had a *political* existence. The very standardisation of the 'solution' to contradiction is itself an enabling condition, the solution's conservatism being counterbalanced by its necessary dramatic inertia. The genres contain and recuperate, but the means by which they do so are partially present *as* convention, and may, in a given case, be foregrounded as such, intentionally or not.

Politicised conflict is susceptible to two forms of treatment in a Hollywood movie – liberal or conservative. In a world in which we are more likely to get an *Ordinary People* or a *Kramer v. Kramer*, we may hope, at best, for a *Coming Home*: we are hardly likely to get a *Christopher Strong* or *The Old Maid*, or even a liberalism as disturbed as that of *Adam's Rib*. The obviously apposite comparison of Hepburn's career with Jane Fonda's can be usefully invoked here. Fonda's context is the appearance of a feminist politics, itself precipitated by, and contributing to, a radical and more generalised crisis in the culture. Her personal life has in the past been notorious for its association with radical politics of various kinds – an association which has frequently made her the object of intense conservative animus and obloquy – and her film work of the 'seventies has consistently sought to engage with explicitly political issues. The characteristic theme of that work (deriving from *Tout Va Bien*, Jean-Luc Godard and Jean-Pierre Gorin, 1972) is the politicisation of a previously uncommitted woman, in the dramatisation of which Fonda is proposed as an identification figure, the spectator being asked to participate in the character's development from unconsciousness or complacency towards a realisation of 'the issues' and corresponding action.

Still: Hepburn and Jane Fonda as Ethel and Chelsea in On Golden Pond.

Fonda has undoubtedly produced interesting and provocative movies, and it is always necessary to steer clear of the kind of self-congratulatory, up-front 'leftism' (most insufferable of petit-bourgeois idioms!) that can pass for film criticism. Nevertheless, the conditions which have enabled Fonda to enact the theme of a woman's politicisation in the commercial cinema have also conduced, in general, to the impossibility of giving the concept of 'politicisation' anything but the most innocuous content – the innocuousness passed off as daringly innovative modernity through the flattery of the spectator's liberal enlightenment. Identification with Fonda in *Coming Home* confirms the belief, which we are presumed to hold in the first place, that acquiring the correct views is essentially a matter of changing our life-style, moving to the beach and becoming vaguely anti-establishment, and that feminism consists of leaving a reassuringly nasty patriarch and going to live with a nice one. These platitudes are mystified by a spurious 'new realism' which suppresses the conventional organisation of the dramatic world. Collective action, in *9 to 5* (Colin Higgins, 1980), turns out to involve the farcically unintentioned zaniness of three lovable kooks, and to issue in an 'improvement of conditions' which is perfectly compatible with the continuation of patriarchy and of capitalism. Fonda's stardom expresses, and corroborates, for a culture which is beyond reform, the ideologies of reformism: the world is seriously out of joint, but it is amenable to progressive adjustment, and political issues exist as, and are resolved in, problems of individual conscience and transformation.

Naturally, given the themes which a contemporary reformism is called upon to dramatise, such projects may have a salutary tendency to founder on their contradictions. One doesn't need to cite Fonda's testimony as corroborative evidence to see that the intention of that remarkable film *Rollover* (Alan J. Pakula, 1982) is deeply conservative – the crisis of capitalism is to be blamed on duplicitous Arabs – but the realisation of the theme, and the drastic lengths to which it is taken, conspire damagingly to exceed the film's brief. The film's disastrous (and, in Fonda's career at the time, unique) commercial failure is plainly significant: *Rollover* does its best, but it is difficult to recuperate coherently the collapse of the international capitalist economy, and the very grandeur of the ambition exposes the film to spectacular internal disturbances. The possibility of such strains and tensions is not, however, the immediate point. What has to be insisted on is that the condition of the 'political' character of the Fonda persona is also the condition of its reformist character.

Hepburn in her films, like all classical stars, is a term of the genres and their interrelation: her work is cast within conventions which, while they serve conservatively to control contradiction, do so in a way which is peculiarly liable to expose it, and may be employed to dramatise it. Like Fonda, she was conspicuously controversial, but the controversy was at once socially significant and socially isolated: it may be necessary to recoup her, because she *is* both significant and unacceptable, but this dialectic of containment isn't immediately implicated in major political lesions in the culture. A complex of factors permits the exceptionalism entailed in the star phenomenon to assume a powerful progressive force: Hepburn's status is as a strikingly aberrant individual who is, however, socially resonant; the absence of popular struggles corresponding to the ideological conflicts dramatised in the persona (the latter being felt at the same time, as conflicts which must be worked through), the existence of popular narrative forms which are both ideologically robust and peculiarly available for the enactment of the tensions which determine their nature as forms. Fonda has been spared the negative consequences of Hepburn's situation: she hasn't made an *Alice Adams* or a *Summertime*, or found herself, as yet, in a position like Hepburn's in 1938, when *The Philadelphia Story* represented the condition on which Hepburn's career could continue. But the same forces that determined these vicissitudes are also the condition of the radical nature of Hepburn's stardom. The proposition that the Hollywood cinema, in the current American context, can produce anything similar, seems dubious in the extreme.

Indeed, Hepburn's status is there to prove it: since the 'seventies, she has functioned, for the first time in her career, as a substantially successful solvent of contradiction at the very moment which has produced the women's movement and the need to defuse and contain it. The answer to the question of how it was possible for her to lend herself to her late films has already been implied. 'She is what she is because that's what she wants to be.' Purely reactionary in its dramatic meaning, the remark tallies with Hepburn's sense of herself: her personal pride in her achievement, and in the self produced through it, have been mythologised *against* the struggles to which both refer. The fact that not only her work, but her self-respect, can be put to such a use should confirm our commitment to their other uses.

Filmography

This filmography consists of the major credits for all Miss Hepburn's film and television work; a brief listing of her theatrical work is also included. Homer Dickens's *The Films of Katharine Hepburn* (*see* Bibliography) gives exhaustive credits.

In the films, the rule has been adopted of putting Miss Hepburn's name first in the cast list. In fact, she was consistently given top billing only in her 'thirties films. Spencer Tracy always insisted on top billing, as did Cary Grant in *The Philadelphia Story*, and in a number of other cases Miss Hepburn's name appeared below that of the leading male actor.

A BILL OF DIVORCEMENT
RKO, 1932, 74 minutes.
With: Katharine Hepburn (Sydney Fairfield), John Barrymore (Hillary Fairfield), Billie Burke (Margaret Fairfield), David Manners (Kit Humphrey), Paul Cavanagh (Gray Meredith), Henry Stephenson (Dr Alliot), Elizabeth Patterson (Aunt Hester).
Directed by George Cukor. Executive producer: David O. Selznick. Script by Howard Estabrook and Harry Wagstaff Gribble, based on a play by Clemence Dane. Photographed by Sid Hickox. Art director: Carroll Clark. Edited by Arthur Roberts. Music director: Max Steiner. Piano concerto by W. Franke Harling.

CHRISTOPHER STRONG
RKO, 1933. 77 minutes.
With: Katharine Hepburn (Lady Cynthia Darrington), Colin Clive (Sir Christopher Strong), Billie Burke (Lady Elaine Strong), Helen Chandler (Monica Strong), Ralph Forbes (Harry Rawlinson), Irene Browne (Carrie Valentin), Jack La Rue (Carlo), Gwendolyn Logan (Bradford).
Directed by Dorothy Arzner. Produced by David O. Selznick. Associate producer: Pandro S. Berman. Script by Zoë Akins, based on a novel by Gilbert Frankau. Photographed by Bert Glennon. Art director: Van Nest Polglase. Edited by Arthur Roberts. Transitions by Slavko Vorkapich. Music by Max Steiner. Special effects by Vernon Walker.

MORNING GLORY
RKO, 1933. 74 minutes.
With: Katharine Hepburn (Eva Lovelace), Douglas Fairbanks, Jr (Joseph Sheridan), Adolphe Menjou (Louis Easton), Mary Duncan (Rita Vernon) C. Aubrey Smith (Robert Harley Hedges), Fred Santley (Will Seymour), Richard Carle (Henry Lawrence), Geneva Mitchell (Gwendolyn Hall), Tyler Brooke (Charles Van Dusen).
Directed by Lowell Sherman. Produced by Pandro S. Berman. Executive producer: Merian C. Cooper. Script by Howard J. Green, based on a play by Zoë Akins. Photographed by Bert Glennon. Art director: Van Nest Polglase. Edited by George Nicholls, Jr. Music by Max Steiner. Costumes by Walter Plunkett.

LITTLE WOMEN
RKO, 1933. 113 minutes
With: Katharine Hepburn (Jo), Joan Bennett (Amy), Jean Parker (Beth), Frances Dee (Meg), Douglass Montgomery (Laurie), Henry Stephenson (Mr Laurence), Paul Lukas (Professor Bhaer), Edna May Oliver (Aunt March), Spring Byington (Marmee), Samuel S. Hinds (Mr March), Mabel Colcord (Hannah), John Davis Lodge (Brooke).
Directed by George Cukor. Executive producer: Merian C. Cooper. Associate producer: Kenneth Macgowan. Script by Sarah Y. Mason and Victor Heerman based on a novel by Louisa M. Alcott. Photographed by Henry Gerrard. Art director: Van Nest Polglase. Edited by Jack Kitchin. Music by Max Steiner. Costumes by Walter Plunkett. Special effects by Harry Redmond.

SPITFIRE
RKO, 1934. 86 minutes.
With: Katharine Hepburn (Trigger Hicks), Robert Young (Stafford), Ralph Bellamy (Fleetwood), Sara Haden (Etta Dawson), Martha Sleeper (Eleanor Stafford), Louis Mason (Bill Grayson), Virginia Howell (Granny Raines), Sidney Toler (Mr Sawyer), Therese Wittler (Mrs Sawyer).
Directed by John Cromwell. Executive producer: Merian C. Cooper. Associate producer: Pandro S. Berman. Script by Jane Murfin and Lula Vollmer, based on the play *Trigger* by Lula Vollmer. Photographed by Edward Cronjager. Art director: Van Nest Polglase. Edited by William H. Morgan. Music by Max Steiner. Costumes by Walter Plunkett.

THE LITTLE MINISTER
RKO, 1934. 110 minutes.
With: Katharine Hepburn (Babbie), John Beal (Gavin), Alan Hale (Rob Dow), Donald Crisp (Dr McQueen), Lumsden Hare (Thammas), Andy Clyde (Wearyworld), Beryl Mercer (Margaret), Billy Watson (Micah Daw), Dorothy Stickney (Jean), Mary Gordon (Nanny), Frank Conroy (Lord Rintoul), Reginald Denny (Captain Halliwell).
Directed by Richard Wallace. Produced by Pandro S. Berman. Script by Jane Murfin, Sarah Y. Mason and Victor Heerman with additional scenes by Mortimer Offner and Jack Wagner, based on a novel and play by J.M. Barrie. Photographed by Henry Gerrard. Art director: Van Nest Polglase. Edited by William Hamilton. Music by Max Steiner. Costumes by Walter Plunkett.

BREAK OF HEARTS
RKO, 1935. 78 minutes.
With: Katharine Hepburn (Constance Dane), Charles Boyer (Franz Roberti), John Beal (Johnny Lawrence), Jean Hersholt (Professor Talma), Sam Hardy (Marx), Inez Courtney (Miss Wilson), Helene Millard (Sylvia), Ferdinand Gottschalk (Pazzini), Lee Kohlmer (Schubert).
Directed by Philip Moeller. Produced by Pandro S. Berman. Script by Sarah Y. Mason, Victor Heerman and Anthony Veiller, based on a story by Lester Cohen. Photographed by Robert De Grasse. Art director: Van Nest Polglase. Edited by William Hamilton. Music by Max Steiner. Costumes by Bernard Newman.

ALICE ADAMS

With: Katharine Hepburn (Alice Adams), Fred
MacMurray (Arthur Russell), Fred Stone (Mr Adams),
Ann Shoemaker (Mrs Adams), Frank Albertson (Walter
Adams), Evelyn Venable (Mildred Palmer), Charles
Grapewin (Mr Lamb), Grady Sutton (Frank Dowling),
Hedda Hopper (Mrs Palmer), Hattie McDaniel
(Malena), Virginia Howell (Mrs Dowling), Jonathan
Hale (Mr Palmer), Janet McLeod (Henrietta Lamb),
Ella McKenzie (Ella Dowling).

Directed by George Stevens. Produced by Pandro S.
Berman. Script by Gladys Unger, John Collier and
Mortimer Offner, based on a novel by Compton
Mackenzie. Photographed by Joseph August. Art
director: Van Nest Polglase. Edited by Jane Loring.
Music by Roy Webb. Costumes by Muriel King and
Bernard Newman.

MARY OF SCOTLAND

RKO, 1936. 123 minutes.

With: Katharine Hepburn (Mary Stuart), Fredric
March (Bothwell), Florence Eldridge (Elizabeth
Tudor), Douglas Walton (Darnley), John Carradine
(Rizzio), Robert Barrat (Morton), Gavin Muir
(Leicester), Ian Keith (James Stuart Moray), Moroni
Olsen (John Knox), Donald Crisp (Huntley).

Directed by John Ford. Produced by Pandro S.
Berman. Script by Dudley Nichols, based on a play by
Maxwell Anderson. Photographed by Joseph August.
Art director: Van Nest Polglase. Edited by Jane Loring
and Robert Parrish. Music by Nathaniel Shilkret.
Costumes by Walter Plunkett.

A WOMAN REBELS

RKO, 1936. 88 minutes.

With: Katharine Hepburn (Pamela Thistlethwaite),
Herbert Marshall (Thomas Lane), Elizabeth Allan
(Flora Thistlethwaite), Donald Crisp (Judge
Thistlethwaite), Doris Dudley (Flora), David Manners
(Alan), Van Heflin (Gerald), Lucile Watson (Betty
Bumble), Piper (Eily Malyon), Lionel Pape (Mr White).

Directed by Mark Sandrich. Produced by Pandro S.
Berman. Script by Anthony Veiller and Ernest Vajda,
based on the novel *Portrait of a Rebel* by Netta Syrett.
Photographed by Robert De Grasse. Art director: Van
Nest Polglase. Edited by Jane Loring. Music by Roy
Webb. Costumes by Walter Plunkett. Ballroom dances
by Hermes Pan.

QUALITY STREET

RKO, 1937. 83 minutes.

With: Katharine Hepburn (Phoebe Throssel), Franchot
Tone (Dr Valentine Brown), Fay Bainter (Susan
Throssel), Eric Blore (Sergeant), Cora Witherspoon
(Patty), Estelle Winwood (Mary Willoughby), Florence
Lake (Henrietta Turnbull), Helena Grant (Fanny
Willoughby), Bonita Granville (Isabella), Joan Fontaine
(Charlotte Parratt), Clifford Severn (Arthur).

Directed by George Stevens. Produced by Pandro S.
Berman. Script by Mortimer Offner and Allan Scott,
based on a play by J.M. Barrie. Photographed by
Robert De Grasse. Art director: Van Nest Polglase.
Edited by Henry Berman. Music by Roy Webb.
Costumes by Walter Plunkett.

STAGE DOOR

RKO, 1937. 92 minutes.

With: Katharine Hepburn (Terry Randall), Ginger
Rogers (Jean Maitland), Adolphe Menjou (Anthony
Powell), Gail Patrick (Linda Shaw), Constance Collier
(Catherine Luther), Andrea Leeds (Kaye Hamilton),
Lucille Ball (Judy Canfield), Eve Arden (Eve), Phyllis

Kennedy (Hattie), Ann Miller (Annie), Samuel S.
Hinds (Henry Sims), Franklin Pangborn (Harcourt),
Elizabeth Dunne (Mrs Orcutt), Margaret Early (Mary).

Directed by Gregory La Cava. Produced by Pandro S.
Berman. Script by Morrie Ryskind and Anthony Veiller,
based on a play by Edna Ferber and George S.
Kaufman. Photographed by Robert De Grasse. Art
director: Van Nest Polglase. Edited by William Hamilton.
Music by Roy Webb. Costumes by Muriel King.

BRINGING UP BABY

RKO, 1938. 102 minutes.

With: Katharine Hepburn (Susan Vance), Cary Grant
(David Huxley), Charles Ruggles (Major Horace
Applegate), May Robson (Aunt Elizabeth), Barry
Fitzgerald (Gogarty), Walter Catlett (Constable
Slocum), Leona Roberts (Hannah Gogarty), Virginia
Walker (Alice Swallow), George Irving (Alexander
Peabody), Fritz Feld (Dr Fritz Lehmann), Ward Bond
(Motor Cop).

Directed and produced by Howard Hawks. Associate
producer: Cliff Reid. Script by Dudley Nichols and
Hagar Wilde, based on a story by Hagar Wilde.
Photographed by Russell Metty. Art director: Van Nest
Polglase. Edited by George Hively. Music by Roy
Webb. Costumes by Howard Greer.

HOLIDAY

FREE TO LIVE/UNCONVENTIONAL LINDA
Columbia, 1938. 95 minutes.

With: Katharine Hepburn (Linda Seton), Cary Grant
(Johnny Case), Doris Nolan (Julia Seton), Lew Ayres
(Ned Seton), Edward Everett Horton (Nick Potter),
Henry Kolker (Edward Seton), Binnie Barnes (Laura
Cram), Henry Daniell (Seton Cram), Jean Dixon
(Susan Potter).

Directed by George Cukor. Associate producer: Everett
Riskin. Script by Donald Ogden Stewart and Sidney
Buchman, based on a play by Philip Barry.
Photographed by Franz Planer. Art director: Stephen
Goosson. Edited by Otto Meyer and Al Clark. Music
by Sidney Cutner. Costumes by Kalloch.

THE PHILADELPHIA STORY

MGM, 1940. 112 minutes.

With: Katharine Hepburn (Tracy Lord), James Stewart
(Mike Connor), Cary Grant (C.K. Dexter Haven),
Ruth Hussey (Liz Imbrie), John Howard (George
Kittredge), Roland Young (Uncle Willie), John
Halliday (Seth Lord), Virginia Wiedler (Dinah Lord),
Mary Nash (Margaret Lord), Henry Daniell (Sidney
Kidd).

Directed by George Cukor. Produced by Joseph L.
Mankiewicz. Script by Donald Ogden Stewart, based
on a play by Philip Barry produced on stage by The
Theatre Guild Inc. Photographed by Joseph
Ruttenberg. Art director: Cedric Gibbons. Music by
Franz Waxman. Costumes by Adrian.

WOMAN OF THE YEAR

MGM, 1942. 114 minutes.

With: Katharine Hepburn (Tess Harding), Spencer
Tracy (Sam Craig), Fay Bainter (Ellen Whitcomb),
Reginald Owen (Clayton), Minor Watson (William
Harding), William Bendix (Pinkie Peters), Dan Tobin
(Gerald), Roscoe Karns (Phil Whittaker), William
Tannen (Ellis), Ludwig Stossel (Dr Martin Lubbeck).

Directed by George Stevens. Produced by Joseph L.
Mankiewicz. Script by Ring Lardner, Jr, and Michael
Kanin. Photographed by Joseph Ruttenberg. Art
director: Cedric Gibbons. Edited by Frank Sullivan.
Music by Franz Waxman. Costumes by Adrian.

KEEPER OF THE FLAME

MGM, 1942. 100 minutes.

With: Katharine Hepburn (Christine Forrest), Spencer Tracy (Steven O'Malley), Richard Whorf (Clive Kerndon), Margaret Wycherly (Mrs Forrest), Donald Meek (Mr Arbuthnot), Horace [Steven] McNally (Freddie Ridges), Audrey Christie (Jane Harding), Percy Kilbride (Orion), Howard Da Silva (Jason Rickards), Darryl Hickman (Jeb Rickards), Forrest Tucker (Geoffrey Midford). Directed by George Cukor. Produced by Victor Saville. Associate producer: Leon Gordon. Script by Donald Ogden Stewart, based on a novel by I.A.R. Wylie. Photographed by William Daniels. Art director: Cedric Gibbons. Edited by James E. Newcom. Music by Bronislau Kaper. Costumes by Adrian.

STAGE DOOR CANTEEN

Sol Lesser (released through United Artists), 1943. 133 minutes.

Katharine Hepburn was one of 65 film and theatre stars who made cameo appearances as themselves in this film about the work of a New York Canteen for the armed forces run by the American Theatre Wing.

Directed by Frank Borzage. Produced by Sol Lesser. Script by Delmer Daves.

DRAGON SEED

MGM, 1944. 147 minutes.

With: Katharine Hepburn (Jade), Walter Huston (Ling Tan), Aline MacMahon (Mrs Ling Tan), Akim Tamiroff (Wu Lien), Turhan Bey (Lao Er), Hurd Hatfield (Lao San), Frances Rafferty (Orchid), Agnes Moorehead (Third Cousin's Wife), Henry Travers (Third Cousin), Jacqueline De Wit (Mrs Wu Lien), J. Carroll Naish (Overseer).

Directed by Jack Conway and Harold S. Bucquet. Produced by Pandro S. Berman. Script by Marguerite Roberts and Jane Murfin, based on a novel by Pearl S. Buck. Photographed by Sidney Wagner. Art director: Cedric Gibbons. Edited by Harold F. Kress. Music by Herbert Stothart. Costumes by Irene and Valles.

WITHOUT LOVE

MGM, 1945. 110 minutes.

With: Katharine Hepburn (Jamie Rowan), Spencer Tracy (Pat Jamieson), Lucille Ball (Kitty Trimble), Keenan Wynn (Quentin Ladd), Carl Esmond (Paul Carrell), Patricia Morison (Edwina Collins), Felix Bressart (Professor Grinza), Emily Massey (Anna), Gloria Grahame (Flower Girl).

Directed by Harold S. Bucquet. Produced by Lawrence Weingarten. Script by Donald Ogden Stewart, based on a play by Philip Barry produced on stage by The Theatre Guild, Inc. Photographed by Karl Freund. Art director: Cedric Gibbons. Edited by Frank Sullivan. Music by Bronislau Kaper. Costumes by Irene and Marion Herwood Keyes.

UNDERCURRENT

MGM, 1946. 116 minutes.

With: Katharine Hepburn (Ann Hamilton), Robert Taylor (Alan Garraway), Robert Mitchum (Michael Garraway), Edmund Gwenn (Professor Hamilton), Marjorie Main (Lucy), Jayne Meadows (Sylvia Burton), Clinton Sundberg (Mr Warmsley), Dan Tobin (Professor Joseph Bangs).

Directed by Vincente Minnelli. Produced by Pandro S. Berman. Script by Edward Chodorov, based on a story by Thelma Strabel. Photographed by Karl Freund. Art director: Cedric Gibbons. Edited by Ferris Webster. Music by Herbert Stothart. Costumes by Irene.

THE SEA OF GRASS

MGM, 1947. 123 minutes.

With: Katharine Hepburn (Lutie Cameron), Spencer Tracy (Colonel James Brewton), Melvyn Douglas (Brice Chamberlain), Phyllis Thaxter (Sara Beth Brewton), Robert Walker (Jock Brewton), Edgar Buchanan (Jeff), Harry Carey (Doc Reid), Ruth Nelson (Selena Hall), James Bell (Sam Hall).

Directed by Elia Kazan. Produced by Pandro S. Berman. Script by Marguerite Roberts and Vincent Lawrence, based on a novel by Conrad Richter. Photographed by Harry Stradling. Art director: Cedric Gibbons. Edited by Robert J. Kern. Music by Herbert Stothart. Costumes by Walter Plunkett.

SONG OF LOVE

MGM, 1947. 118 minutes.

With: Katharine Hepburn (Clara Wieck Schumann), Paul Henreid (Robert Schumann), Robert Walker (Johannes Brahms), Henry Daniell (Franz Liszt), Leo G. Carroll (Professor Wieck), Elsa Janssen (Bertha), Gigi Perreau (Julie).

Directed and produced by Clarence Brown. Script by Ivan Tors, Irmgard Von Cube, Allen Vincent and Robert Ardrey, based on a play by Bernard Schubert and Mario Silva. Photographed by Harry Stradling. Art director: Cedric Gibbons. Edited by Robert J. Kern. Music by Bronislau Kaper. Piano recordings by Artur Rubinstein. Costumes by Irene, Walter Plunkett and Valles.

STATE OF THE UNION

THE WORLD AND HIS WIFE

MGM/Liberty Films, 1948. 122 minutes.

With: Katharine Hepburn (Mary Matthews), Spencer Tracy (Grant Matthews), Van Johnson (Spike McManus), Angela Lansbury (Kay Thorndyke), Adolphe Menjou (Jim Conover), Lewis Stone (Sam Thorndyke), Howard Smith (Sam Parrish), Maidel Turner (Lulubelle Alexander), Raymond Walburn (Judge Alexander), Charles Dingle (Bill Hardy), Margaret Hamilton (Norah).

Directed and produced by Frank Capra. Associate producer: Anthony Veiller. Script by Anthony Veiller and Myles Connolly, based on a play by Howard Lindsay and Russell Crouse. Photographed by George J. Folsey. Art director: Cedric Gibbons. Edited by William Hornbeck. Music by Victor Young. Costumes by Irene.

ADAM'S RIB

MGM, 1949. 101 minutes.

With: Katharine Hepburn (Amanda Bonner), Spencer Tracy (Adam Bonner), Judy Holliday (Doris Attinger), Tom Ewell (Warren Attinger), David Wayne (Kip Lurie), Jean Hagen (Beryl Caighn), Hope Emerson (Olympia La Pere), Clarence Kolb (Judge Reiser), Eve March (Grace).

Directed by George Cukor. Produced by Lawrence Weingarten. Script by Ruth Gordon and Garson Kanin. Photographed by George J. Folsey. Art director: Cedric Gibbons. Edited by George Boemler. Music by Miklos Rozsa. Costumes by Walter Plunkett. Song *Farewell Amanda* by Cole Porter.

THE AFRICAN QUEEN

Horizon/Romulus (released through United Artists). 103 minutes.

With: Katharine Hepburn (Rose Sayer), Humphrey Bogart (Charlie Allnut), Robert Morley (Reverend Samuel Sayer), Peter Bull (Captain of the *Louisa*), Theordore Bikel (First Officer).

Directed by John Huston. Produced by S.P. Eagle [Sam Spiegel]. Script by James Agee and John Huston, based on a novel by C.S. Forester. Photographed in Technicolor by Jack Cardiff. Second unit photography by Ted Scaife. Edited by Ralph Kemplen. Music by Alan Gray. Costumes by Doris Langley Moore and Connie de Pinna.

PAT AND MIKE
MGM, 1952. 95 minutes.
With: Katharine Hepburn (Pat Pemberton), Spencer Tracy (Mike Conovan), Aldo Ray (Davie Hucko), William Ching (Collier Weld), Sammy White (Barney Grau), George Matthews (Spec Cauley), Charles Buchinski [Bronson] (Hank Tasling), Jim Backus (Charles Barry),Frank Richards (Sam Garsell).
Directed by George Cukor. Produced by Lawrence Weingarten. Script by Ruth Gordon and Garson Kanin. Photographed by William Daniels. Art director: Cedric Gibbons. Edited by George Boemler. Music by David Raksin. Miss Hepburn's wardrobe by Orry-Kelly.

SUMMERTIME
SUMMER MADNESS
Lopert Films (released through United Artists), 1955. 99 minutes.
With: Katharine Hepburn (Jane Hudson), Rossano Brazzi (Renato Di Rossi), Isa Miranda (Signora Fiorini), Darren McGavin (Eddie Yaeger), Mari Aldon (Phyl Yaeger), Jane Rose (Mrs McIlhenny), Macdonald Parke (Mr McIlhenny), Jeremy Spenser (Vito Di Rossi), André Morell (Englishman), Gaitano Audiero (Mauro).
Directed by David Lean. Produced by Ilya Lopert. Associate producer: Norman Spencer. Script by David Lean and H.E. Bates, based on the play *Time of the Cuckoo* by Arthur Laurents. Photographed in Technicolor by Jack Hildyard. Art director: Vincent Korda. Edited by Peter Taylor. Music by Alessandro Cicognini.

THE RAINMAKER
Paramount, 1956. 122 minutes.
With: Katharine Hepburn (Lizzie Curry), Burt Lancaster (Starbuck), Wendell Corey (File), Lloyd Bridges (Noah Curry), Earl Holliman (Jim Curry), Cameron Prud'homme (H.C. Curry), Wallace Ford (Sheriff Thomas), Yvonne Lime (Snookie).
Directed by Joseph Anthony. Produced by Hal B. Wallis. Script by N. Richard Nash, based on his own play. Photographed by Charles Lang, Jr. Art director: Hal Pereira. Edited by Warren Low. Music by Alex North. Costumes by Edith Head.

THE IRON PETTICOAT
Benhar (released through MGM), 1956. 89 minutes.
With: Katharine Hepburn (Vinka Kovelenko), Bob Hope (Chuck Lockwood), James Robertson Justice (Colonel Sklarnoff), Robert Helpmann (Ivan Kropotkin), David Kossoff (Dubratz), Alan Gifford (Colonel Tarbell), Paul Carpenter (Lewis), Noelle Middleton (Connie), Sidney James (Paul).
Directed by Ralph Thomas. Produced by Betty E. Box. Script by Ben Hecht [name removed from credits at his request], based on a story by Harry Saltzman. Photographed in Technicolor by Ernest Steward. Art director: Carmen Dillon. Edited by Frederick Wilson. Music by Benjamin Frankel. Costumes by Yvonne Caffin.

DEST SET
HIS OTHER WOMAN
20th Century-Fox, 1957. 103 minutes.
With: Katharine Hepburn (Bunny Watson), Spencer

Tracy (Richard Sumner), Gig Young (Mike Cutler), Joan Blondell (Peg Costello), Dina Merrill (Sylvia), Sue Randall (Ruthie), Neva Patterson (Miss Warringer).
Directed by Walter Lang. Produced by Henry Ephron. Script by Phoebe Ephron and Henry Ephron, based on a play by William Marchant produced on stage by Robert Fryer and Lawrence Carr. Photographed in De Luxe Color by Leon Shamroy. Art director: Lyle Wheeler. Edited by Robert Simpson. Music by Cyril J. Mockridge. Costumes by Charles Le Maire.

SUDDENLY, LAST SUMMER
Horizon (GB) Ltd/Academy Pictures/Camp Films (released through Columbia), 1959. 114 minutes.
With: Katharine Hepburn (Violet Venable), Elizabeth Taylor (Catherine Holly), Montgomery Clift (Dr Cukrowicz), Albert Dekker (Dr Hockstader), Mercedes McCambridge (Mrs Holly), Gary Raymond (George Holly), Mavis Villiers (Miss Foxhill), Patricia Marmont (Nurse Benson).
Directed by Joseph L. Mankiewicz. Produced by Sam Spiegel. Script by Gore Vidal and Tennessee Williams, based on a play by Tennessee Williams. Photographed by Jack Hildyard. Art director: William Kellner. Edited by Thomas G. Stanford. Music by Buxton Orr and Malcolm Arnold. Costumes by Jean Louis and Norman Hartnell.

LONG DAY'S JOURNEY INTO NIGHT
Embassy, 1962. 174 minutes (UK release version 136 minutes).
With: Katharine Hepburn (Mary Tyrone), Ralph Richardson (James Tyrone, Sr), Jason Robards, Jr (James Tyrone, Jr), Dean Stockwell (Edmund Tyrone), Jeannne Barr (Cathleen).
Directed by Sidney Lumet. Produced by Ely Landau and Jack J. Dreyfus, Jr. Script: play by Eugene O'Neill. Photographed by Boris Kaufman. Edited by Ralph Rosenblum. Music by André Previn. Costumes by Motley.

GUESS WHO'S COMING TO DINNER?
Columbia, 1967. 108 minutes.
With: Katharine Hepburn (Christina Drayton), Spencer Tracy (Matt Drayton), Sidney Poitier (John Prentice), Katharine Houghton (Joey Drayton), Roy E. Glenn Sr (Mr Prentice), Beah Richards (Mrs Prentice), Cecil Kellaway (Monsignor Ryan), Isabell Sanford (Tillie), Virginia Christine (Hilary St George).
Directed and produced by Stanley Kramer. Associate producer: George Glass. Script by William Rose. Photographed in Technicolor by Sam Leavitt. Production designer: Robert Clatworthy. Edited by Robert C. Jones. Music by Frank DeVol. Costumes by Joe King. Song *Glory of Love* by Billy Hill, sung by Jacqueline Fontaine.

THE LION IN WINTER
Avco Embassy, 1968. 134 minutes.
With: Katharine Hepburn (Eleanor of Aquitaine), Peter O'Toole (Henry II), Jane Merrow (Princess Alais), John Castle (Geoffrey), Anthony Hopkins (Richard), Timothy Dalton (King Philip), Nigel Terry (John), Nigel Stock (William Marshall).
Directed by Anthony Harvey. Produced by Martin Poll. Executive producer: Joseph E. Levine. Associate producer: Jane C. Nusbaum. Script by James Goldman, based on his own play. Photographed in Eastmancolor by Douglas Slocombe. Art director: Peter Murton. Edited by John Bloom. Music by John Barry. Costumes by Margaret Furse.

THE MADWOMAN OF CHAILLOT
Warner/Seven Arts, 1969. 142 minutes.
With: Katharine Hepburn (Countess Aurelia), Edith Evans (Josephine), Margaret Leighton (Constance), Giulietta Masina (Gabrielle), Charles Boyer (Broker), Claude Dauphin (Dr Jadin), John Gavin (Reverend), Paul Henreid (General), Oscar Homolka (Commissar), Nanette Newman (Irma), Richard Chamberlain (Roderick), Yul Brynner (Chairman), Donald Pleasance (Prospector), Danny Kaye (Ragpicker).
Directed by Bryan Forbes. Produced by Ely Landau. Executive producer: Henry T. Weinstein. Associate producer: Anthony B. Ungar. Script by Edward Anhalt, based on a play by Jean Giraudoux, translated by Maurice Valency. Photographed in Technicolor by Claude Renoir and Burnett Guffey. Art director: Georges Petitot. Edited by Roger Dwyre. Music by Michael J. Lewis. Costumes by Rosine Delamare. Song *The Lonely Ones* by Michael J. Lewis and Gil King.

THE TROJAN WOMEN
Josef Shaftel/Cinerama, 1971. 111 minutes.
With: Katharine Hepburn (Hecuba), Vanessa Redgrave (Andromache), Geneviève Bujold (Cassandra), Irene Papas (Helen), Patrick Magee (Menelaus), Brian Blessed (Talthybius), Alberto Sanz (Astyanax).
Directed by Michael Cacoyannis. Produced by Michael Cacoyannis and Anis Nohra. Executive producer: Josef Shaftel. Script by Michael Cacoyannis, based on a play by Euripides, translated by Edith Hamilton. Art director: Nicholas Georgiadis. Edited by Michael Cacoyannis, Music by Mikis Theodorakis. Costumes by Annalisa Rocca.

A DELICATE BALANCE
American Express Films (New York)/Ely Landau Organisation (London)/Cinevision (Montreal), 1974, Produced for The American Film Theatre. 134 minutes.
With: Katharine Hepburn (Agnes), Paul Scofield (Tobias), Lee Remick (Julia), Kate Reid (Claire), Joseph Cotten (Harry), Betsy Blair (Edna).
Directed by Tony Richardson. Produced by Ely Landau. Associate producer: Henry T. Weinstein. Executive producer: Neil Hartley. Script by Edward Albee, based on his own play. Photographed in colour by David Watkin. Art director: David Brockhurst. Edited by John Victor Smith.

THE GLASS MENAGERIE
Talent Associates/Norton Simon Inc., 1974. 100 minutes.
With: Katharine Hepburn (Amanda Wingfield), Joanna Miles (Laura Wingfield), Sam Waterston (Jim O'Connor), Michael Moriarty (Tom Wingfield).
Directed by Anthony Harvey. Produced by David Susskind. Associate producer: Cecil F. Ford. Script by Tennessee Williams, based on his own play. Photographed by Billy Williams. Art director: Alan Tomkins. Edited by John Bloom. Costumes by Betty Adamson. Production designer: Terry Marsh.

LOVE AMONG THE RUINS
ABC Entertainment Inc., 1975. 120 minutes.
With: Katharine Hepburn (Jessica Medlicott), Laurence Olivier (Sir Arthur Granville-Jones), Colin Blakely (J.F. Devine), Richard Pearson (Druve), Joan Sims (Fanny Pratt), Leigh Lawson (Alfred Pratt), Gwen Nelson (Hermione Davis), Robert Harris (The Judge), Peter Reeves (Malden), Ian Sinclair (Pratt's Solicitor), John Dunbar (Clerk of the Court).
Directed by George Cukor. Produced by Allan Davis. Executive producer: Denis L. Judd II. Script by James

Costigan. Photographed by Douglas Slocombe. Art director: Carmen Dillon. Edited by John F. Burnett and Dev Goodman. Costumes by Maggie Furse. Music by John Barry.

ROOSTER COGBURN
Universal/CIC, 1975. 120 minutes.
With: Katharine Hepburn (Eula Goodnight), John Wayne (Rooster Cogburn), Anthony Zerbe (Breed), Richard Jordan (Hawk), John McIntyre (Judge Parker), Strother Martin (McCoy), Paul Koslo (Luke), Jack Colvin (Red), Jon Lormer (Reverend Goodnight), Richard Romancito (Wolf), Lane Smith (Leroy), Warren Vanders (Dagby).
Directed by Stuart Millar. Produced by Hal B. Wallis. Associate producer: Paul Nathan. Script by Martin Julien, suggested by the character Rooster Cogburn from the novel *True Grit* by Charles Portis. Photographed in Technicolor by Harry Stradling, Jr. Art director: Preston Ames. Edited by Robert Swink. Costumes by Luther Bayliss. Music by Laurence Rosenthal.

OLLY, OLLY, OXEN FREE
THE GREAT BALLOON ADVENTURE
Rico Lion (released only for television), 1978. 83 minutes.
With: Katharine Hepburn (Miss Pudd), Kevin McKenzie (Alby), Dennis Dimster (Chris), Peter Kilman (Mailman).
Directed and produced by Richard A. Colla. Executive producer: Don Henderson. Script by Eugene Poinc, based on a story by Maria L. De Ossio, Eugene Poinc and Richard A. Colla. Photographed in Metrocolor by Gayne Rescher. Production design: Peter Wooley. Edited by Lee Burch. Music by Bob Alcivar.

THE CORN IS GREEN
Warner Brothers TV, 1979. 100 minutes.
With: Katharine Hepburn (Miss Moffat), Ian Saynor (Morgan Evans), Bill Fraser (Squire), Patricia Hayes (Mrs Watty), Anna Massey (Mrs Ronberry), Artro Morris (John Goronwy), Dorothy Phinnis (Sarah Pugh), Toyah Wilcox (Betty Watty), Huw Richard (Idwal), Bryn Fon (Robbart).
Directed by George Cukor. Produced by Neil Hartley. Script by Ivan Davis, based on a play by Emlyn Williams. Photographed in colour by Ted Scaife. Art director: Carmen Dillon. Music by John Barry.

ON GOLDEN POND
ITC/IPS, 1981. 109 minutes.
With: Katharine Hepburn (Ethel Thayer), Henry Fonda (Norman Thayer), Jane Fonda (Chelsea), Doug McKeon (Billy), Dabney Coleman (Bill), William Lanteau (Charlie), Peter Turgeon (Minister).
Directed by Mark Rydell. Produced by Bruce Gilbert. Script by Ernest Thompson, based on his own play. Photographed in colour by Billy Williams. Production designer: Stephen B. Grimes.

THE ULTIMATE SOLUTION OF GRACE QUIGLEY
Golan Globus/Northbrook (released through MGM/UA and Cannon Films). 102 minutes as shown at Cannes Film Festival, later edited and reshot; prints vary between 87 minutes and 95 minutes.
With: Katharine Hepburn (Grace Quigley), Nick Nolte (Seymour Flint), Elizabeth Wilson (Emily Watkins), Chip Zien (Dr Herman), Kit Le Fever (Muriel), William Duell (Mr Jenkins), Walter Abel (Homer Watkins).

Directed by Anthony Harvey. Produced by Menahem Golan and Yoram Globus. Executive producers: A. Martin Zweibeck and Adrienne Zweibeck. Associate producer: Christopher Pearce. Script by A. Martin Zweibeck. Photographed in MGM Color by Larry Pizer. Edited by Bob Raetano. Costumes by Ruth Morley. Music by John Addison.

MRS DELAFIELD WANTS TO MARRY
Schaefer-Karpf Productions, 1986. 100 minutes.
With: Katharine Hepburn (Mararet Delafield), Harold Gould (Marvin Elias), Denholm Elliott (George Parker), David Ogden Stiers (Horton), Kathryn Walker (Sarah), John Pleshette (David Elias), Charles Frank (Chipper), Suzanne Lederer (Shirley), Brenda Forbes (Gladys), Bibi Besch (Doreen), Tom Heaton (Harrison), Robert Sidley (Digby).
Directed by George Schaefer. Script by James Prideaux. Photographed by Walter Latz. Music by Peter Matz.

LAURA LANSING SLEPT HERE
Schaefer-Karpf Productions, 1988. 100 minutes.
With: Katharine Hepburn (Laura Lansing),Joel Higgins (Walter Gomphers), Karen Austin (Melody Gomphers), Lee Richardson (Larry Baumgartner), Nicholas Surovy (Conway Reed), Moira Walley (Violet), Schuyler Grant (Annette Gomphers), Sean Harmon (Walter Jr).
Directed by George Schaefer. Script by James Prideaux. Photographed by Paul Lohman.

THIS CAN'T BE LOVE
Davis Entertainment, 1994. 100 minutes.
With: Katharine Hepburn (Marion Bennett), Anthony Quinn (Michael Reyman), Jason Bateman (Grant). Jami Gertz (Sarah), Maxine Miller (Wilma) Lynda Boyd (Latrice), Morris Paynch (Gordon), Lori Ann Triolo (Marvel).
Directed by Anthony Harvey. Script by Duane Poole.

LOVE AFFAIR
Warner Brothers/Mulholland Productions. 108 minutes.
With: Katharine Hepburn, Warren Beatty, Annette Bening, Pierce Brosnan, Garry Shandling, Chloe Webb, Kate Capshaw, Paul Mazursky, Brenda Vaccaro, Glenn Shadix, Barry Millar, Harold Ramis.
Directed and produced by Glenn Gordon Caron. Executive producer: Andrew Z. Davis. Screenplay by Warren Beatty and Robert Towne from a script by Glenn Gordon Caron, based on the films Love Affair (1939) scripted by Delmer Daves and Donald Ogden Stewart from a story by Leo McCarey and Mildred Cram and An Affair to Remember scripted by Delmer Daves and Leo McCarey. Photographed by Conrad Hall. Edited by Robert C. Jones. Production designer: Ferdinando Scarfiotti. Art director: Geoffrey S. Grimshaw. Music by Ennio Morricone.

ONE CHRISTMAS
1994. 100 minutes.
With Katharine Hepburn (Cornelia Beaumont), Julie Harris (Sook), T.J. Lowther (Buddy), Tonea Stewart (Evangeline), Henry Winkler (Dad), Swoozie Kurtz (Emily), Troy Simmons (Toby).
Directed by Tony Bill. Produced by Duane Poole. Executive producers: John Philip Dayton, Merril Karpf, John Davis. Script by Duane Poole, based on a short story by Truman Capote. Photographed by Thomas Del Ruth and Donald Morgan. Production design: Robert Holloway. Edited by Duane Hartzell. Music by Van Dyke Parks.

STAGE WORK

Debut with the Edwin H. Knopf Stock Company, Baltimore, Maryland, 1928. Played a lady-in-waiting in The Czarina by Melchior Lengyel and Lajos Biro, and a flapper in The Cradle Snatchers by Russell Medcraft and Norma Mitchell.

The Big Pond (George Middleton and A.E. Thomas) The Great Neck Theatre Long Island, August 1928. Directed by Edwin H. Knopf. With Marius Rogati (Francesco), Reed Brown Jnr (Ronny Davis), Marie Curtis (Mrs Billings), Doris Rankin (Mrs Livermore), Katharine Hepburn (Barbara), Harlan Briggs (Henry Billings).

These Days (Katherine Clugston) Cort Theatre, New York, November 1928. Directed by Arthur Hopkins. With Mary Hall (Rosilla Dow), Mildred McCoy (Virginia MacRae), Gertrude Moran (Pansy Larue Mott), Katharine Hepburn (Veronica Sims), Gladys Hopeton (Miss Guadaloupe Gorhan), Bruce Evans ('Chippy' Davis), Helen Freeman (Miss Signhild Valdemir Van Alstyne).

Holiday (Philip Barry) Plymouth Theatre, New York, November 1928. Directed by Arthur Hopkins. With Hope Williams (Linda Seton - understudied by Katharine Hepburn), Ben Smith (Johnny Case), Dorothy Tree (Julia Seton), Monroe Owsley (Ned Seton), Barbara White (Susan Potter), Donald Ogden Stewart (Nick Potter).

Death Takes a Holiday (Alberto Casella, adapted by Walter Ferris) Touring production, November 1929. Directed by Lawrence Marston. With Florence Golden (Cora), Thomas Bate (Fedele), James Dale (Duke Lambert), Ann Orr (Alda), Olga Birkbeck (Stephanie), Viva Birkett (Princess of San Luca), Katharine Hepburn (Grazia), Philip Merivale (His Serene Highness, Prince Sirki, of Vitalba Alexandri).

A Month in the Country (Ivan Turgenev, translated by M.S. Mandell.) Guild Theatre, New York, March 1930. Directed by Rouben Mamoulian. With Charles Kraus (Herr Shaaf), Minna Phillips (Anna Semenova), Alla Nazimova (Natalia Petrovna), Elliot Cabot (Mikhail Aleksandrovich Rakitin), Eda Heinemann (Lizaveta Bogdanovna), Eunice Stoddard (Viera Aleksandrovna - understudied by Katharine Hepburn), Hortense Alden (Katia - replaced by Katharine Hepburn in the second month), Henry Travers (Afanasi Ivanych Bolshintsov).

Summer Stock, The Berkshire Playhouse, Stockbridge, Massachusetts: Hepburn appeared in A Romantic Young Lady by G. Martinez Sierra (translated by Helen and Harley Granville-Barker) and The Admirable Crichton by J. M. Barrie.

Art and Mrs Bottle or **The Return of the Puritan** (Benn W. Levy) Maxine Elliot Theatre, New York, November 1930. Directed by Clifford Brooke. With G.P. Huntley Jr (Michael Bottle), Katharine Hepburn (Judy Bottle), Joyce Carey (Sonia Tippet), Walter Kingsford (George Bottle), Jane Cowl (Celia Bottle).

Summer Stock with the Ivoryton Players, Ivoryton, Connecticut, 1931. Appeared in Just Married by Adelaide Matthews and Anne Nichols, The Cat and the Canary by John Willard and The Man Who Came Back by Jules Eckert Goodman.

The Animal Kingdom (Philip Barry) Pittsburgh,

September 1931. Directed by Gilbert Miller. With G. Albert Smith (Owen Arthur), Frederick Forrester (Rufus Collier), Lora Baxter (Cecelia Henry), William Gargan (Richard Regan), Leslie Howard (Tom Collier), Katharine Hepburn (Daisy Sage, replaced by Frances Fuller after the Pittsburgh opening), Ilka Chase (Grace Macomber).

The Warrior's Husband (Julian Thompson) Morosco Theatre, New York, March 1932. Directed by Burke Symon. With Virginia Volland (Buria), Bertha Belmore (Caustica), Dorothy Walters (Heroica), Jane Wheatley (Pomposia), Irby Marshall (Hippolyta), Katharine Hepburn (Antiope), Colin Keith-Johnston (Theseus), Don Beddoe (Homer), Al Ochs (Hercules), Porter Hall (Gaganius, the Herald), Alan Campbell (Achilles), Randolph Leymen (Ajax).

Summer Stock, Ossining, New York. Played Psyche Marbury in *The Bride the Sun Shines On* by Will Cotton.

The Lake (Dorothy Massingham and Murray MacDonald) Martin Beck Theatre, New York, December 1933. Directed by Jed Harris. With Frances Starr (Mildred Surrege), Blanche Bates (Lena Surrege), Lionel Pape (Henry Surrege), Katharine Hepburn (Stella Surrege), Colin Clive (John Clayne), Philip Tonge (Stephen Braite), Wendy Atkin (Dotty Braite), Audrey Ridgwell (Jean Templeton).

Jane Eyre (Charlotte Brontë, dramatised by Helen Jerome) Toured December 1936 - April 1937. Directed by Worthington Miner. With Viola Roache (Mrs Fairfax), Phyllis Connard (Leah), Katharine Hepburn (Jane Eyre), Dennis Hoey (Mr Rochester), Teresa Dale (Grace Poole), Teresa Guerini (The Maniac), Barbara O Neil (Diana Rivers), Stephen Kerr Appleby (St John Rivers).

The Philadelphia Story (Philip Barry) The Shubert Theatre, New York, March 1939. Directed by Robert B. Sinclair. With Lenore Lonergan (Dinah Lord), Vera Allen (Margaret Lord), Katharine Hepburn (Tracy Lord), Forrest Orr (William Tracy), Shirley Booth (Elizabeth Imbrie), Van Heflin (Macaulay Connor), Frank Fenton (George Kittredge), Joseph Cotten (C.K. Dexter Haven), Nicholas Joy (Seth Lord).

Without Love (Philip Barry) St James Theatre, New York, November 1942, and tour. Directed by Robert B. Sinclair. With Elliot Nugent (Patrick Jamieson), Tony Bickley (Quentin Ladd), Ellen Morgan (Martha Ladd), Katharine Hepburn (Jamie Coe Rowan), Audrey Christie (Kitty Trimble), Robert Shayne (Peter Baillie), Sherling Oliver (Paul Carrel).

As You Like It (William Shakespeare) Cort Theatre, New York, January 1950, and tour. Directed by Michael Benthall. With William Prince (Orlando), Ernest Graves (Oliver), Cloris Leachman (Celia), Katharine Hepburn (Rosalind), Bill Owen (Touchstone), Dayton Lummis (Frederick), Aubrey Mather (Duke), Ernest Thesiger (Jacques).

The Millionairess (George Bernard Shaw) Shubert Theatre, New York, June 1952, and tour. Directed by Michael Benthall. With Campbell Cotts (Julius Sagamore), Katharine Hepburn (Epifania, the Lady), Cyril Ritchard (Adrian Blenderbland), Robert Helpmann (The Doctor).

Summer tour of Australia with Robert Helpmann and

the Old Vic Company, 1955. Played Portia in *The Merchant Of Venice*, Katherina in *The Taming Of The Shrew* and Isabella in *Measure For Measure*.

The Merchant of Venice (William Shakespeare) American Shakespeare Festival Theatre, Stratford, Connecticut, July 1957. Directed by Jack Landau. With Richard Waring (Antonio), Donald Harron (Bassanio), Katharine Hepburn (Portia), Lois Nettleton (Nerissa), Morris Carnovsky (Shylock), Dina Doronne (Jessica).

Much Ado About Nothing (William Shakespeare) American Shakespeare Festival Theatre, Stratford, Connecticut, August 1957. Directed by John Houseman and Jack Landau. With Morris Carnovsky (Antonio), Larry Gates (Dogberry), John Colicos (Leonato), Katharine Hepburn (Beatrice), Lois Nettleton (Hero), Stanley Bell (Don Pedro), Alfred Drake (Benedick), Richard Waring (Don John).

Twelfth Night (William Shakespeare) American Shakespeare Festival Theatre, Stratford, Connecticut, June 1960. Directed by Jack Landau. With Donald Davis (Orsino, Duke of Illyria), Katharine Hepburn (Viola), Loring Smith (Sir Toby Belch), Sada Thompson (Maria), O.Z. Whitehead (Sir Andrew Aguecheek), Morris Carnovsky (Feste), Margaret Phillips (Olivia), Richard Waring (Malvolio), Clayton Corzatte (Sebastian),

Antony and Cleopatra (William Shakespeare) American Shakespeare Festival Theatre, Stratford, Connecticut, July 1960. Directed by Jack Landau. With Robert Ryan (Antony), Katharine Hepburn (Cleopatra), Douglas Watson (Canidius), Donald Davis (Enobarbus), Rae Allen (Charmian), Anne Fielding (Iras) John Ragin (Octavius Caesar), Clifton James (Pompey), Sada Thonpson (Octavia).

Coco (Book and lyrics by Alan Jay Lerner; music by André Previn) Mark Hellinger Theatre, New York, December 1969, and tour. Directed by Michael Benthall. With Maggie Task (Helene), George Rose (Louis Greff), Katharine Hepburn (Coco), Shirley Potter (Varne), Lynn Winn (Marie), Rita O'Connor (Jeanine), Graciela Daniele (Claire), Rene Auberjonois (Sebastian Baye).

A Matter of Gravity (Enid Bagnold) Broadhurst Theatre, New York, Febuary 1976, and tour. Directed by Noel Willman. With Katharine Hepburn (Mrs Basil), Christopher Reeve (Nicky), Paul Harding (Herbert), Wanda Bimson (Elizabeth).

The West Side Waltz (Ernest Thompson) Ethel Barrymore Theatre, New York, Febuary 1981, and tour. Directed by Noel Willman. With Katharine Hepburn (Margaret Elderdice), Dorothy Loudon (Cara Varrum), David Margulies (Serge Barrescu), Regina Baff (Robin Bird), Don Howard (Glen Dabrinsky).

Bibliography

1. Stars

Any contemporary work on the star system must be indebted to the pioneering studies of Richard Dyer – the monograph on *Stars* (British Film Institute, 1979) and the essays on Lana Turner (*Movie* 25, Winter 1977/78) and Marilyn Monroe (British Film Institute, 1980). While I am by no means in agreement with all Dyer's particular judgements, and while he sometimes seems unhelpfully equivocal theoretically, the value of his work as an exposition of the issues involved in studying stars cannot be doubted, and I have drawn on it gratefully, venturing to offer in the process, tacitly or explicitly, a number of criticisms of it. *Stars* contains an invaluable bibliography on the star system generally and on specific stars.

2. Directors

George Cukor, Hepburn's most regular director, has been the unfortunate victim of an unusual number of inept monographs. His book-length interview with Gavin Lambert, *On Cukor* (W.H. Allen, 1972), contrives to give some interesting answers to some rather uninspired questions and includes discussions of all the films with Hepburn. Frank Capra's autobiography, *The Name Above The Title* (Macmillan, New York, 1971), contains fascinating material on the shooting of *State of the Union*. The anthology *Women and Film*, edited by Gerald Peary and Karyn Kay (Dutton, New York, 1978), prints a cryptic interview with Dorothy Arzner in which she gives a strange account of *Chriistopher Strong*.

3. Katharine Hepburn

Books on Katharine Hepburn or with substantial coverage of her are listed on the next page.

Homer Dickens's *The Films of Katharine Hepburn* has no critical pretensions, but is useful for its exhaustive credits of Hepburn's film and stage work and for its liberal selection of extracts from contemporary reviews (mainly American) of the movies. It is also, like all the books in the Citadel Press series, admirably illustrated. B.H. Fussell's article 'Hepburn: All that Glitters . . .' (*1,000 Eyes*, vol.2, no.4, 1976, pp.4-5) is impressionistic and studiously non-theoretical, but also perceptive and provocative in a mode which has the virtues and limitations of epigram. Molly Haskell discusses Hepburn's work at length in *From Reverence to Rape*. I disagree with much of what she says, and I do not share her (implied) interpretive framework. Nevertheless, her book remains the only attempt of which I'm aware to write about Hepburn in some kind of historical context, and provides, at the very least, a stimulus for dissent.

The rest of the material on Hepburn which I have encountered is not merely deplorable but unusable. Charles Higham's biography, *Kate*, is everything the pretension implied in the title would lead one to expect, and fails to come up – as even the most banal and hagiographic Hollywood biographies usually manage to do – with interesting data about either the life or the films. Alvin H. Marrill's *Katharine Hepburn* is one of the weakest of an uneven series of monographs.

Since this book was written, the literature on Hepburn has been increased with the appearance of two books by Hepburn herself, the memoir *The Making of The African Queen: or How I Went to Africa with Bogart, Bacall and Huston and Almost Lost My Mind* and the autobiography *Me, Stories of My Life*. There has also been a lengthy biography by Barbara Leaming. A useful review of this and of the problems of show business biographies in general, 'Getting A Life' by David Thomson, appears in *Sight & Sound*, vol.5, no.8, August 1995.

Anderson, Christopher *Young Kate*, Henry Holt, New York, 1988

Bryson, John *The Private World of Katharine Hepburn*, Victor Gollancz, London, 1990

Carey, Gary *Katharine Hepburn: A Biography*, Robson Books, London, 1983

Dickens, Homer *The Films of Katharine Hepburn*, Citadel Press, New York, 1971; revised edition, Carol Publishing, New York, 1990

Edwards, Anne *A Remarkable Woman: A Biography of Katharine Hepburn*, New York, 1985

Freedland, Michael *Katharine Hepburn*, W.H. Allen, London, 1984

Haskell, Molly *From Reverence to Rape*, Penguin, New York, 1974

Hepburn, Katharine *Me, Stories of My Life*, Alfred A. Knopf, New York, 1981

Hepburn, Katharine *The Making of The African Queen: or How I Went to Africa with Bogart, Bacall and Huston and Almost Lost My Mind*, Century, London, 1987

Higham, Charles *Kate: The Life of Katharine Hepburn*, W.W. Norton, New York, 1975

Huston, John *An Open Book*, New York, 1972

Kanin, Garson *Tracy and Hepburn*, Angus & Robertson, New York, 1971

Leaming, Barbara *Katharine Hepburn*, Weidenfeld & Nicholson, London, 1995

Marrill, Alvin H. *Katharine Hepburn*, Pyramid, New York, 1973

Morley, Sheridan *Katharine Hepburn: A Celebration*, Pavilion/Michael Joseph, London, 1984; revised edition, 1989

Navarro, Marie-Louise *Katharine Hepburn dans l'objectif*, Paris, 1981

Newquist, Roy *A Special Kind of Magic*, New York, 1967

Parish, James Robert *The RKO Gals*, Ian Allan, London, 1974

Rosen, Marjorie *Popcorn Venus*, New York, 1973

Smith, Milburn (ed.) *Tracy and Hepburn*, Barven Press, New York, 1971

Spada, James *Hepburn: Her Life in Pictures*, London, 1984

Wallis, Hal, & Higham, Charles *Starmaker*, New York, 1980

Index